To my beloved N

'Teach me thy love to know;
That this new light, which now I see,
May both the work and workman show:
Then by a sunne-beam I will climbe to thee.
                                    See that ye love one another.'

CONTENTS

CONTENTS

INTRODUCTION

Who are we?

For we British, that's an oddly difficult question. Although our national self-assessment usually notes a number of good points (we're inventive, tolerant, and at least we're not French), it lists a torrent of bad ones too. Our society is fragmented, degenerate, irresponsible. Our kids are thugs, our workers ill educated, our managers greedy and incompetent. We hate our weather. Our public services are abysmal. Our society is rude and unfriendly. We drink too much and in the wrong way. Our house prices are crazy, our politicians sleazy, our roads jammed, our football team rubbish. When *The Times* invited readers to put forward new designs for the backs of British coins, one reader wrote in saying, 'How about a couple of yobs dancing on a car bonnet or a trio of legless ladettes in the gutter?'

All this denigration may not be good for our self-esteem, but it does at least suggest the existence of some sort of national identity, however humble. But scratch below the surface and that identity quickly starts to unravel. Take the nationality issue, for example. How many countries are there whose name is as confused as ours? Are we best called Great Britain? The British Isles? The United Kingdom? Or none of these? The technically correct title is the United Kingdom of Great Britain and

Northern Ireland – a composite term which makes reference to a second composite term (Great Britain) and a chunk of land (Northern Ireland) that was until recently claimed by another sovereign state.

Confused? It gets worse. Take sport. The English mostly cheer the team of any 'home nation', including the Republic of Ireland, which isn't a home nation at all. Meanwhile the Scots cheer the Welsh and vice versa, while both will cheer anyone at all if they're playing against England. Ryan Giggs, the best Welsh footballer of his generation, once captained the English Schoolboys. One of the leading 'English' bowlers is Simon Jones, a Welshman. In rugby, Ireland plays as one team, in football as two, in cricket as one team occasionally masquerading as an English county.

It's sometimes said that our identity confusion has been exacerbated by today's multicultural society. Anyone reading today's newspapers would almost certainly come away with an impression of a society uneasy with itself, a land where racial and religious tension seethes only inches beneath the surface. But if this is the case – and I doubt it – it's certainly nothing new. Contemporary multiculturalism may pose challenges, but infinitely fewer than it posed in the past. The Viking version of multiculturalism generally involved a sword in the belly. The sixteenth-century version of a multi-faith society involved bonfires, stakes and heretics.

In any case, our national confusion goes far wider and deeper than simply national, ethnic or religious issues. Recent reactions to the war in Iraq exposed long-standing divisions about the country's attitudes to its past. When the British government chose to go to war, was it acting in its old role of imperialist bully? Or in its equally old role of global policeman and bringer of freedom? The national debate displayed both responses, both equally impassioned. The rise of the British Empire is arguably the most salient fact in the history of the modern world. Should we be proud of it or ashamed? Or perhaps the empire has nothing to do with us any more? For all our love of military adventure, are we perhaps just a glorified adjunct of the United States, a kind of East Atlantic Puerto Rico?

Our own government is hardly keen to boast on our behalf. The Home Office recently published a booklet called *Life in the United Kingdom*, aimed at helping immigrants navigate the path to citizenship. It's not a bad publication at all. It begins with a twenty-five-page history of the country, from Roman times to the present. The survey is balanced and accurate, if a bit on the bland side. But what it leaves out is peculiar. It does say, 'British industry came to lead the world in the nineteenth century.' But that hardly gets the point across. The fact is that at the peak of our industrial power, we dug two-thirds of the world's coal, refined half its iron, forged five-sevenths of its steel, manufactured two-fifths of its hardware, and wove half its commercial cotton cloth. That's not simply leading others. That's being so far ahead of others that we were, in effect, imagining an entire new world into existence, a world that has utterly altered human expectations of health, wealth and technological possibility.

Likewise, the booklet comments that 'the railway engine [was] pioneered by George and Robert Stephenson'. Well, yes, so it was, but British inventors have also played key roles in developing the steam engine, the telegraph, aeronautics, the steam turbine, the microscope, the screw-driven iron ship, industrial steel, multiple-print photography, the electric light, the chain-driven bicycle, the electric generator, pneumatic tyres, the telephone, television, radar, the fax machine, the computer, the jet engine, the pocket calculator, and the World Wide Web. Those medical and public health innovations which Britons were most instrumental in developing – vaccination, integrated mains sewerage, antiseptic surgery and antibiotics – have saved far more lives than all other medical innovations put together. Are these facts really not worth a mention?

And why stop there? The British empire covered a quarter of the earth's surface, but used an army smaller than that of Switzerland to exert its rule. The world speaks our language. Our scientists have won vast numbers of Nobel Prizes, more than those in any country except the United States. The evolution of such things as habeas corpus, trial by jury, due process, the abolition of torture, and the rule of law aren't purely British in inspiration, but owe more to us than to anyone else. Our parliamentary democracy has been hugely influential in spreading ideals of liberty and representative government around the world. At the Royal Navy's peak, it owned more than half of the world's warships and made possible the nineteenth-century globalization of trade and finance.

These aren't small things. In fact, not to put too fine a point on it, the modern world has been more deeply shaped by Britain than by any other country. And we brought some good stuff to the party. Democracy, the limited state, the rule of law, free trade, industrialization, modern agriculture, modern finance, international law – none of these is exclusively British, but they're all sticky with our fingerprints. To the (very considerable) extent that the world is now shaped by American power and American values ... well, we know which country gave her birth. If the modern world is richer, freer, more peaceful, more democratic and healthier than it was, then Britain has played a leading role, often *the* leading role, in that transformation.

This book is about just that. What follows is a series of observations about very particular aspects of our culture and history. But underlying these observations is a broader theme, that of British exceptionalism: the ways in which our history is most strikingly different from that of our neighbours. This book takes a particular interest in the many things that we did first, or best, or most, or were the only ones ever to do. It focuses especially on those of our oddities which spread across the world – everything from football to the rule of law.

This isn't meant to be a balanced way to view ourselves. A balanced view would take into account the many ways in which we were identical to our neighbours, or borrowed ideas and institutions from them. It would look at the ways in which we were last or worst or feeblest. Yet those viewpoints already have wide expression in our culture. Those ladettes in the gutter or the yobs dancing on the bonnet symbolize all that we already dislike in ourselves. This book is a reminder of the other side, the side that our grumbling too often ignores.

Along the way, a picture of Britain emerges: one possible answer to the conundrum of Britishness, one way of answering that question, '*Who are we?*' And if the book skates over much of what is least praiseworthy in our culture, then at least it aims to do justice to our joint creation: a world inconceivably better now than it was four hundred years ago. A world that, compared with that earlier age, is (mostly) prosperous, (mostly) free, (mostly) technically advanced. In short, a world that is (mostly) British.

Before proceeding farther, a few caveats are in order. Readers wanting to race straight through to the action should do just that.

The first caveat has to do with the horrendous complexity of the term 'British'. Britain in its current shape dates from only 1707, and that's to ignore all the complexities of Britain's relationship with Ireland, and indeed its relationships with the overseas colonies and dominions. Before the Act of Union, there was a century in which the crowns of Scotland and England were joined, albeit with one or two rude interruptions, yet those two countries and Ireland were all importantly separate from one another. That separateness, indeed, was a crucial complicating factor during the turbulence of that century. Prior to 1603, old-fashioned histories of Britain are generally content to talk about England almost exclusively until a British identity starts to flicker into life in the early-modern era. This approach is a nonsense, of course. If Britain means anything at all prior to 1603, then it designates a geographical area that certainly includes Scotland. The most recent history to take these issues seriously was called simply *The Isles*, a title that squarely places geography ahead of politics.

The complications of Britishness are perhaps most evident in relation to Ireland. That country was colonized by the British, and its citizens were for a long time both Irish and British. Which identity is paramount? It all depends on who you ask. When called an Irishman, the Dublin-born, London-dwelling Duke of Wellington is said to have replied that 'Being born in a stable does not make one a horse.' On the other hand, the Ulster-born, Dublin-dwelling Seamus Heaney refused to have his work included in a book of British verse, writing, 'Be advised, my passport's green. / No glass of ours was ever raised / To toast *The Queen*.'

In this book, I haven't attempted to solve this or any other identity problem. Indeed, I've simply avoided definitions altogether. If Scottish soldiers in Canada develop the sport of ice hockey, then that, for me, is an example of Britishness in action. If a French-born king of England (but not Wales or Scotland) develops the common law, then that too, for the purposes of this book, counts as an example of Britishness in action. There's no neat logic in action here, but then if it's logic you were after, you shouldn't have bought a book about Britain.

I've a further confession to make, namely that Scotland, Wales and Ireland don't figure much in my account of exceptionalism in the pre-modern era. There are two reasons for that, one good, one bad. The bad one is simply that this is a short book with a lot to do. By focusing on England, I was able to narrow the amount I needed to read about and write about. It was a labour-saving device, and nothing more. The better reason is that, in those earlier centuries, the most important elements of exceptionalism to arise anywhere in the British Isles had to do with the English language, the English common law and the rise of the English parliament. Since England would become the dominant partner in the subsequent political unions, those English oddities would prove more lastingly influential than comparable oddities elsewhere in the archipelago. In any event, it's possible to get too hung up about all of this. I live in England, but spent huge chunks of my childhood in Wales. My grandfather was Protestant Ulster, his ancestors Scots and his wife Manx. My wife's maiden name is Moroney, and her father Catholic Irish. I'm hardly exceptional in being this much of a mixture. If football fans of one home nation want to get all steamed up with those of another, then that's up to them, but it's not much different from the liver yelling insults at the pancreas, the heart giving aggro to the gall bladder.

Finally, one last caveat. This book is rather unfashionable in celebrating British achievement. It suggests that the nation's part in shaping the modern world exceeds the role played by any other country, not only in terms of the scale of its impact, but in terms of its benefits too. (That's not to say there weren't disbenefits also. There were, and very significant ones at that.) Any such celebratory tone can easily seem rather embarrassing, a display of bad taste akin to having a flagpole in your front garden or enjoying the poetry of Rudyard Kipling. Personally, though, I'm not sure that questions of taste should determine what history to remember. The naval historian, Nick Rodger, had this to say about his own field of expertise:

> Many modern writers implicitly assume that the functions of the Navy were essentially aggressive, to win territory overseas. It seems for them to follow that sea power is nowadays both uninteresting, except to specialists in imperial history, and morally disreputable, something that the honest historian ought to pretend does not exist.

A similar comment could be made more broadly about any view of Britain which lays too much emphasis on the positive, on the distinctive and on the world-shaping. This book certainly does lay too much emphasis on these things. I hope I've made it crystal clear that it is not intended as an even-handed survey. Yet honest historians ought never to pretend or imagine things away. History, like life, doesn't make for easy moral conclusions. Any historian wanting to avoid a 'morally disreputable' and intellectually shallow patriotism risks biasing the picture in the other direction, overlooking facts that should not be overlooked. If this book has a serious purpose, then it's this: to thump down on the table a whole collection of such facts. Included in the collection are some obvious but under-emphasized ones, such as British naval predominance, and some less obvious ones too – for example, facts connected with social welfare, homicide, sports or the health transition.

What one makes of this collection is another matter altogether: a business for professional historians, not rank amateurs like myself. Having written a book built entirely on the scholarship of others, I'm as keenly aware as it's possible to be of how much remarkable work is being done by historians today. I'm not just indebted to their work, I'm in awe of it.

LANGUAGE

SHAW'S POTATO

The playwright and would-be spelling reformer George Bernard Shaw famously pointed out that, using only common English spellings, we could write the word *fish* as *ghoti*:

> **F**: *gh* as in *rough*
> **I**: *o* as in *women*
> **SH**: *ti* as in *nation*

Shaw couldn't have been trying very hard, if this was the best he could come up with. If he'd turned his attention to the other half of Britain's national dish, he could perfectly well have come up with *ghoughbteighpteau* for potato:

> **P**: *gh* as in *hiccough*
> **O**: *ough* as in *though*
> **T**: *bt* as in *debt*
> **A**: *eigh* as in *neighbour*
> **T**: *pt* as in *pterodactyl*
> **O**: *eau* as in *bureau*

Other languages have their eccentric spellings, of course, but English is in a league of its own. French, German, Spanish, Italian and Russian all spell more or less as they sound. English just isn't like that. If you heard individual words from this paragraph and were asked to write them out, how would you know to choose *more* rather than *moor* or *maw*? *Know* rather than *no*? *Would* rather than *wood*? *Write* rather than *right* or *rite*? *Or* rather than *oar*, *ore* or *awe*? *Their* rather than *they're* or *there*? *You* rather than *ewe*? *Course* rather than *coarse*? *But* rather than *butt*? *In* rather than *inn*? *For* rather than *four*, *fore* or even (for those acquainted with the archaic term for Scottish gypsies) *faw*? The answer is that, of course, you couldn't. But nothing happens without a reason, and the strange spellings of English have their reasons too, lurking deep in the heart of Shaw's potato.

P as in hiccough

The first point to make is that language is human. It's fallible. Or, not to beat about the bush, it's full of cock-ups. One such error is hiccough. The word first pops up in Elizabethan English as *hickop* or *hikup*, an adaptation of the earlier *hicket* or *hicock*. Now it's pretty clear from all these versions that the word was onomatopoeic, a fair attempt to catch the sounds of a hiccup in letters. But no sooner had the word decided to settle down than people started to assume that a hiccup was some sort of cough. And if a hiccup was a cough, then shouldn't it be written that way: *hiccough*, not *hiccup*? The answer was no, it shouldn't. Not then, and not now. The error grew nevertheless, until *hiccough* became at least as common as *hiccup*. The error is rejected by most dictionaries, but is still common enough that my computer spellcheck accepts both versions. Since people not dictionaries are the ultimate appeal court in these matters, then *hiccough* is certainly a real enough word, a mistake that's passed the test of time.

O as in though

Most oddities of English have little to do with straightforward errors. A bigger problem is that English is a living language, and its strangest spellings are often left as residues, like tree rings marking out past phases of growth.

English spellings largely derive from a particular period in British history, the fourteenth and fifteenth centuries. It's possible to be as precise as this for the simple reason that for the three hundred years or so following the Norman Conquest English had mostly disappeared as a written language. When official documents needed to be written, they'd been written in French or Latin. Thus by the time that English began to re-emerge from its long hiding, it was faced with the challenge of adopting a writing system almost, as it were, from scratch.

This could easily have been a recipe for disaster. People tended to spell as they pronounced, and regional accents of the time were very varied. There are more than five hundred spellings recorded for the word *through*. The word *she* had more than sixty, including:

Scae

Sse

Sche

Shae

Se

Che
Shee
Zhee
Sheea
Sheh
Shey
Sha
Sso
Sco
Scho
Schoe
Show
Sho
Shoy
Schew
Schw
Shoe
Shou
She
Su
Scheo
Sheo
Zhe

If you were writing just for your own friends, or to conduct business locally, perhaps none of this might have mattered. But as soon as official records and legal proceedings began using English too, then this kind of variation began to matter a lot; a common approach was called for. Naturally enough, London, home to the court and the senior echelons of the national bureaucracy, became dominant in imposing its spellings, in particular through the most senior bureaucrats of them all, the Masters of Chancery. Over time, they began to stamp their authority on the chaos. Out went all those *scheo*s and *sheea*s and *zhe*s, to be replaced by *she*. Out went *ich* (and many others) to be replaced by *I*. Because the movers and shakers of London spoke an English drawn mostly from London and the Midlands, our spelling is based largely on those accents.

Those early bureaucrats did a good job. Fifteenth-century English spelling was increasingly systematic and rational – a typical European language. Alas, however, no sooner had the spellings been fixed than pronunciations shifted. The spelling of words like *through*, *rough* and *right* is a perfectly accurate guide to the way these words used to be spoken. But the language has moved on, leaving these old medieval relics behind.

T as in debt

The silent B in debt is another tree ring.

When the Masters of Chancery were working to fix the language, there was a debate between those who thought that all spellings should be phonetic, and those who wanted them to be based on sound etymology. The phonetic camp won out in most cases, but not in all. Debt has a silent B, simply because medieval scholars wanted to point out that the word has its origins in the Latin *debere*, to owe. So a silent B was added – and never mind the fact that the word actually came from the French *dette*, which never had a B anywhere near it.

This was a quirky way to justify introducing a totally needless letter, and it was based on a more than generous interpretation of etymology, but there was, at least, an etymological connection, however thin. Medieval scholars were, however, prone to finding connections to the Latin where none actually existed, so our language is littered with plenty of spellings that are unjustifiable on any level. *Island* doesn't come from the Latin *insula*; it comes from an s-free Germanic root. (Compare modern German Eiland.) *Anchor, rhyme, scythe, island, numb, ghost* and many others derived their oddness from other errors fixed and perpetuated by Renaissance dictionaries.

A as in neighbour

All the problems so far mentioned fade into insignificance compared with the one identified by the A in Shaw's potato.

Just as the Masters of Chancery were producing the first rational spelling system in English, something was going on to turn all their fine work on its head. This was the Great Vowel Shift, which did exactly what it said on the tin. Before the shift, English vowels had been much the same as their Continental neighbours. The word *fine* in English used to be pronounced with an 'ee' sound, like the Italian *fino* ('fee-no'). If a four-teenth-century speaker of English had encountered a sentence like '*I see my goat is lame – my cow too*', they'd have pronounced it approximately as: '*Ee say mee gawt ays lahm – mee coo toe.*'

This sounds odd to us, but only because we're not used to it. At least English used its vowels in more or less the way you'd expect given its ancestry. Then, for no known reason, the vowels decided to get up from their fixed positions and wander round till they settled again in new places. The Chaucerian 'ee' sound became the modern 'eye' sound, the Chaucerian 'ay' became the modern 'ee', and so on.

The process was both strange and not strange at the same time. In some ways, nothing much could be more ordinary.

Language changes. If you want a *scone*, do you ask for a *scohne* or a *sconn*? If you talk about *dust*, do you use the southern 'uh' sound, or the shortened Yorkshire 'oo' sound? If a Brummie moves to a new part of the country – Liverpool, say, or Glasgow or Cornwall – they may well start to modify their vowel sounds, almost without noticing it. The Great Vowel Shift was in a way no odder than that – and bear in mind that it took place over two centuries, or the space of five or six medieval lifetimes.

On the other hand, the process is also a little odd. Why did English change so much and its closest neighbours little or not at all? And what propelled the movement? There is no shortage of theories. Social upheavals following the Black Death is one possibility. Another is that as the French-speaking ruling class came to speak English, there was a vogue for a kind of patriotic hypercorrection of French vowel sounds. But no one knows for sure. It's just one of those things.

The one certainty, however, is that English spellings were fixed before, during and after the shift. A word like *polite* (around before the shift) simply saw its pronunciation change, from something like *pol-eet* to the modern *pol-ite*. But an almost identical word – *police* – which entered the language after the shift reflects the Continental 'ee' sound of its origin. The result, of course, is that there's no way to tell in advance how a word should be spelled, or how a spelling should be spoken. Fine for those who grow up with the language; murder for those who have to learn it.

T as in pterodactyl

The first recorded reference to a pterodactyl is in Sir Charles Lyell's *Principles of Geology*. In it, Lyell predicts, 'The ptero-

dactyle might flit again through umbrageous groves
of tree-ferns.' Whether pterodactyls could ever
have been described as flitting is open to
doubt, but what's significant here
is that new words have to be coined
for new uses, and that one of the
biggest creators of new words
is science.

Scientists are only human. They want their coinages to have
a bit of class – and what could be more classy than a bit of Latin
or (still better) Greek? And since the ancient Greeks were fond
of their initial Ps, our language is now adorned with *pterodactyls* and *ptomaine* and *psychology* and many others. The
trouble with these introductions, of course, is that English
tongues can't really wrap themselves around such (to us) exotic
constructions. So the pronunciation tends to be anglicized,
while the spelling resolutely isn't.

O as in bureau

The final great complicating factor for English is highlighted by
the final letter of Shaw's potato. *Bureau* is a French word. It has
entered English with its pronunciation and spelling more or
less intact, but because the French match up vowel sounds and
letter combinations differently from us, their words only serve
to baffle and complicate our spellings.

That's not the only problem that can arise, however. Sometimes a new word entered the language – for example, *nation*,
another French borrowing – and English tongues weren't able
to wrap themselves around the foreign sounds. So the French
pronunciation, roughly *na-see-o(n)*, becomes corrupted to the

comfortable English *nay-shun*. Creations like this are hideously common. Do you want to guess how many ways there are to create the *sh* sound in English? You might play safe and say two or three. Or perhaps go wild and suggest five or six. The correct answer is in fact thirteen, as in *shed, sure, issue, mansion, passion, ignition, suspicion, ocean, conscious, chaperone, schedule, pshaw* and *fuchsia*.

Potato as in 𐑴𐑑𐑱𐑑𐑴

That's now every letter of Shaw's potato accounted for. Shaw himself so disliked the mess of spellings that he left money in his will for a prize to be awarded for the best new alphabet to take care of English spelling. The winner was a chap called Kingsley Read. As Read saw it, a big part of the problem with English spellings is that there are too few letters for the number of sounds they need to make. There are forty-eight distinct sounds in English, and only twenty-six letters to do their work. The letter A, for example, has at least four jobs to do: *ay* as in *able, a* as in *at, ah* as in *alms* and *or* as in *all*. If English is to be easy to spell, then there should be one sound to a letter, one letter to a sound. Read's alphabet, the Shavian alphabet, is a rather beautiful creation. It looks like this:

𐑨𐑤 𐑣𐑿𐑥𐑩𐑯 𐑚𐑰𐑦𐑙𐑟 𐑸 𐑚𐑹𐑯 𐑓𐑮𐑰 𐑯 𐑰𐑒𐑢𐑩𐑤 𐑦𐑯 𐑛𐑦𐑜𐑯𐑦𐑑𐑦 𐑯 𐑮𐑲𐑑𐑕. 𐑞𐑱 𐑸 𐑧𐑯𐑛𐑬𐑛 𐑢𐑦𐑞 𐑮𐑰𐑟𐑩𐑯 𐑯 𐑒𐑪𐑯𐑖𐑩𐑯𐑕 𐑯 𐑖𐑫𐑛 𐑨𐑒𐑑 𐑑𐑫𐑢𐑹𐑛𐑟 𐑢𐑳𐑯 𐑩𐑯𐑳𐑞𐑼 𐑦𐑯 𐑩 𐑕𐑐𐑦𐑮𐑦𐑑 𐑝 𐑚𐑮𐑳𐑞𐑼𐑣𐑫𐑛.

(That's the start of the Universal Declaration of Human Rights, in case you missed it.) Alas, however, no one ever used Read's alphabet. No one ever used Quickscript, his later modification of it. No one has ever used Readspel, Read's final attempt to get people on his side. And no one ever will.

In the end, weird spellings are only a problem if that's how you choose to see them. Part of the beauty of English is that its history is visible for all to see. It's a hybrid between Anglo-Saxon rootstock and Franco-Latinate blooms. It's a magpie language, acquisitive and reckless. It's a human language, strewn with errors and eccentricities. It's a living language, with vowels and pronunciations that shift from age to age. That won't ever change. The question really is, who'd want it to?

DECLINING TO CONJUGATE

For English speakers, one of the most striking facts about learning other languages is how bloomin' complicated they seem to be. A perfectly regular French verb has five different forms in its present tense alone. Adjectives have to vary depending on whether a noun is singular or plural, masculine or feminine. And French is easy. German has three genders, five cases. The Polish struggle with three genders and seven cases, and if that weren't enough, their nouns, adjectives, numbers and pronouns all decline differently. Italian has fifty forms for each verb, ancient Greek more than three hundred, modern Turkish an eye-popping two *million*.

For we Brits, this complexity seems simply astonishing. We have two standard noun forms, singular and plural – *dog* and *dogs*, for example. We have four standard verb forms: *bark*, *barks*, *barking* and *barked*. Our adjectives don't vary at all.* When we encounter a language with the complexity of Polish or Turkish, most of us find it simply stunning. It seems a wonder that Polish or Turkish toddlers ever manage to master the tongue at all.

To a linguist, however, the puzzle is a rather different one. English is a Germanic language, and the only one of its family

---

* With one exception: *blond* and *blonde*.

to have lost almost all inflections. English is, in fact, about the least inflected language ever known. The reason for this has nothing to do with some form of linguistic evolution, from 'primitive' inflected languages to 'modern' uninflected ones. Rather, the answer has to do with that most English of solutions to precarious situations: muddle, fudge and compromise.

Back in 878, Alfred the Great defeated the Danish army at Edington. The battle checked the hitherto unstopped Viking advance, and enabled Alfred to go on to negotiate a peace agreement which divided the country into two. A line was drawn diagonally across England, running roughly from Chester to London. The area to the south of the line would remain under English rule; the northern part (the 'Danelaw') would be ruled by the Danes (though most of those ruled, of course, would be English).

Trade carried on across the line, very much as before. After Alfred's son, Edward, had won back the Danelaw, then a common authority existed across the whole country, though pockets of Danish settlers were still widespread. Although frustratingly little is known about the pattern of Danish settlement, the likelihood is that significant numbers of Danes contined to come and settle across the eastern seaboard for the next two hundred years or so. Indeed, as late as the nineteenth century, linguists were recording language communities in Lincolnshire whose speech contained entire sentences that were effectively in Danish, not English. Old habits die hard.

Under these conditions – and largely in the east – Danes and English came into regular, daily, routine contact. The two communities would have been able to communicate with relatively little difficulty. Although the English spoke Old English and the Danes spoke Old Norse, the two languages were extremely close, rather in the way Norwegian and Swedish are today. The sentence 'I'll sell you the horse that pulls my cart' translates as:

OLD ENGLISH: *Ic selle the that hors the draegeth minne waegn*
OLD NORSE: *Ek mun selja ther hossit er dregr vagn mine*

The main words of this sentence are pretty close. *Sell* translates as *selle / selja*. Horse is *hors / hossit*, and so on. The speakers of one group could fairly easily have guessed the broad meanings of the other party's words. But what about all those word endings? The cases and genders, tenses, moods and the rest? The chances of a non-native speaker being able to guess the subtle implications of all those word endings would have been approximately nil.

So – and still only in the east – the word endings started to disappear. As traders and others sought to do business, Dane with English and vice versa, they simply started to drop the parts of the language that didn't function for them. The process moved furthest and farthest in the areas where Dane and English lived closest together. In the west of the country, where Danish influence was minimal, a highly inflected version of English lasted right into the fifteenth century.

In the end, though, the Easterners had the advantage of geography. London, Oxford and Cambridge all fell, more or less, into the eastern zone, and those three centres of cultural power ended up dictating the language the rest of the country would speak. In consequence, English went from being an ordinarily inflected language to one with almost no variation at all: the pidgin product of an uneasy peace.

How should one interpret this change? Almost certainly as a historical-linguistic quirk. Just one of those things. Yet it's hard to avoid a nagging sense of something further. There have been plenty of instances in which two similar linguistic communities have travelled and traded, mixed and mingled, yet English is exceptional in its lack of inflection. Were those early English exceptional in their desire to trade rather than fight, in their willingness to rub along with alien folk? The evidence falls a mile short of being conclusive, yet those same traits would prove to be reasonably prominent national characteristics many centuries down the road. Possibly, and only just possibly, those same traits were present way back in Anglo-Saxon times; that linguistic oddity their only surviving trace.

Whatever the answer to that particular conundrum, the inflections never came back. They are still eroding, very slightly, today. *Whom* has almost given way to *who*. The regional dialect *thou makes(t)* for the standard *you make* has just about vanished too. Those wonderful Danish-speaking Lincolnshire folk have been obliterated by the BBC and universal education and the internal combustion engine. (Though Lincolnshire dialect is still rich in words and phrases from Old Norse.)

This simplified, simplifying language offers one huge benefit to the world. To its billion and a half non-native speakers, English spelling is nothing but a plague and a torment. English inflections, by contrast, are now so simple you could learn them all in a minute, and still have time to put the kettle on.

A WORLD OF SQUANTOS

In November 1620, the Pilgrim Fathers made landfall off Plymouth Rock in Massachusetts. It wasn't the best time of year to arrive. The New England winter was more ferocious than anything the predominantly East Anglian settlers were used to. Nor were the precedents exactly encouraging. The first British settlement in North America had disappeared without trace. The second (in Jamestown, Virginia) had survived, but only after terrible loss of life. The Pilgrim Fathers weren't even well equipped. They were missing basic tools, and were astonishingly ignorant of both agriculture and fishing. Their prospects were lousy, and they knew it. In the words of the colony's first governor, William Bradford:

> And for the season it was winter, and they that know the winters of that country know them to be sharp and violent and subject to cruel and fierce storms, dangerous to travel to known places, much more to search an unknown coast. Besides, what could they see but a hideous and desolate wilderness, full of wild beasts and wild men?

From that hideous wilderness stepped forth a miracle. In the words of William Bradford again:

> Whilst we were busied hereabout, we were interrupted, for there presented himself a savage which caused an alarm. He very boldly came all alone and along the houses straight to the rendezvous, where we intercepted him, not suffering him to go in ... He saluted us in English and bade us 'welcome'.

The 'savage' who emerged from the Massachusetts woods had picked up a few words of English from visiting sailors, but the miracle hadn't yet taken place. The man who bade the settlers welcome took them to meet a second man, Tisquantum, abbreviated to Squanto. And Squanto spoke English; not just a few words, but fluently. Captured by British fishermen some fifteen years before, Squanto had been carried off to London, where he'd learned English and received training as a guide and interpreter, before managing to escape home again on a returning boat.

The unlikelihood of this sequence of events is simply astounding. What are the odds that a bunch of under-skilled and under-equipped Englishmen should pitch up and find perhaps the most fluent native American speaker of English anywhere on the continent? Squanto didn't just offer a taste of home. He taught the settlers the things they needed to know. He showed them how to sow their corn seeds with little bits of chopped fish for fertilizer. He taught them how to fish and how to distinguish what was edible from what was not. It's quite likely that Squanto saved the colony.

The story makes a point. Back then, English was a minor language, with limited projection beyond England's own boundaries. Today, it is the world's own language. Back then, it was the unlikelihood of finding a Squanto which made his appearance so miraculous. Today, a traveller could pitch up almost anywhere – any country, any coast, any continent – and hope to find some words of English spoken, by at least some members of the local community. The miracle today is not the rarity of English, but its universality.

That doesn't mean, of course, that English has become the world's most commonly spoken language. It hasn't. A billion Mandarin Chinese speakers dwarf the 350 million or so native English speakers. But that misses the point. To be a global language is to be the preferred means of communication between two parties from different language communities, and it's here where English is exceptional. On top of the 350 million native speakers, there are perhaps another 400 million speakers in former colonies, plus a billion or so speakers – from Japanese tourists to Swedish businessman – who have simply adopted the language as the simplest means of international communication. This number is growing all the time, not least in China, which will soon have more English speakers than the combined total of all English-speaking countries. No other language remotely compares with the global significance of English. Its lead is increasing all the time.

It's always tempting to romanticize the language's dominance, to start muttering about Shakespeare and Chaucer, the flexible euphony of our tongue. But Shakespeare, Schmakespeare. The world speaks English because of British gunboats (and emigrants) in the nineteenth century and American hegemony in the

twentieth. If those Mayflower settlers had happened to speak Ubykh, a Caucasian language with eighty-one consonants and only three vowels, or perhaps Rotokas, a Papua New Guinea language with just six consonants and five vowels, then the world would quite likely be speaking those fine languages today.

Meanwhile, English is spreading in other ways too. The Oxford English Dictionary currently lists about half a million words. Its American equivalent, Webster's, comes up with a roughly similar figure of 450,000. The two dictionaries have, however, much less of an overlap than you might guess. The OED contains more archaic or regional British terms, Webster's more Americanisms. Putting the two dictionaries together would probably produce an expanded word count of some 750,000 words. (I say probably: no one has ever bothered to work it out.) But even this total excludes huge swaths of English. It excludes terms from the various world Englishes (Singapore English, Jamaican English, Indian English, etc.). It excludes much slang and regional dialect. It excludes acronyms, even those that are usually used as words (CIA, NATO, the EU, and so on). It excludes most flora and fauna. If all these were added in, the word count would probably reach a million. If all scientific and technical terms were added, the count might be twice that. By comparison, French has an 'official' dictionary-based word count of less than 100,000 words, German around 190,000.

The sheer scale of its vocabulary is one of the key reasons why other languages are fighting a hopeless battle to keep English terminology out. It is all very well for the Académie Française to invent new French terms to replace Anglo-Saxon intruders, *autofinancement* for *cashflow*, for example. But what about those million or so technical and scientific terms – *bluetooth protocol*, *polypropylene*, *iPod*, *troposphere*? Is the Académie really going to invent new terms for those and all 999,997 others? In 2004, *The Economist* quoted research which suggested that two-thirds of all Internet content is in English. Scientific and technical journals are also disproportionately anglophone. English isn't just pushing other languages back, it's eating into them too.

What of the future? There are roughly two schools of thought. The first takes Latin as its example. The break-up of the Roman Empire led to the break-up of the language. Romanian, Italian, French, Spanish and Portuguese litter the linguistic map, the ruined remains of a once great empire. Romanian and Portuguese speakers may both be speaking linear descendants of the same language, but the languages have long since become mutually unintelligible.

Is this the fate of English? There's plenty of evidence to suggest it. After all, it's already slightly misleading to speak of one single language called 'English'. We have at the very least Indian English, American English, British English, Nigerian English, Philippines English, Canadian English, Pakistani English, Australian English, and so on. (The order of terms in that list might not be a conventional one, but it's perfectly logical: the terms are arranged in descending order, by size of the English language community.) But this list describes broad types only. Within every genus, there is an abundance of species. Not just Scouse English, but Caribbean Scouse, Pakistani Scouse, Irish Scouse, and so forth. If you sat in a Singaporean student café, among students speaking their version of English, you probably wouldn't understand what was being said. Perhaps the English break-up is already happening. Perhaps the rot has already set in.

Or then again, perhaps not. The counter-argument is simple: call it the eBay paradigm. In a world of highly competitive markets, eBay is rare and extraordinary in having virtually no meaningful competition. How come? Simply because eBay was the first, and as such it started out with the most buyers and the most sellers. Buyers naturally flock to the system with the most products to choose from. Sellers naturally gravitate to the outlet with the largest number of buyers. Unless eBay does something horrendous to mess up, its position is and will remain unrivalled. What's true of beanie toys and second-hand clothes is all the more true of a universal language. If you're an ambitious student keen to acquire a second tongue, which one does it make most sense to master? Obviously the one that gives access to the largest possible number of fellow speakers. So the larger the number of English speakers, the greater the incentive for others to to learn it. Dominance feeds dominance.

There perhaps lies the real point about that Singaporean café. If you were sitting there, sipping your *bandung* and picking at your fish-head curry, it's likely that your fellow diners would notice your difficulty in making sense of their conversation. So they'd probably just shift the way they spoke. From the idiosyncrasies of Singaporean youth English to something like an international Standard English. That Standard English would still be noticeably local in flavour. It would certainly be American tinted. But you'd understand it. They'd understand you. That's the point of a universal language. It makes one world of us all: a world of Squantos.

LITERATURE

LASHINGS OF POP

I am – or was, until this book – a novelist by trade. I've sold five novels, each of which has been translated into a fair number of different languages. Every contract I sign stipulates that I'm sent a royalty statement, and each royalty statement contains information on books sold. So does that mean I know how many books I've sold in total? No. Nothing of the sort. I couldn't even say to the nearest 10,000 copies.

In large part, that's due to my laziness. To work out an answer I'd have to crunch a lot of numbers, in order to produce a statistic that has no direct effect on my life and which will be out of date by the time I've crunched it. But in part too it's because the system doesn't make things simple. You'd think that a royalty statement from publisher to author would somewhere contain one simple figure equating to the total number of books sold. Not so. My own dear publisher sends me stats that make a phone bill from BT look like a model of limpid clarity. Nowhere on any document they've ever sent me is a single number that says, 'We've sold this many of your books'– the one stat that authors are likely to be most interested in.

When PR folk representing the likes of Dan Brown or J.K. Rowling claim that so many zillion copies have been sold, they probably have a pretty decent idea of the total, but decent isn't the same as accurate. Does Dan Brown's agent really know how many B-format paperbacks have been sold in the Ukraine? Or the exact number of cute little Japanese hardbacks, complete with facsimile signature and sash? Or the number of books printed in Braille for the Brazilian market? Personally, I doubt it.

All this poses a problem. There is no systematic way of knowing which authors have sold the largest numbers of books. No central agency monitors such things. Even the *Guinness Book of Records*, whose job it is to know such things, ends up using well-informed guesstimates. For those of us who are list maniacs at heart, this dearth of information falls rather hard.

Luckily, however, there is an alternative route to much the same goal. Ever since the advent of the printing press, books have been translated at the initiative of individual publishers and booksellers. In most markets, such practice would be regarded as normal, but to the orderly minds of the world's national librarians, the system seemed little short of anarchy. In the absence of some central register, national collections, such as the British Library, would struggle to keep track of all the published translations of major authors, such as Dickens and Shakespeare. Consequently, back in 1931, the League of Nations was pressured into setting up the first systematic record of translations, the *Index Translationum*. Fifteen years and one world war later, the United Nations took over the chore. In 1979, the system was computerized and a true cumulative database began to take shape. The world may have kept no record of books sold, but we do now possess excellent data on the next best thing: the number of translations made from them.

The statistics as presented by UNESCO don't always make the most perfect logical sense. UNESCO's top fifty includes a fair old number of authors who aren't really authors at all (Walt Disney Inc., different versions of the Bible). It also counts the two Grimm brothers separately though they wrote together, and it takes seriously the output of authors (Lenin, Marx, Engels, John Paul II) whose translations owed more to supply-push than the demand-pull of eager consumers. If these oddities are tidied away, then just forty-one authors remain.

Once cleaned up, the statistics confirm something that's been easy to sense but hard to prove: that no country on earth writes like we British. Of the forty-one most translated authors in the world, no less than fourteen, a full third of the total, are British. The next most translated country is the United States, whose much larger population has contributed just eleven names to the list. The entire rest of the world, with sixteen names on the list, barely counts for more than our little islands.

Authors by country
(rank in brackets, correct at time of writing)

Britain & Ireland	United States	Rest of World
Agatha Christie (1)	Danielle Steel (6)	Jules Verne (2)
Enid Blyton (3)	Stephen King (8)	Hans Christian Andersen (7)
William Shakespeare (4)	Mark Twain (10)	Grimm brothers (9)
Barbara Cartland (5)	Isaac Asimov (11)	Georges Simenon (12)
Arthur Conan Doyle (14)	Jack London (15)	Alexandre Dumas (13)
Robert Louis Stevenson (19)	Robert Stine (22)	Fyodor Dostoevsky (16)
Charles Dickens (20)	Nora Roberts (24)	René Goscinny (17)

Britain & Ireland	United States	Rest of World
Victoria Holt (23)	Sidney Sheldon (28)	Leo Tolstoy (18)
Oscar Wilde (25)	Ernest Hemingway (29)	Astrid Lindgren (21)
Alistair MacLean (27)	Robert Ludlum (33)	Rudolf Steiner (26)
James Hadley Chase (32)	Edgar Allan Poe (37)	Hermann Hesse (30)
J.R.R. Tolkien (34)		Honoré de Balzac (31)
Ruth Rendell (35)		Charles Perrault (36)
Rudyard Kipling (40)		Plato (38)
		Franz Kafka (39)
		Anton Chekhov (41)

It doesn't require a very long look at the table above to see that what's in question here isn't a battle fought out between the greats of literature. Although Shakespeare and Dickens, Tolstoy and Dostoevsky all make the grade, the table is dominated by popular authors of every stripe. Hercule Poirot beats Hamlet. The Famous Five and their lashings of ginger pop have sold better than Chekhov, Kafka and Plato put together. English literature (the normal, if patronizing, term for English, Welsh, Scots and Irish literature in English) may well be among the strongest of world literatures, but it's the success of Britain's more commercial authors which is particularly striking.

This success deserves to be celebrated rather than sneered at. British literature has given the world its most famous detectives: Hercule Poirot, Miss Marple and Sherlock Holmes. It has given the world its best-known spy, James Bond,* and its most literarily successful one, John le Carré's Smiley. It has given the world its seminal work of fantasy literature: *The Lord of the Rings*. Walter Scott, in his day, was one of the very first novelists

---

* Also its most famous secretary, Miss Moneypenny.

of genuinely international appeal. Robinson Crusoe and Jekyll & Hyde both added bold new archetypes to the imaginative resources of literature. It was a Briton, Wilkie Collins, who wrote the first true detective novel. Children around the world have thrilled to *Alice in Wonderland*, the Famous Five, Winnie-the-Pooh, Harry Potter, Peter Pan. These achievements are different from, and lesser than, the achievements of the Shakespeares and Chaucers, Dickenses and Austens – but they're achievements all the same.

It's tempting to ascribe these popular literary successes to the dominance of English as an international language. So universal has English become that it is surely easier for foreign translators to pick from English-language texts than ones in, say, Norwegian, Portuguese or Uzbek. UNESCO certainly appears to believe just that. On its website, it commented: 'This is perhaps one way of controlling the market and maintaining the cultural dominance of English and the market is controlled through what is on offer, through the availability of products sold by the industry of culture – whether it is music, or films or books.' (The atrociously mangled syntax of this sentence suggests that the 'industry of culture' would be in mortal danger if left to writers such as this.)

UNESCO, however, is just plain wrong. Just who exactly is thought to be 'controlling the market'? A conspiracy of top executives at News International and Walt Disney? An undercover alliance between the CIA and MI6? A secret society headed by Dan Brown and J.K. Rowling, his trusty lieutenant? The point about the book market is that it's a *market*. Readers buy whatever they want to read. Publishers publish anything that looks like selling. It's true that English acts as a convenient international clearing house. Japanese publishers wanting to translate a Danish text will most likely translate from the English version, not the Danish. In that sense, though, the universality of English makes works in minor tongues *more* available than they were before, not less. When great books come along in those minor tongues, they sell. The Danish language *Miss Smilla's Feeling for Snow* was a big hit. So was the Norwegian book *Sophie's World*. Contrary to what UNESCO might think, these books sold not because of a slip-up in the CIA's operating procedure, but because they were good to read. That, funnily enough, is what readers care about.

In the end, why should it seem so odd to argue that British writers do so well because they're good at what they do? Nobody has a problem accepting that the German musical tradition is (vastly) richer than the British one, that the Italians have done (infinitely) more for opera, that the French have done very much more for painting, and so on. We Brits aren't awful at these other art forms, but we don't excel. In literature, however, whether popular or highbrow, we do excel. It is *our* art form, the one that, for whatever reason, speaks more deeply to our national consciousness than any other.* It has done so since the time of Alfred the Great, when English vernacular literature was the most developed in Europe. It does so now.

---

* I'm using the word 'national' in a very broad sense here, since Ireland has made a quite disproportionate contribution to 'English' literature. Since the death of Shakespeare, the greatest dramatists of the British Isles have arguably been Congreve, Sheridan, Wilde, Synge, Shaw and Beckett – every one of them Irish.

OF COWS AND BEEF

The word *Welsh* derives from an Anglo-Saxon root, *Wealas*, which means slave or foreigner. There, in a nutshell, is all you need to know about the politics of sixth-century Britain. The incoming Angles, Jutes and Saxons had turned the native British Celts into foreigners in their own land; not quite slaves perhaps, but humiliatingly subject all the same.

Anglo-Saxon rule didn't extend merely to land and territory; it covered language too. Although a certain amount of inter-marriage must have taken place between invaders and 'slaves', that intermarriage was reflected hardly at all in the spoken word. Virtually no Celtic words survived the onslaught, and those that did are telling. Modern English words such as *tor*, *crag*, *combe*, *cairn*, *cromlech*, *dolmen* and *loch* are all Celtic, and they all describe features of the landscape which simply hadn't existed in the flatlands from which the invaders had come. The newcomers took the words they absolutely needed and ditched the rest. Only a few dozen Celtic words survive in English today.

While the Celts always referred to their invaders as Saxons,* the newcomers themselves began to call themselves *Anglii*, their new country *Anglia*, and (in due course) their language *Englisc*. It's that language which we speak today. Of the hundred most

---

* They still do. That's what the Scots word *Sassenach* means.

commonly used words in modern English, almost all are Old English in origin, including all but one of the top twenty-five. (In order: *the, of, and, a, to, in, is, you, that, it, he, was, for, on, are, as, with, his, they, I, at, be, this, have, from.* The Old Norse intruder in this list is *they.* The word *the* appears in this book some 5,850 times.) These twenty-five words make up about one third of all printed material in English. The top hundred words make up about a half. The first French-derived word doesn't appear until *number* at seventy-six.

You can tell a lot about a society from the language it speaks. The language of the *Anglii* was domestic, rural, warlike, concrete. Words such as *man, daughter, friend* and *son* are Old English. So are *dog, mouse, wood, swine, horse.* So are *plough, earth, shepherd, ox, sheep.* So are *love, lust, sing, night, day, sun.* So are words such as *so, are, words, such, as.* The one linguistic invasion of real significance in those years was Christianity. As the pagan Anglo-Saxons began to convert to the new religion, new words (mostly Greek or Roman in origin) crept in to handle the new concepts: *bishop, monk, nun, altar, angel, pope, apostle, psalm, school.* The number of new words was small, less than 1 per cent of the existing vocabulary, but they extended the language by giving it ways of expressing new thoughts, new concepts.

With the language to do it, the Anglii began to produce a literature of their own, probably a great one. If people wanted to preserve their work, they wrote not in English but in Latin. As a consequence, most work that was written in English has been lost for ever. Fortunately, though, enough of the old literature has survived for us to get a feel of what was lost. *Beowulf* is the first great surviving work of literature written in English, a story of strange monsters and Dark Age realpolitik. Here, in

Seamus Heaney's translation, is the arrival of the monster Grendel at the feasting hall:

> In off the moors, down through the mist-bands
> God-cursed Grendel came greedily loping.
> The bane of the race of men roamed forth,
> hunting for a prey in the high hall.
> Under the cloud-murk he moved towards it
> until it shone above him, a sheer keep
> of fortified gold. Nor was that the first time
> he had scouted the grounds of Hrothgar's dwelling –
> although never in his life, before or since,
> did he find harder fortune or hall-defenders.

This extract gives us the true feel of Anglo-Saxon: gritty, alliterative, forceful, direct. In Heaney's words: 'What I had always loved was a kind of four-squareness about the utterance … an understanding that assumes you share an awareness of the perilous nature of life and are yet capable of seeing it steadily and, when necessary, sternly. There is an undeluded quality about the Beowulf poet's sense of the world.'

Warrior-like it may have been, but Anglo-Saxon almost died nevertheless – not just once, but twice. The first major threat came with the Viking invasions when, but for Alfred the Great, we might well have ended up speaking Norse, not English. The second near-death experience came with the Norman Conquest in 1066. Because the new king, William, had been hard up for cash, he'd paid for much of his help with pledges of English land. When victory came, those pledges were redeemed. All of a sudden, every position of power in England was filled by French speakers. The new noblemen spoke French. Bishops and abbots spoke French. The court spoke French. The king made a short-lived effort to learn English, then gave up and stuck to French. As an official language, English completely vanished. In its written form, its disappearance was almost total.

For centuries, a kind of linguistic apartheid reigned. English peasants continued to speak English. The court continued to speak French. But in between the top and bottom layers of society, mixing was inevitable, as Normans married English, as French babies were cared for by local women. At the level where the two societies met, the English language underwent the most rapid – and important – transformation of its life.

A torrent of new words poured in from the French, thousands of them, far more than had ever come from Norse or Celtic. The Normans brought a new kind of justice and administration to the land. *Arrest, attorney, bail, bailiff, felony, fine, pardon, perjury* and *verdict* all come from the French. They brought new concepts of chivalry: *courtesy, damsel, honour, romance, tournament, chivalry*. The arts, science, the domestic scene – all borrowed heavily from French words: *music, paper, melody, grammar, calendar, ointment, pantry, lamp, curtain, chimney*. And while the English worked the fields tending the *oxen* or *cows, sheep, calves, deer* and *pigs* (all English words), it was as often as not their French masters who got to eat the resulting *beef, mutton, veal, venison* and *pork* (all French ones).

On the whole, these new words didn't replace the older English ones, they sat alongside them. That's why the language now has so many alternatives: the fancy French model and the plainer English one. For example, the English *ask* sits beside the French *question, interrogate, demand*. The English *king* rubs shoulders with *royal, regal, sovereign*. We have English *hands* but do French *manual* work. For three hundred years such words poured over the Channel, leaving English immeasurably enriched, a different language.

It wasn't just new words, it was new ways of writing too. Compare these two bits of verse, one French, one English.

> Foy porter, honneur garder
> Et pais querir, oubeir
> Doubter, servir, et honnourer
> Vous vueil jusques au morir
> Dame sans per.

(I want to stay faithful, guard your honour / Seek peace, obey / Fear, serve and honour you / Until death / Peerless lady –
Guillaume de Machaut.)

And the English one:

> Summer is y-comen in,
> Loude sing, cuckoo!
> Groweth seed and bloweth mead
> And spring'th the woode now –
> Sing cuckoo!
> Ewe bleateth after lamb,
> Low'th after calfe cow.
> Bullock starteth, bucke farteth.
> Merry sing, cuckoo! (*Anon*)

The French verse is smooth, melodious, liquid. It is clever writing. Its themes are courtly love, honour and chivalry; its principal sound effect coming from that smoothly repeated soft rhyme. The English verse is the exact opposite. It's earthy, lusty and crude. It talks about animals and farts. It's a language at home in the fields, not the court. It uses rhyme, but does so not in a smooth and flowing way like the French, but in a way designed to make the most of the natural swing and rhythm of spoken English. That old Anglo-Saxon taste for alliteration is still there (*calf / cow, bullock / buck*). This is a language that enjoys its own sound effects; the one thing it won't do is stay polite and well mannered.

The point isn't that one form of writing is better than the other. The point is that English writers suddenly faced a huge expansion in their *choice* of how to write. They could be lusty, earthy, crude, jaunty. Or they could be Latinate, posh, abstract, clever. Or, like Chaucer and Shakespeare, they could mix and match, moving from the earthy to the sublime and back again. That expressive richness has been the language's greatest resource, and it has been core to the achievements of its greatest writers.

That choice of how to write is still with us today. Britain's two best-known poets of recent times have been Ted Hughes and Philip Larkin. Here is Ted Hughes, writing about a ewe having problems giving birth:

> I caught her with a rope. Laid her, head uphill
> And examined the lamb. A blood-ball swollen
> Tight in its black felt, its mouth gap
> Squashed crooked, tongue stuck out, black-purple,

> Strangled by its mother. I felt inside,
> Past the noose of mother-flesh, into the slippery
> Muscled tunnel, fingering for a hoof …

This is Anglo-Saxon in modern clothes. Hughes is earthy, concrete, in-yer-face. He uses compound nouns, alliteration and thumping stresses. It's verse that lives in the fields, and raises two fingers to the court.

Here, in contrast, is the way Philip Larkin writes about animals – in his case, retired racehorses.

> Yet fifteen years ago, perhaps
> Two dozen distances sufficed
> To fable them: faint afternoons
> Of Cups and Stakes and Handicaps,
> Whereby their names were artificed
> To inlay faded, classic Junes …

This is pure French. The language is Latinate, high-flown, smooth and elegant; a language comfortable with the Royal Enclosure, not the dung and straw of the stable yard.

In short, English became – and remained – a language in which you could swear like a German, or seduce like a Frenchman. You could make war using one vocabulary, and philosophize with another. No other European language has that suppleness, that blend of Germanic directness and Latinate elegance. If our literary tradition is as great as any in the world, then that greatness owes much to the language that gave it birth.

HALF-CHEWED LATIN

It began with the Black Death.

In Bristol, where it struck first in 1348, some 45 per cent of the population died. Across the country, the death toll was lower, but still vast. As the country fell dying, the only growth industry was that of burial, and since priests were constantly in contact with the sick and dying, the death rate among the clergy probably exceeded even that of the general population. In January 1349, the Bishop of Bath and Wells wrote, 'Priests cannot be found for love nor money … to visit the sick and administer the last sacraments.' Since those last sacraments would have been viewed as of vital importance in Catholic England, the problem was a serious one. Dreadful times bring drastic remedies. The bishop went on to say that, in the absence of a priest, it would be proper for the dying to confess their sins to a lay person or even (steady on!) 'to a woman if no man is available'.

Perhaps it was this new DIY approach to dying which fostered new ways of thinking, or perhaps it was simply the collision between hard times and a complacent Church. At all events, the age produced its revolutionary, an Oxford scholar named John Wyclif. Wyclif began to compare the Church he saw around him with the words of scripture, and he found the Church wanting. He wrote, 'Were there a hundred popes and all the friars turned to cardinals, their opinions on faith should not be accepted except in so far as they are founded on scripture itself.'

Logically, then, if scripture was so important, it should be available to everyone – and available in English, not Latin. In our own secular times, it's hard to get overexcited by such a suggestion, but in a world where it was not altogether clear whether Church or state exerted more power, Wyclif's proposal was revolutionary, a clear threat to the status quo.

Wyclif didn't just talk about what ought to be done, he made sure that it was done. A group of scholars, working in line with Wyclif's doctrines, began to translate the Bible. It was by no means the first time in European history that a vernacular translation had been produced, but it was the first time that a complete translation had been produced by serious scholars working in explicit defiance of Church doctrine. To offer a contemporary analogy, it was as if Wyclif and his fellows were seeking to introduce the freedoms of the Internet to a society that had long known only state-owned media. The English language was the battering ram. The result, one day, would be the Protestant Reformation itself.

Yet for all Wyclif's thundering denunciations of the Church, those first attempts at translation were oddly timorous. It was just as if, when it came to the point, the translators didn't quite have the nerve to leave the original text behind. Here, for instance, is a chunk taken from the first psalm.

> Blisful the man, that went not awei in the counseil of unpitouse, and in the wei off sinful stod not; and in the chayer of pestilence sat not, But in the lawe of the Lord his wil; and in the lawe of hym he shal sweteli thenke dai and nygt.

Even putting aside the archaic spellings, this text reads more like half-chewed Latin than proper English. But it was a start. Its authors must have recognized the weakness of that early version, because no sooner had the first translation been finished than a new and better one was begun. Those translations were transcribed by hand, then disseminated by wandering Lollard preachers. (Lollard, from the Middle Dutch word meaning 'a babbler of nonsense', came to be applied pejoratively to all Wyclif's followers, who then came to embrace the term enthusiastically.)

In a land where books were rare and precious, where the language of salvation had always been incomprehensible to the vast bulk of the population, those Bibles must have been the most extraordinary experience: liberating, poetic, exciting, inspiring. Many parish priests, indeed, would have understood next to nothing of the Latin that they had so solemnly intoned in church. With Wyclif's new Bibles, weavers and housewives were suddenly being let into knowledge of God's word itself, secrets that had previously been the property of only a tiny handful.

Inevitably, of course, the movement was suppressed. Wyclif's manuscripts were burned and the Lollards themselves arrested, often killed. But just as today the tide of technology tends to favour the Internet over those seeking to erect barriers against it, so too did the invention of the printing press shift things decisively in favour of revolution. Wyclif's translations had had to be copied, slowly and painfully, by hand. Those that came after him in England and (particularly) Germany could churn out copies by the thousand. Costs fell, print runs increased. By 1526, William Tyndale, heavily influenced by Martin Luther, printed three thousand copies of his English language New

Testament, then sold each copy for as little as four shillings. The authorities could no more track down and burn each copy than they could order trees to hold their leaves in autumn. An English-speaking God had finally, decisively arrived.

As far as British exceptionalism is concerned the story ends there. An Englishman, John Wyclif, inaugurated a movement that would lead to the most important development in the Christian Church since the split between Catholic and Orthodox. That movement then shifted its centre of gravity eastwards to Germany, and England played no more than a secondary role in what followed. Yet to end the story at that point leaves off, at least from a literary point of view, its conclusion.

As we know, Henry VIII broke with Rome and, on his death, the Archbishop of Canterbury, Thomas Cranmer, converted the English Church into a genuinely Protestant one, something it had not been during Henry's reign. During the six-year reign of Edward VI, around sixty new versions of the Bible were released. More followed under Elizabeth, then James.

Compared with the old days, this was liberation indeed, but a troubling one all the same. It was all very well to write the gospels in the language of ploughboys, but the translations couldn't all be equally good. Which ones were right, which wrong? It was time to set up a committee.

The committee in question was a bureaucrats' daydream. Fifty-four translators were appointed, split across six working groups, who toiled away for six years. The results were fed into yet another committee, a review committee, comprising scholars from Oxford, Cambridge and London. The review panel spent nine months in honing their texts. The result of their labours, the Authorised Version of the Bible (or the King James Bible), could have been a bureaucratic disaster, a hotch-potch of muddle and compromise. It was nothing of the sort. It has become, deservedly, one of the great monuments of English.

The secret of its success was a simple one. All the committees, but most especially the final review committee, paid close attention to what would *sound* good when read aloud. Furthermore, keeping to their mandate of making scriptures accessible, the translators stuck to a honed-down lexicon of just eight thousand words. (Shakespeare, by contrast, uses some twenty thousand.) The result was grand, spare, sonorous and easy to understand. Here, for example, are the famous words from John's Gospel, given in some of the major versions of the Bible up to this point:

AN ANGLO-SAXON VERSION (995): '*God lufode middan-eard swa, dat he seade his an-cennedan sunu, dat nan ne forweorde de on hine gely ac habbe dat ece lif.*'

WYCLIF (1380): *'For god loued so the world; that he gaf his oon bigetun sone, that eche man that bileueth in him perisch not: but haue euerlastynge liif.'*

TYNDALE (1534): *'For God so loveth the worlde, that he hath geven his only sonne, that none that beleve in him, shuld perisshe: but shuld have everlastinge lyfe.'*

KING JAMES (1611): *'For God so loved the world, that he gave his only begotten Sonne: that whosoever beleeveth in him, should not perish, but have everlasting life.'*

Among these different versions, Wyclif's words, with their strange spellings and disconcerting rhythms, seem to us like ancient history. The Anglo-Saxon *is* ancient history. Tyndale's version rings out almost as clear and modern as the King James version. But it is only in its final appearance that these lines find their feet; meaning, rhythm and weight coming together in perfect balance.

That Bible in that version is one of the great monuments of our, or any, literature.* It, every bit as much as Shakespeare, has shaped the language we use today. Whether we are *fruitful and multiply* or are *at our last gasp*, whether we *serve two masters* or *cast our pearls before swine*, whether we *live by bread alone* or off *the fat of the land* that *flows with milk and honey*, then in this *den of thieves* (for *by their fruit shall we know them*) we are quoting the Bible. If *we have ears to hear*, if *nation should rise against nation*, if we *pass by on the other side*, if we *kick against*

---

* The same could be said of Luther's 1534 German-language Bible, as much a literary landmark as a religious one.

the pricks, if we are *full of good works* or a *law unto ourselves*, if we say, '*Doctor, heal thyself*,' and if *we take up our beds and walk* (doubtless escorting *the poor whom we have always with us*), if we are *present in spirit*, if we *suffer fools gladly*, if we cry '*Oh death, where is thy sting?*' then (*be of good cheer*) we are quoting the Bible. In short, *where two or three are gathered together*, we can but find that we *live, move and have our being* in the world that Wyclif, Tyndale and the King James translators created.

The influence of that Bible lies in far more than just a couple of hundred famous phrases. As I was writing this chapter, I happened to pick up a copy of my third novel, *The Sons of Adam*, where I came across the following sentence: 'Tom would be happy if all the kings of the earth had been turned overnight into ordinary people: shoe-shine boys, oil-riggers, commercial travellers, bums.' That phrase 'the kings of the earth' is straight from the Authorised Version (Revelation 6:15 if you care to check) and it isn't standard English today. 'All the kings in the world' would be more normal, or perhaps even 'Every king on the planet'. But I had wanted a grander phrase than that, something to point up a contrast with the 'ordinary people' that followed. I've probably never read the relevant bit of Revelation and I certainly didn't consciously reach for the language of King James, yet because I was after something sonorous, grand and spare, my subconscious took me there anyway – just as thousands of other writers have been led, wittingly or unwittingly, to the exact same source. That's influence. That's greatness.

A WILDERNESS OF MONKEYS

Shakespeare. What is there to say about him that hasn't already been endlessly said? How to find a new angle on this most talked-about figure? In the end, mightn't it be best just to sidestep the Bard and talk about other things instead?

Except that one can't. In a book on British exceptionalism, Shakespeare simply insists on being heard. In the onrushing torrent of history, his is one of the few individual rocks to jut out above the waters: not simply the man of his moment, a product of time and place, but a genius for all time. As far as Britain is concerned, only Newton occupies a similar place. Perhaps, at a long stretch, Darwin too. To avoid Shakespeare just because he's too hard to talk about would leave an absence in this book so loud as to be deafening.

Shakespeare was, of course, one of the greatest writers of his or any other age. The infuriating thing about him is his perfection. Most writers, even great ones, have their strengths and weaknesses. Dickens is, for all his glories, also sentimental and vulgar. Jane Austen, for all hers, wrote confidently only within very narrow limits and almost never strayed beyond them. Wordsworth is often pedestrian, Tennyson often stupid. That's not to diss those writers, it's just to note their human foibles. Shakespeare, curse the man, appeared to have none. Whether you want lyrical, stirring, witty, clever, romantic, sad, spiritual, angry, psychologically perceptive, evocative – anything at all – Shakespeare is up there with the very best of English or any other literature. He wrote in verse so totally unstrained you'd swear he drank pentameters with his mother's milk. With other poets, even great ones like Milton, there's always a sense of effort. The result may be wonderful, but you can smell the sweat. Not so with Shakespeare.

The Bard, however, did something more for art than simply illuminate it for one shortish lifetime. He altered it – not just English literature, but Western literature – for ever. In particular (and this is a point brilliantly made by John Carey in his *What Use Are the Arts?*) he was the first writer ever to understand fully the possibilities of *indistinctness* in language – a blurry allusiveness, a sideways leap into the non-rational, the sudden electric crackle of subconscious connection. To see what I mean, consider (as Carey does) the following two snippets, both talking about jewels, both written by English playwrights, both dating from the 1590s.

Bags of fiery opals, sapphires, amethysts,
Jacinth, hard topaz, grass-green emeralds,
Beauteous rubies, sparkling diamonds

CHRISTOPHER MARLOWE, *The Jew of Malta*

Thou torturest me Tubal, – it was my turquoise, I had it of Leah when I was a bachelor: I would not have given it for a wilderness of monkeys.

WILLIAM SHAKESPEARE, *The Merchant of Venice*

The Marlowe passage is perfectly decent writing. The length of his list suggests the depth and richness of the treasure. His adjectives bring in hints of feel, colour, light, even temperature. If you studied a how-to book on good writing, a decent student would probably come up with something like the bit from Marlowe.

Shakespeare, however, simply overleaps these more pedestrian qualities. First, there's that 'thou torturest me Tubal'. All of a sudden, that turquoise isn't just a precious stone, it's become an instrument of psychic torture. Just four words in, and Shakespeare's already outclassed Marlowe by a country mile. But then comes the phrase that makes Shylock's turquoise really flash into being. Shylock says he wouldn't surrender that stone 'for a wilderness of monkeys'. What on earth does he mean? What wilderness? What monkeys? Why would monkeys be likely to inhabit a wilderness? More to the point, why should a wilderness of monkeys be valuable currency in any case? Cold logic would rate a wilderness of monkeys rather low down on any list of financial assets, so Shylock's expostulation hardly suggests that the turquoise has value. Except that it does. Cold logic has nothing to do with it. Shylock cares so much about that damn stone that his reason almost deserts him, and it's the inexpressible genius of that phrase to make us feel the stone, and Shylock, and the intensity of the moment, as though we were right there in the man's head.

That's what Shakespeare can make of a one-off phrase. When he brings that same extra-logical suggestiveness into a sustained passage of poetry, no writer has ever touched him. Here's a piece from *Antony and Cleopatra*, in which Cleopatra is mourning and praising her now-dead lover:

> His legs bestrid the ocean; his reared arm
> Crested the world; his voice was propertied
> As all the tuned spheres, and that to friends;
> But when he meant to quail and shake the orb,
> He was as rattling thunder. For his bounty,
> There was no winter in't; an autumn 'twas
> That grew the more by reaping; his delights
> Were dolphin-like, they showed his back above
> The element they lived in; in his livery
> Walked crowns and coronets, realms and islands were
> As plates dropped from his pocket.

There's no question that this is writing of the very highest quality. But could anyone paint a picture of the Antony that Cleopatra is talking about? His legs straddle the ocean, but only his dolphin-like back appears to be above water. His bounty is autumnal, although (perhaps because of all that orb-shaking) he has a habit of dropping island-sized dinner plates from his back pocket, presumably biffing those crowns and coronets on the way. Taken at face value, the passage is nonsense. This is mixed metaphor taken to the max. In Shakespeare's hands, however, it (inevitably) works.

Such work, however strange it must first have sounded, was too self-evidently brilliant to leave literature unaltered. On the contrary, however hard it was for other writers to follow that

first example, follow it they would strive to do. The consequence has been that Shakespeare brought the vast richness of
the inexplicable and extra-logical not just to English but to
world literature. Writers since him may not have touched those
heights, but they have a new resource to make use of, a new
mode of expression, a new way to communicate meaning. In
twenty-first-century writing, be it in English or Japanese, those
methods are now routinely deployed. Though it would be easy
for us to forget that such things have to be discovered,
perfected and disseminated, we shouldn't do so. Shakespeare
was literature's benefactor; that 'wilderness of monkeys' his
remarkable gift.

LAW

THE RUSTICS OF ENGLAND

In 1154, England acquired a new king: Henry II.

Henry, grandson of William the Conqueror, was about as English as *saucisson* and *baguettes*. Not being English, he also had a very un-English drive for centralization and order. He put the barons in their place, knocking down any castles that hadn't obtained regal planning permission; he streamlined the tax system; he overhauled record-keeping; and he turned his attention to the courts.

From Anglo-Saxon times on, England had enjoyed the most developed state apparatus in Europe, including a set of shire and local 'hundred' courts. These courts did their job, up to a point. The laws they applied were mostly unwritten, customary hand-me-downs,

passed from one generation to the next. The methods of trial were somewhat confused, being a mixture of the traditional trial-by-ordeal and the newfangled trial-by-jury, or indeed, sometimes by a hybrid of the two. If this was confusing, then so too was the law itself. The lack of clear central control meant that the law in Exeter represented something different from the law in Carlisle. No one had ever experienced or expected anything else, and the system worked at least as well as it did anywhere else, and quite likely a fair bit better.

Yet Henry wasn't a king willing to put up with anything so ramshackle. Legal disputes had a habit of ending up with the king himself. Although a court system existed, Henry could hardly delegate authority to it with a great degree of confidence that the system would actually deliver the effects expected of it. In place of those variable, regional, hard-to-control courts, he therefore instituted a new system of royal judges who roved the land, dispensing justice. The new judges combined local reach and royal power. Although justice came to the people just as it had always done, it now came with explicit royal authority and, particularly on the civil side, a common set of procedures and practices. No other European country had such an advanced or complete system. It was an English first.

Yet the reform was a partial one, all the same. The courts had certainly been shaken up but, in terms of criminal proceedings, neither the laws nor modes of trial were much affected. Jury trial continued slowly to displace those trials-by-ordeal, which had been falling out of fashion not just in England but elsewhere. (And to begin with juries were asked only to decide questions of fact, not those of guilt or innocence. These things develop slowly.) The laws enforced were the same hand-me-downs as before. Yet no one argued for more radical reform.

Back in twelfth-century England, no one was expecting or asking for any more – indeed, there wasn't even a concept of what 'more' might be. So Henry left the system to bed in, while he rushed off to do other things, such as have Thomas à Becket chopped to pieces in Canterbury Cathedral.*

For the English, the period of radical change was over. For Europe, it was only just beginning. European monarchs faced the same problems as Henry, but they came up with a sharply different solution. Scholars at the Continent's first true universities began to blow the dust off old Roman codes of law, and they liked what they saw. Roman law looked like the real deal: a universal law code; formal rules of evidence; professional judges – and the whole thing sanctified by its posh Roman origin.

The 'new' Roman codes swept across the Continent like wildfire. In places like Sweden and northern France, where jury trials had once been used, such outmoded things were swept aside in the modernizing rush. And why not? The new Roman model was logical, scholarly, professional and modern. The system that had evolved in England looked rustic, antiquated, lowbrow and embarrassing.

But which was better?

Roman law contained one very liberal-sounding provision. In the effort to avoid false convictions, an accused man could only be convicted if (i) he made a full confession, or (ii) there were two sworn eyewitnesses to the crime. The provision sounded surprisingly liberal for the age, but it concealed a nasty catch. On the whole, criminals weren't so monumentally stupid

---

* Becket's murder could just have been a teeny misunderstanding, of course. History is as yet undecided.

as to commit their crimes in the presence of two eyewitnesses, so, in most cases, the only route to conviction was via confession. But who would be so stupid as to confess? No one, of course – unless inducements were put in their way, and the inducement of choice was torture. In effect, Roman law was a law of torture. An entire jurisprudence of torture was concocted. Who could be tortured and for how long, by what methods, for which crime? Answers needed to be found to such questions – and were. Torture remained commonplace for centuries, lasting well into the eighteenth century.

Meanwhile, England had no torture. It was unknown – indeed, forbidden – under the common law. It was down to juries to determine guilt or innocence, on the basis of evidence and common sense. The consequences of this difference are simply enormous. First, there's quite simply the question of obtaining verdicts that made sense. A thirteenth-century English court was no doubt a pretty rudimentary place but, if you stood in the dock, you could at least rely on the fact that you were being judged by twelve ordinary blokes, sworn to a standard of truthful enquiry, considering matters on the basis of ordinary reason and evidence. On the Continent, by contrast, guilt or innocence was determined mostly by the accused's capacity to resist torture. Hardened criminals with strong nerves could escape scot-free. The innocent with weaker nerves would be tortured, then convicted. Furthermore, whether or not guilt was ever determined, the accused had *already* been punished, in one of the least pleasant ways imaginable. Just as bad, Roman law established a system whereby paid agents of the state regularly inflicted cruelty of the worst sort on its citizens. The entire relationship of the individual to the state was imprinted by that basic power relationship. It was a terrible, terrible system and it endured for centuries.

Nor was it only a characteristic of the state. The Church's codes of justice were also Roman in inspiration, and the Church came to regard torture as an essential part of its soul-protection duties.* When Philip IV wanted to crush the supposedly heretical Templar movement in France, he used torture widely and indiscriminately, with the knowledge and blessing of the Church. English kings too were under an obligation to eliminate heresy, but more or less refused to do so via torture. This English intransigence risked annoying the Holy Father. Pope Clement V wrote to Edward II, saying, 'We hear that you forbid torture as being contrary to the laws of your land; but no state can override Canon Law, Our Law; therefore I command you at once to submit these men to torture … You have already imperilled your soul as a favourer of heretics … Withdraw your prohibition and we grant you remission of sins.' The Pope, in other words, was *ordering* an English king to torture supposed heretics on pain of damnation. Edward formally gave way, but the Inquisition failed to establish itself in England: English soil would remain alien to its practices. Torture remained uncommon. The death penalty from religious courts remained rare.

As for the provincialism of England's rustic little methods, time was to change all that. Where the British Empire led, the common law followed. The United States has a version of common law. So do most other former colonies, including Canada, Australia, New Zealand, India, Pakistan, Malaysia and

---

* Nobody had anticipated this outcome when Roman codes were first introduced – but as we know, *no one* expects the Spanish Inquisition.

numerous others. What's more, Enlightenment Europe came to have a growing moral revulsion to its reliance on torture. The existence of the English model proved that there were other ways to do things; ways that didn't involve a collapse of law and order. The English system was widely cited, widely copied. The Continent retained its civil law traditions, of course, but it adapted them. Torture went out; new evidential procedures came in. Cruelty began to drain out of that basic relationship between individual and the state. In the strange and unpredictable way of history, those old English rustics ended up shaping the law not merely of England, but half the world besides.

'NO FREE MAN ...'

It was the early thirteenth century. England was at war, the enemy was France, and England was coming off worse. When John, the English king, returned home, he faced an unprecedented degree of resentment from his barons, who were angry about a number of things, not least John's failure to fulfil that most basic requirement of English kingship: to give the French a good walloping. Worse still, he'd managed to lose Normandy, home to many an Anglo-Norman *grand-père* and *grand-mère*. Resentment led to rebellion. The rebellion was no moral crusade, and most barons either supported the king or remained studiedly neutral. The leading rebels, indeed, were lawless men with deep personal animosity towards the king, and interests stretching not much farther than their wallets.

John, like any half-competent medieval monarch, knew just what to do: he wouldn't negotiate with the rebels, he'd slaughter them. Events, however, ran away from him. The rebels seized London and forced John into a negotiated settlement. A treaty was drawn up, and incorporated into a legal agreement known as the Great Charter, or Magna Carta. On 15 June 1215, the king's Great Seal was affixed to the final draft 'in the meadow which is called Runneymede between Windsor and Staines'.

The moment is one of those defining moments of English history: up there in 'name recognition' with the battles of

Hastings and Waterloo, comfortably exceeding such seismic events as the Glorious Revolution for sheer memorability. But what exactly had happened? It wasn't obvious then and isn't so now.

The answer, on the face of it, is not a lot. There are very few sweeping political statements in the charter. Most of its articles are yawn-inducingly dull, and virtually every clause has been repealed. We no longer rejoice at the freedoms given us by Clause 23:

No town or person shall be forced to build bridges over rivers.

Clause 31 doesn't cause the Queen too many sleepless nights:

Neither we nor any royal official will take wood for our castle … without the consent of the owner.

Clause 35 is now mostly honoured in its breach:

There shall be a standard width of dyed cloth, russett, and haberject, namely two ells within the selvedges.

And the de Athée family has probably recovered from the humiliation of Clause 50:

We will remove completely from their offices the kinsmen of Gerard de Athée … namely, Engelard of Cigogne, Peter, Guy, and Andrew of Chanceaux, Guy of Cigogne, Geoffrey of Martigny with his brothers, Philip Mark with his brothers and his nephew Geoffrey, and the whole brood of the same.

What's more, there was
nothing especially unusual
about the idea of a written
charter between king and
nobles. Medieval states across
Europe lived in constant
tension between the power of
the centre and the power of
the warlord-barons. As a
result, kings were constantly
drawing up agreements with
their nobles. They had done
so on the Continent and had
done so in England, where precedent
stretched back at least to Henry I.

This particular charter seemed doomed
from the start. John himself had only ever
used the document as a kind of stalling
tactic. His aim, still, was to repudiate the
charter and slaughter the rebels. The rebels too hardly treated
the treaty as sacrosanct, reneging instantly on their agreement
to hand over London. For both sides, Magna Carta was a diversion from the real business, which would have to be settled at
sword point. Sure enough, less than three months after Magna
Carta, king and barons were at war again. The charter seemed
to be dead and buried.

It was nothing of the sort. The same realpolitik that had
created the treaty in the first place brought it back from the
dead. In 1216, a French army was on English soil, chasing John
northwards through the country. The French seemed certain to
succeed, but then John did the most brilliant thing of his career

so far: he died. His son was speedily proclaimed Henry III, and the regency council reissued Magna Carta in order to rally support. The reissue may have been little more than a PR stunt, but if so it was one with stunning results. Backing for the French invaders flooded away. The French were forced to go back home. England had been spared a second conquest.

For all this cynicism, the charter nevertheless remained about more than realpolitik and effective PR. No other medieval charter, in England or elsewhere, had ever contained such sweeping freedoms for the ordinary man. The very document had been addressed not only to nobles, in the manner of most such charters, but to all free men. Here in Article 1 comes the ringing statement from a king to his people:

> … We have also granted to all the free men of Our realm, for Ourselves and Our heirs forever, all the liberties written below, to have and to hold by them and their heirs from Us and Our heirs.

It's hard to know quite why the men negotiating Magna Carta had chosen to include such language. The rebel barons didn't care a fig about the liberties of the man on the Clapham horse-and-cart. Most of the liberties mentioned had little enough to do with him anyway. But some did, two in particular. Articles 39 and 40 run as follows:

> 39: No free man shall be taken or imprisoned or disseised [unlawfully dispossessed of land or property] or outlawed or exiled or in any way ruined, nor will we go or send against him, except by the lawful judgement of his peers or by the law of the land.

40: To no one will we sell, to no one deny or delay right or justice.

At the time, these clauses meant less than now appears. For one thing, they applied to free men only, and many Englishmen were villeins bound to the manor and therefore not technically free. Furthermore, the two clauses initially had less significance than they came to accrue. Article 39 was not intended to guarantee trial by jury – it just came to mean that. Article 40 was not meant to prevent indefinite imprisonment without trial – but it too came to mean that. One of the most striking things about the agreement is precisely how it came to take on a deeper significance with every passing century.

Arguably, though, the most startling innovation of Magna Carta lies in the largely forgotten Article 61. Almost the last article in the whole agreement, this clause set up a panel of twenty-five barons who would, in effect, supervise the king's adherence to the agreement. If the king was found to fail then:

> … those five-and-twenty barons shall, together with the community of the whole land, distrain and distress us in all possible ways, namely, by seizing our castles, lands, possessions, and in any other way they can, until redress has been obtained as they deem fit, saving harmless our own person, and the persons of our queen and children; …

In the political climate of the age, this proposal was simply nuts: a recipe for civil war. But, in the most dramatic way conceivable, it drove home the fact that the king was subject to the law. His 'castles, lands, possessions' were at stake if he broke the rules. This was a shockingly novel position. Under Roman law – the emerging law of continental Europe – the king *was* the rule-maker. It was no more possible for a king to bind himself than it was for the sun to scorch itself. In England, by contrast, the law was the law of the land, the common law, the semi-mythical law of Edward the Confessor and his Saxon predecessors. If the law had been there for centuries before the king and would be there for centuries after, then how could the king possibly claim a greater place? Clause 61 was dropped from every subsequent reissue of the agreement, but its spirit persisted and grew.

Virtually all modern states today either practice the rule of law or pretend that they do. It's perhaps the most revered political ideal in the world, more elemental than representative democracy, almost as ancient an ideal as political thought itself. But while the ancient Greeks may have originated the theory, the actual, effective practice was to come very much later. If you're looking for the practical, rather than theoretical, origin of the rule of law, then there you have it, in Article 61 of Magna Carta. For the first time in the post-Roman world, a king had become a subject in his own kingdom, servant to the law and the 'community of the whole land'. It was an example that first England, then the rest of the world, would come to respect and emulate; a Runnymede acorn whose roots now cover the globe.

A HANDFUL OF FEATHERS

Theft is illegal. It always has been. If you nick something and get caught, you will be prosecuted under the Theft Act of 1968, which says in the very first sentence of the very first paragraph:

> A person is guilty of theft if he dishonestly appropriates property belonging to another with the intention of permanently depriving the other of it.

Easy, huh? But what if you stole something in 1967, the year before the act was passed? Well, prior to the 1968 act, there was the Larceny Act of 1916. That act didn't have one neat way to categorize theft. In fact, you don't need to get very far into its definitions before the eyes start to goggle:

> A person steals who, without the consent of the owner, fraudulently and without a claim of right made in good faith, takes and carries away anything capable of being stolen with intent, at the time of such taking, permanently to deprive the owner thereof; provided that a person may be guilty of stealing any such thing notwithstanding that he has lawful possession thereof, if, being a bailee or part owner thereof, he fraudulently converts the same to his own use or the use of any person other than the owner:

The expression 'takes' includes obtaining the possession (a) by any trick; (b) by intimidation; (c) under a mistake on the part of the owner with knowledge on the part of the taker that possession has been so obtained; (d) by finding, where at the time of the finding the finder believes that the owner can be discovered by taking reasonable steps; The expression 'carries away' includes any removal of anything from the place which it occupies, but in the case of a thing attached, only if it has been completely detached; ...

All this just seems weirdly complex – 'completely detached' from reality, indeed – and so it was. The contorted definitions arose, however, because the 1916 act was trying to bring order not simply to previous acts of parliament, but to the entire area covered by the common law. And what *was* the common law? Quite simply this: it was the laws of the land as judges had found and interpreted them. Edwardian judges looked at the precedents laid down by Victorian judges, who in turn had looked at the precedents set by Georgian judges, who in turn had looked at the precedents set by their predecessors, who in their turn ...

Although the unbroken chain of precedent does not run as far back as the courts of the twelfth century and Henry II, the mode of deciding cases has always looked to the past. Questions of fact were decided by juries or by ordeal; questions of law always relied on a kind of collective memory of the unwritten law, the laws and customs of the land. In effect, those judges of Henry's court determined that theft was illegal because theft had been illegal for as long as anyone could remember. As with theft, so with most other offences. It wouldn't even be true to say that the origins of English law are lost in the mists of time.

That implies that if we only knew more, we'd be able to locate a source. And we wouldn't. No such unitary source has ever existed. Little wonder that by the time of the 1916 Larceny Act, the law of theft had become a tangled jungle almost too dense to pierce.

Because we're used to it, the oddness of all this is easy to miss. A modern parliament is a huge law-passing machine, and the cases adjudicated by today's courts are constantly bumping up against the rules laid down by some act of parliament. Yet this modern rule-making is a very recent phenomenon. When did parliament first outlaw theft in its most general form? In 1300?; 1500?; some time in the seventeenth century? Not a bit of it. The first really general attempt to outlaw theft was in that Theft Act of 1968 – everything else had just been an attempt to get old common law practices and the mish-mash of parliamentary statutes into some sort of order.

Even now, there are giant areas of law where common, not statute, law rules entirely. I'm on the point of selling the house I'm now writing in. When my buyer and I sign the contract of sale, that contract will be binding on us both, and enforceable through the courts. That does not mean, however, that I'm protected by some act of parliament. I'm not. There simply *is* no basic law of contract on the statute books. It doesn't exist, and most likely never will. My fundamental protection is that when Henry's royal judges came to systematize the law, they thought that contracts should be honoured and made sure that they were.

No one would ever choose to build from scratch a legal system that looks like ours, any more than you'd choose to build a skyscraper by starting with a henhouse and then just improvising. Britain, however, is a country where very few of our most important institutions have been built from scratch. They tend to be ramshackle affairs: cobbled together, patched, altered, repaired, made to last another few years. At the heart of most institutional skyscrapers in Britain – the law, parliament, the monarchy – you'll find splintering timbers and a handful of feathers. No one in their right minds would set out to do things like this. But – as long as you're British – it's an approach that works.

FROM THE SAME MUD

There's a joke doing the rounds which, in one of its versions, goes something like this. In a recent survey, those living in England/Wales/Scotland were asked whether they thought of themselves primarily as British or as English/Welsh/Scots. An overwhelming 68 per cent of respondents replied, 'Polish.'

Five hundred years ago, similar jokes wouldn't have involved the answer 'Polish', but they might well have named the Welsh, or Cornish, or Irish, or any other regional grouping. Then as now, migration was feared. Then as now, migrants were seen (by some people, some of the time) as bearers of disease, crime and immorality; speakers of funny-sounding English; thieves of jobs and women; scroungers too idle to work. Inevitably also, then as now, there were people keen to make a bob or two by exploiting these fears.

One such person was a Kentish tax-collector, Thomas Harman, who in 1566 published his *Caveat or Warning for Common Cursetors, vulgarly called Vagabonds.* The book, which seems to have been something of a publishing sensation, categorized the scams, frauds and deceptions of these wandering migrants. Among many other types, Harman identified:

ABRAM MEN (or *Abraham men, Bethlem men, Poor Toms*)
Those feigning madness and claiming to have been resident in Bedlam.

PALLIARDS (or *Clapperdudgeons*)
Those begging alms, but selling what they're given. Often Irish with false passports, or Welshmen using herbs to raise wounds on their legs, thus counterfeiting infirmity.

UPRIGHT MEN
Skilled professional thieves and beggars, though both able-bodied and experienced at a trade or in service.

JARKMAN (or *Patrico*)
Forger of licences.

WHIPJACKS
Those pretending to be shipwrecked sailors on their way home.

PRIGGERS OR PRANCERS
Horse thieves.

DUMMERERS
Beggars pretending deafness.

COUNTERFEIT CRANKS
Those pretending to suffer from the 'falling sickness'. Often use false testimonials from Shropshire.

Harman's categorization of women was particularly complex. *Kinchin morts* were young female rogues, *dells* virginal ones, *doxies* those who had had their virginity taken by an upright man. *Walking morts* were unmarried female rogues, *autem morts* their married (but still promiscuous) equivalents. *Bawdy baskets* were female pedlars of any marital status.

Most of the concerns that Harman was keenest to fan into life are recognizable to us today. Foreignness was much feared. Egyptians or gypsies were probably the scariest outsiders, the

Irish next, then perhaps the Welsh. Harman gives a lot of prominence to accusations of crime, fraudulent claims on charity, and immorality. The unreliability of identity documents strikes a chord today, as does the deep unease of the settled at the presence of the mobile in their midst. Harman also sounds another note, however, so disconcertingly contemporary that we hardly expect to find it in the mid-sixteenth century. The opening sentence of the book's dedication reads:

> As of auncient and long tyme there hath bene, and is now at this present many good godly profitable lawes and actes made and set forth in this most noble and flourishing realme, for the reliefe, succour, comfort and sustenacion of the pore, nedy, impotent and miserable creatures, beeing and inhabiting in all partes of the same.

Harman (who never used one word when half a dozen would do) goes on to make the point that the rogues outlined in the book are preying on these 'good godly' laws to the detriment of everyone else. The upright men, for instance, know 'Sommerset shyre, Wyll shyre, Barke shyre, Oxforde shyre, Harforde shyre, Myddilsex, Essex, Suffolke, Northfolke, Sussex, Surrye, and Kent as the chiefest and best shyres of relief', and 'have so good lyking in their lewde lecherous loyteringe' for these places that they'll brave any possible punishment to remain. At its core, in fact, Harman's book is an attack on benefit fraud.

Eh? We tend to think of benefit fraud as being very much a by-product of the twentieth-century welfare state. To the extent that there were any measures at all for the relief of the poor in centuries before that, we think of them as so utterly awful – all gruel, whippings and the workhouse – that the idea that anyone might seek out such relief seems far fetched to the point of loopy. Not so. Although Harman (like his modern-day descendants) is hardly a reliable guide to the social scene he claims to describe, he was absolutely right to suggest that the Tudor welfare state was very much alive and kicking.

Its roots ran deep. Back in the thirteenth century, the state played little or no role in ensuring social welfare, but the Church most certainly did. Everyone was required to pay one tenth of their income to the Church, of which one third was – at least in theory – reserved for the relief of the poor. For additional requirements, such as Christian burial of the indigent, additional collections were held. The arrangements mixed compulsion with volunteerism, backed by a powerful medieval Christian ideology of charitable work that would find its reward in the afterlife. Different localities found different ways to tackle the problem, but whatever the methods, broadly speaking, they worked. One historian has suggested that no century until the wealthy twentieth century was kinder to its poor.

Changing times, however, brought changing problems. As the pace of change in agriculture picked up, displacing the landless and swelling the towns, it became increasingly clear that large swaths of the poor had been made poor through acts of man, not God, and that the older methods of poor relief were no longer sufficient. The time-honoured ideology of the *societas christiana*, the Christian society, wasn't replaced, but it became buttressed by an emphasis on *civitas*, the responsibility of civil society to make good its own failures. In 1536, a new poor relief bill was brought before parliament. Although parliament had considered and passed numerous poor relief measures in the past, this one was newly radical in its scope. The bill acknowledged that poverty might have causes other than 'visitation of God' and the pauper's 'own default'. It aimed at relieving poverty of every kind. A national council would provide wages, food and medical care for the able unemployed, who would be given employment on public works, mostly transport related. The whole project would be financed by the king and his wealthier subjects, with further voluntary contributions from everyone in every parish.

The bill was too much. It went too far for the spirit of the age, and parliament ended up settling for a more traditional bill – urging charity for those in genuine need, while at the same time imposing tough measures on the able-bodied vagabond. A succession of further bills prodded restlessly at the same barrage of issues. Should vagabonds be whipped, stocked or bound over as slaves? Should the impotent poor be prohibited from begging, allowed to beg freely or permitted to beg only under licence and if wearing a badge? But for all parliament's vacillation, the drift was towards a more organized social response to need. In 1570 – that is, while Harman's *Caveat* was still selling like hot buns on a cold night – the city of Norwich launched a sweeping anti-poverty crusade that offered skills training, education, health-care, work and custodial support. The city employed thirty-four physicians and other practitioners (one third of them women) to offer care. A census was taken to establish who was sick, who old and who disabled, in order that the city authorities could take due responsibility for their care. Norwich was ahead of the game, but the country was moving fast in the same direction.

A bout of poor harvests in the 1580s, then again in the 1590s, brought matters to a head. The displaced poor had become a serious social problem. Would the country choose to act decisively or ignore the problem? It chose to act. The Poor Laws of 1598 and 1601 were a radical step forward in the state care of the poor. Overseers were to be appointed in every parish to dispense funds for poor relief, which were to be raised by compulsory taxation. Overseers were to provide cash for food, and, if needed, medical care and housing as well. Work was to be provided for those who were poor but able-bodied.

This was no mere paper law. The system actually did what was asked of it. Overseers were appointed, taxes were levied, poor relief funds were distributed. The Elizabethan Poor Laws – themselves the product of a long-established parish-centred tradition – formed the most generous, the most comprehensive and the most uniform system of social welfare anywhere in Europe. Indeed, one of its most striking features was its endurance. It was inevitable, for example, that from time to time those in power would become anxious about the cost of the system, and seek to restrict the payments made by parish overseers. Yet those overseers stuck to their task, and were more often than not supported by magistrates in so doing. The law required them to relieve poverty. To a highly impressive degree, that's exactly what they tried to do. In 1696 (the date of the earliest vaguely reliable estimate), the system distributed just under 1 per cent of national income, or enough to help about 3.5 per cent of the population. A hundred years later, the system swallowed 2 per cent of national income and reached 10–15 per cent of the population. Private charitable and Church-mediated endeavours would have added signficantly to these totals.

Migrants continued to arouse fear and suspicion. One of the great themes of poor law reform would be the tension between returning vagabonds to their parish of origin and seeking to permit the labour force enough mobility to keep up with a changing economy. But such concerns, as is amply clear to us, will never go away. Economies change. Labour moves. Generous benefit provision simultaneously helps the poor and attracts the cheats. Those Polish jokes (or Irish, Welsh or Cornish ones), like the poor, will be always with us.

There's a broader lesson in all this, though, and one that touches on one of the roots of British identity. One of the themes of this book is how very capitalist England, and later Britain, was. Long before the Industrial Revolution, England was the most capitalist society in Europe. Yet where is the red-in-tooth-and-claw energy of that capitalism now? The other day I listened to a radio phone-in that was discussing the need for proper regulation of estate agents. (In my defence, I should point out that it was a long journey and the only alternative was *The Archers*.) The presenter took it for granted that estate agents should be better regulated. The professional body of estate agents, whatever that is, agreed that regulation was needed. Every caller to the programme agreed that regulation was overdue. Not a single dissenting voice was raised. Why not? Had this been the USA, wouldn't someone have phoned in to say something along the lines of: 'Now I don't like realtors any more than the next guy, but if there's one thing I hates worse than a goldarn realtor, it's the goldarn government poking its cotton-pickin' nose into other people's business'? In America, the market's ability to weed out the scammers and incompetents is trusted more widely than the government's. Why is this voice more or less inaudible in Britain? What has happened to those capitalist ultras of the past?

The answer is that those capitalist ultras never forgot their social responsibilities. Ours has been a radically capitalist society for sure, but it also led the way in the protection of the needy. In part, it stood at the forefront of things because its state institutions functioned very well, very early. In Elizabeth's England, it was possible to pull a parliamentary lever and effect the proper response in virtually every parish in the country. Less well-functioning states couldn't have achieved that trick, even if they'd wanted to. But the English parliament didn't simply have the power to pull that lever: it actually pulled it and made sure that it stayed pulled. Although members of parliament were property owners, and therefore would be pay-ing for the Poor Law rather than profiting from it themselves, the swell of opinion remained solidly in favour of effective poor relief. In short, as a society, our national ideology has long been both that the government should protect the vulnerable and that it's more than capable of doing so.

William Bromyard, an English Dominican of the fourteenth century, wanting to remind his readers that social rank had nothing to do with intrinsic value, wrote that all 'are descended from the same first parents and all come from the same mud'. As a society, we believed that then and very largely still believe it now, whether we're English, Welsh, Scots – or Polish.

THE LAWMAKERS

A BETTIR LAWE

To judge them by their constitutions, most states are short-lived creatures, generally living no longer than a single human lifespan. Germany, Italy and Japan all acquired their founding documents in the wake of the Second World War. Since the fall of the Bastille, France has been through two empires and five republics, and has existed in its current incarnation only since 1958. Canada, being somewhat British, is something of an oddity and only formally acquired authority over its own constitution in 1982. Seen through this lens, the 'New World' of the United States is really no such thing, as the country boasts the oldest written constitution still operative today.

And Britain? It's a conventional politeness to say that we have no *written* constitution, but the phrase is a figleaf, concealing nakedness. The point of a constitution, after all, is to place limits on politicians. Ordinary legislative acts generally need just a simple majority to get them into law. Changes to the constitution require something much more significant: two-thirds majorities, approval by states or provinces, plebiscites or whatever. Britons enjoy no such protections. If a prime minister wanted to repeal Magna Carta or the Bill of Rights or any of the Representation of the People Acts, he could do so, with no more legal machinery in his way than would exist if he wanted to tinker with the last Fisheries Act but one.

If our attitude to our own state machinery looks almost shockingly laid back, then the state opening of parliament suggests one possible reason: namely that the whole thing is just some giant kitsch pantomime thrown together as a joke played on passing Americans. The cast list includes the Lord Great Chamberlain, Black Rod, the Serjeant-at-Arms, the Lord Privy Seal and the Yeomen of the Guard (who are made to hunt for imaginary barrels of gunpowder in the cellars). The props list incorporates the Royal Standard, the Great Sword of State, the Imperial State Crown, the Cap of Maintenance, the Mace and very much more. All this sounds like Harry Potter crossed with *Alice in Wonderland*; it certainly seems like no way to run a modern state.

That shouldn't come as a surprise. If the system *looks* medieval, that's because it *is* medieval. If an unwritten con- sitution seems dangerously lax, that's because our traditions arose aeons before anyone had thought of putting such things in writing. If we agree for a moment to permit the oxymoron of an unwritten constitution, then Britain's constitution is by far the oldest in the world, its parliamentary tradition so old that, as with so many British things, it's meaningless even to ask when it first arose. To get a sense of how far and deep this tra- dition stretches, consider the way acts of parliament are passed. The conventional preamble to a modern act of parliament reads as follows:

Be it enacted by the Queen's most Excellent Majesty, by and with the advice and consent of the Lords Spiritual and Temporal, and Commons, in this present Parliament assem- bled, and by the authority of the same, as follows ...

The first Statute of Westminster, passed in 1275, opened in almost exactly the same way:

> These are the Acts of King Edward, son to King Henry, made at Westminster at his first general parliament after his coronation … by his council and with the assent of the archbishops, bishops, abbots, priors, earls, barons and the community of the realm being thither summoned …*

Those archbishops, bishops, abbots and priors equate to today's 'Lords Spiritual'. The earls and barons represent today's 'Lords Temporal'. The 'community of the realm' may not have had a precise formal meaning, but Edward's parliament on that occasion contained commoners – knights and burgesses – from which seed the modern House of Commons would grow.

The similarities between the parliament now and its predecessor of seven centuries back don't end there. It would be easy, for instance, to dismiss those commoners at Edward's parliament as merely bystanders to

---

* The passage has been translated from Norman French, and was the first statute not to have been written in Latin. Since change for change's sake is not a British vice, medieval French is still in use today. When the Lords assent to a bill sent from the Commons, the endorsement is phrased: '*A ceste Bille les Seigneurs sont assentus.*' The standard formula for royal assent is, '*La Reyne le veult.*'

the main event, as inconsequential to proceedings as the pretence of ballot boxes in Soviet Russia. Yet it would be wrong to do so. That 1275 parliament was significant because it brought into being the Statute of Westminster, which ordered, among other things, that, 'because elections ought to be free, the king commandeth on pain of his great forfeiture that no one, great man or any other person, by force of arms, nor by malice shall disturb any from making free elections'. Those elections were genuinely national affairs. Edward had, after all, summoned, 'from each of the cities, boroughs and market towns of your bailiwick six or four citizens, burgesses or other good men', all of whom were to be elected. Indeed, at that 1275 parliament, elected representatives would have been in a clear majority of those present. That's not to suggest, of course, that English government back then was an entirely democratic affair. It plainly wasn't, yet it remains a stunning thought that the principle of free elections in England is more than seven hundred years old.

Although parliament as we recognize it today had its birth in medieval times, our tradition of consultative government arose far earlier still. When King Ine of Wessex passed a new set of laws in around 694, they were documented as having been enacted by:

> Ine, by the grace of God, king of the West Saxons, with the advice and instruction of ...[my bishops] along with all my ealdormen and the chief councillors of my people.

Queen Elizabeth hardly says anything different today. That's as far back as we can trace this particular formula for enacting laws, but the tradition of consultation goes as far back into the past as it is possible to peer. When King Edwin of Northumbria encountered the Christian gospel in 627, he was moved to accept it, but was well aware that such a decision, in a king, was a matter not merely of private faith, but of public policy too. Edwin therefore did what any Anglo-Saxon monarch would have done: he took advice. Bede reports the moment as follows:

> [King Edwin] answered that he was both willing and bound to receive the faith which [Bishop Paulinus] taught; but that he would confer about it with his principal friends and counselors, to the end that, if they also were of his opinion, they might all be cleansed together in Christ, the Fountain of Life. Paulinus consenting, the king did as he said; for holding a council with the wise men, he asked of every one in particular what he thought of the new doctrine and the new worship that was preached …

Edwin's counsellors advised in favour. The rest is history: approximately fourteen Christian centuries of it. Before the seventh century, the Angles, Saxons and Jutes (mostly sitting at home in Angeln, Saxony* and Jutland) were non-Christian and non-literate. Although their consultative traditions certainly long pre-dated Christianity, we just don't have the written records to say much about that earlier period.

The age of our constitutional tradition is exceptional enough, but its nature perhaps still more so. Ours was that rarest of things: a political custom by which the supreme ruler was meant to listen to his counsellors *and actually did so*. The

---

* Or, strictly speaking, at home in Angeln, *Friesland* and Jutland. The area now called Saxony is not actually where the Anglo-Saxon Saxons came from. Got that?

Norman Conquest came closest to snuffing the idea out for ever. William the Conqueror, coming from a politically unsophisticated and relatively young state, was too savvy an operator simply to dismantle the political institutions of England, already the most politically developed country in Europe. But the institutions he did most to retain (the hundred and shire, the shire court and sheriff, the Anglo-Saxon writs, and so on) were all valuable to a king seeking firm political control. The key mechanism by which a king consulted his people was the old Anglo-Saxon *witan*. In William's day, those *witan*s were still used (though under the new name of council), but they had undergone a subtle yet important shift. Though William certainly had advisers and listened to what they had to tell him, the idea that the king might be *constrained* by any such advice would have struck him as barmy. William, like the current governor of California, was no 'girlie-man', and he wasn't about to start acting like one.

Nevertheless, as time passed, the older pre-Norman tradition bubbled up again, too strong to be resisted. Partly, it was necessity. All across late medieval Europe, the existence of weak kings and strong barons virtually demanded some kind of formal body to reconcile arguments between the two. Institutions that enabled kings to treat with their principal subjects as a group were a more or less standard feature of late medieval states. The French had their *parlement* and Estates-General. Comparable structures existed in Spain, the Netherlands, Scotland, the Holy Roman Empire and elsewhere. Such similarities shouldn't, however, disguise the way in which England was utterly exceptional. The Estates-General might look a bit like an English parliament, but it wasn't the same beast at all. It was more like a tool of royal propaganda, a megaphone that allowed the king to project his voice farther and louder than he otherwise could.

Not so in England. The English parliament, uniquely in Europe, came to possess an iron grip over taxation. Although the king controlled his own ordinary revenues (from his estates, the sale of lands and offices, and so forth), any special tax required consent, and that consent was by no means always forthcoming. The English parliament likewise came to have legal authority too. No law would be recognized unless passed by both houses of parliament – including, vitally, the elected representatives of the people – and agreed by the king. In 1327, a parliament even went so far as to depose a king,* more than three centuries before a later parliament would come to execute one.

* Edward II was the unfortunate monarch, and the circumstances surrounding his deposition were of murky constitutionality at best.

English parliaments also reached much farther down the social strata than any comparable European body. In the (admittedly exceptional) moment of Simon de Montfort's victory in 1265, commoners were called upon to deliberate on issues of the very highest statecraft. As Simon Schama puts it: 'So a cloth merchant or a Suffolk knight with a few acres now got to judge the terms on which the son of the king might safely be released from captivity!' In short, that Anglo-Saxon tradition of consultation ran so deep that the incoming Normans never managed to quash it. Rather the opposite: kings learned to use it as a way of resolving disputes and overcoming crises. The more the old tradition was revived and re-established, the more impossible it became to imagine other ways of doing things.

The English system wasn't just different, it was better: better at conveying the people's feelings to the monarch, better at making sure that the monarch respected them. 1470, Sir John Fortescue wrote that there were two different sorts of kingdom: the absolute monarchy and the constitutional one, represented for him by France on the one hand, England on the other.

The first kynge mey rule his peple bi suche lawes as he makyth hym self. And therefore he may sett uppon thaim tayles [taxes] and other imposicions, such as he wol [desires] hymself, with owt thair assent. The secounde kynge may not rule his peple bi other lawes than such as thai assenten unto. And therfore he mey sett upon thaim non imposicions with owt thair owne assent ... Blessyd be God, this lande [England] is rulid under a bettir lawe; and therfore the peple therof be not in such peynurie, nor therby hurt in thair persons, but ... have all thinges nescessarie to the sustenance of nature.

This book is about British exceptionalism, forty-three short chapters picking out various aspects of our history where the British way has differed sharply from the ways of others. The book ranges across everything from Anglo-Saxon English to the development of men's fashion. But if you want to know where the very heart of our exceptionalism lies, then it's right here, in John Fortescue's 'bettir lawe': a people's right to assent to the laws that govern them, Britain's chiefest protection through the ages, her most important contribution to the world.

NO REMOTE IMPASSIVE GAZE

War is, and always has been, alarmingly expensive. In the period after about 1500, however, and for reasons that are still being debated, those costs began to grow at an explosive rate.

Military manpower

Date	Spain	Dutch Republic	France	Sweden	Russia
1470s	20,000	–	40,000	–	–
1590s	200,000	20,000	80,000	15,000	–
1630s	300,000	50,000	150,000	45,000	35,000
1700s	–	100,000	400,000	100,000	170,000

The Dutch and Russian armies grew five times over, the Swedish almost sevenfold, the French tenfold; the Spanish army grew by a multiple of fifteen times to its peak. A cost explosion of this sort was without precedent, and it forced a simple choice on European states of the era: keep up or go under. Those states that played the game successfully survived. Those that didn't were swatted from existence.

Unsurprisingly, statesmen of the time were well aware of the problem, well aware of the threat. But the issue posing the deepest challenge was not military but political in nature. After all, seventeenth-century armies were pretty basic affairs. To put together an army you needed a lot of unemployed peasants for men, some unemployed noblemen for officers, and a large number of fairly basic weapons. If you wanted a bigger army, you simply needed more peasants, more nobles, more weapons, more cash.

It was assembling the men and the cash which proved the trickiest part of the challenge. In the late 1400s, most European states functioned via representative institutions that had grown and developed through medieval times. Those bodies didn't have the clout that parliament had grown to possess in England, but they still mattered enough to cause a problem. How, after all, was a king to go about building a massive army, if he constantly needed to bargain with his noblemen and taxpayers for manpower and resources? The thing couldn't be done and the state adapted accordingly. Traditional liberties were done away with. Those old medieval bodies were either abolished or emasculated. Kings became supreme monarchs: absolute, centralized, powerful. In effect, countries themselves came to take on the command structures of armies: always top-down, never bottom-up. A purely military problem – how to keep up with the army of the Joneses – became one with political ramifications of the greatest possible consequence.

This then was the pattern for Europe: bigger armies, political strain, then either collapse (if you failed the challenge) or autocracy (if you didn't). Every major country to survive followed this pattern. Except England. Far from becoming more autocratic over the two hundred years from 1500, England became the exact opposite: a country under firm parliamentary rule, whose king was ever more firmly excluded from real power. By the time George I came to the British throne in 1714, the country had a king who couldn't speak English, and a parliament that didn't want him to. As so often before, and as so often later, England was the solitary exception to an otherwise solid European rule.

How come? The answer certainly has nothing to do any lack of military spending. True enough, the English army grew less than most: it went from being 25,000 strong at its (temporary) peak in the 1470s to some 87,000 strong in the 1700s, a three-and-a-half-fold increase. But it's an error to focus on the army, when it was England's navy which most counted. In 1509, Henry VIII's England had no navy at all. Ships, when needed for royal purposes, were simply borrowed or commandeered from the private sector. There were no royal shipyards, no permanent bureaucracy, no fixed naval hierarchy of officers and men. Scroll forwards to 1688, and James II vacated the throne leaving behind a navy of 151 seriously expensive ships, second in power only to the French navy, and even then not by much. This battle fleet was supported by a vast and costly hinterland of dockyards, victualling yards, shipbuilders, administrators, financiers, and so forth. In short, if all defence spending is taken into account, not just the purely military part, then England experienced a cost explosion every bit as dramatic as those found elsewhere. If cost pressure alone was enough to drive nations into autocracy then England should have ended up with one of the most centralized and absolutist monarchies in Europe. Should have, but didn't. So why not?

The first point, of course, is that England's starting point was different. In 1485, the English parliament had tight control over tax and legislation, and it boasted a level of social inclusiveness unknown on the Continent. To a large extent, the survival of parliament through two centuries of ever more costly warfare has a lot to do with the strength of its position at the start. A weaker parliament might well have gone under.

There's a second point, however, more intriguing and perhaps more persuasive too. Armies and navies are both expensive, but the costs involved are of a very different sort. Armies – those simple agglomerations of peasants, noblemen, pikes and muskets – could simply be ordered into existence, assuming that the command structure and the cash existed so to order them. Navies were never like that. Not then, and not now. A naval fighting ship was a formidably *complex* piece of equipment. She needed to be built by experienced shipwrights; serviced in suitable dockyards; supplied with cordage, spars, victuals, sailcloth, ammunition and powder; manned by skilled and experienced seamen; managed by experienced officers. All this meant that a navy was far more intensive in capital and skills than any army. Such a complex animal simply couldn't be coerced into being. What a navy required was, to quote N.A.M. Rodger, Britain's leading naval historian:

> a system of government which involved the maximum participation by those interest groups whose money and skills were indispensable to sea-power – not just the nobility and the peasants whom absolutism set to work, but the shipowners and seafarers, the urban merchants and financiers, the industrial

investors and managers, the skilled craftsmen; all the classes in short, which absolutist government least represented and least favoured ... A military regime could sustain itself by force, but a navy had to earn public support. Autocracy was adequate for an army, but navies needed consensus.

Rodger is surely right – so right, indeed, that the creator came to take on the shape of the created. Army discipline emphasized drill above all else. The object was to have men move, turn, stand and fire with the oiled predictability of a machine. The effectiveness of men in land combat depended on precisely that element of predictability and obedience to command. The autocracies of the Continent came to operate in a very similar way themselves – disciplined, hierarchical; the political echoing the military.

Command, of course, was important for navies too, but the purpose of naval discipline was never to produce automatons. A ship's crew was skilled and specialized, with its own master (navigator), carpenter, bosun, gunner, cook, purser and petty officers. Even the humble seaman was skilled to a degree that would astonish us today. An 'able' seaman was one able to 'hand, reef and steer' – no small accomplishment this, when the necessity for reefing might involve climbing a hundred feet above deck to battle flying canvas in a gale-torn night. These seamen were responsive to command, but also proactive, resourceful, independent and skilled. They also, and unlike soldiers, had other employers, the merchant marine, willing to pay a good price for their particular brand of skill – a fact of life that forced the navy to compete for talent, in a way that armies never quite had to.

The contrast between army and navy is brought to life by Patrick O'Brian in *The Far Side of the World*. (The action is set in the navy of Nelson rather than Blake, but the contrast drawn would have been true of either era.) The ship's captain, Jack Aubrey, is inspecting his men, just after they have managed to rescue him from a deserted island.

Jack ... turned aft, to where the Marines were standing as straight as ramrods in their scarlet coats: their cross-belts were brilliant with pipeclay, their muskets and side-arms shone again, their hair was powdered to a turn, their leather stocks were as tight as stocks could well be and allow a little circulation of the blood; and although awnings had been rigged, the eastern sun, not yet at its height, beat on their backs with shocking force. They might not be beautiful, but they were certainly suffering. Accompanied by Howard [the captain of Marines], and by Mowett [the ship's first lieutenant], he passed along the rows of faces, many of them nameless to him even now and all of them impersonal, gazing out beyond him, wholly without expression.

'Very creditable, Mr Howard,' said Jack ... Then, still with Mowett and with each of the divisional officers in turn, he went round the rest of the ship.

This was quite a different ceremony. Here he knew every man, many of them – indeed most of them – intimately well, knew their virtues, vices, particular skills, particular failings. And here there was no remote impassive gaze, no eyes trained to avoid the charge of familiarity or dumb insolence. Far from it: they were very pleased to see him and they smiled and nodded as he came by – Davis even laughed aloud. Furthermore it was perfectly obvious to all concerned that a rescued captain, just returned to his ship by a combination of extraordinary luck and extraordinary exertions, could not decently find fault with his ship's company. As an inspection his tour was therefore a matter of pure though amiable form; and it very nearly turned into a farce when the bosun's cat joined them and marched steadily in front of the Captain, its tail in the air.

Naval vessels didn't just tolerate this kind of mutually respectful intercourse between officer and sailor, they required it, just as the effectiveness of armies (and Patrick O'Brian's marines) depended on their total submission to command. In lurching towards democracy, England, like its neighbours, came to resemble the creatures that each had conjured into existence: armies on the Continent, the navy in Britain.

This line of thought is intriguing for two reasons. The first is the obvious one. England was, as so often, exceptional in a way that mattered, and understanding the causes of that uniqueness is of interest in its own right. The second reason is this. Modern historical scholarship is an astonishingly specialized affair. This chapter is largely based on arguments presented in N.A.M. Rodger's *Safeguard of the Sea*. That book, the first in a three-volume history of British seapower, contains a 'select' bibliography that is fifty pages long. The successor volume offers a further 'select' list which runs to almost ninety. To a jackdaw mind like mine, scholarship of this depth is almost impossible to conceive; it's certainly no longer possible for a single historian to combine a profound grasp of, say, British naval history with an equally detailed view of, say, parliamentary history. The resultant, inevitable specialization means that history can often seem over-compartmentalized. (Rodger, I might add, is a notable exception to the rule.)

Yet everything is connected. Britain's naval exceptionalism can't be divorced from its unique path on the parliamentary front, or the industrial and commercial fronts, or the later imperial front. Connections have a habit of existing even where they might be least expected. I doubt that anyone has ever written a book about the English constitutional upheavals in the seventeenth century and dedicated a large chunk of their discussion to naval developments, but perhaps it's high time that someone did. That the navy has long protected our borders is obvious. That it acted as midwife to our fledgling democracy is so little obvious that almost no one suggests it – yet for all that, it may be every bit as true.

GOOD KING FRANK

Willy, Willy, Harry, Ste,
Harry, Dick, John, Harry three,
One, two, three Neds, Richard two,
Henries four, five, six – then who?
Edwards four, five, Dick the bad,
Harries twain and Ned the lad,
Mary, Bessie, James the vain,
Charlie, Charlie, James again,
William & Mary, Anna Gloria,
Four Georges, William and Victoria,
Ted, George, Ned, then George were seen
And now it's Liz – God Save Our Queen.

When our present queen dies, then her eldest son, all being well, will ascend to the throne. The line of succession would then pass to Charles's eldest son, William, who would in due course expect to become King William V. Or so convention has it. But the convention hides a slightly embarrassing truth: that Kings William I, II and III weren't really Williams at all.

The first monarch with any name remotely like William was a certain Guillaume of Normandy, known as Le Bâtard. Guillaume le Bâtard was born in France, christened in France and spent most of his life in France. He spoke French. When he invaded England, he brought with him a French-speaking court, French-speaking nobles and French-speaking churchmen. King Guillaume was definitely not called William, just as his son (Guillaume II le Roux) was not called William either.

Of course, many European names have equivalents in other languages. John translates as Ian, Iáin, Evan, Ieuan, Eóin, Jean, Juan, João, Giovanni, Johann, Jan, Ivan and many other variants. But we don't call Ivan the Terrible, John the Terrible. Johann Sebastian Bach isn't John Bach. Likewise, given that Guillaume I and II were never christened William, called William or thought of themselves as William, it seems perverse to insist on calling them that. Indeed, it's worth remembering that when the French arrived in England in 1066, typically English names included such splendours as Æðelfrid, Ceolwulf, Earpwald, Hlothere, Thrydwulf and (my favourite) Yffi. Though we may think of names like Tom, Dick and Harry as quintessentially English, they're simply anglicizations of French originals. In 1066, the name William didn't exist.

The new court was foreign, and so it stayed. Schoolchildren used to learn the kings and queens of England with a version of the rhyme quoted at the start of this piece, a comfortable verse that sounds like a roll-call of names in some Edwardian classroom. But let's call a spade a spade (or rather *bêche*). The kings of England from the Norman Conquest to Henry V were as follows:

1066–87 Guillaume I le Bâtard
1087–1100 Guillaume II le Roux
1100–35 Henri I Beauclerc
1135–54 Etienne de Blois
1154–89 Henri II Courtmanteau

1189–99	Richard I Coeur de Lion
1199–1216	Jean Sans Terre
1216–72	Henri III
1272–1307	Edouard I
1307–27	Edouard II
1327–77	Edouard III
1377–99	Richard II
1399–1413	Henri IV
1413–22	Henry V

What's more, the wives (and therefore mothers) of the kings were mostly as foreign as the kings themselves. Guillaume I was married to Mathilde de Flandre. Henri II was married to Aliénor de Guyenne. From Jean Sans Terre to Edouard III, the queens comprised Isabella d'Angoulême, Aliénor de Provence, Leanor de Castilla, Margarete de France, Isabelle de France and Philippa de Hainault (the place in Belgium, that is; not the stop on the London Underground). Even that most English of kings, Henry V, married one Catherine de Valois. Only in the late fifteenth century did there come a period when most English monarchs had two native English speakers for parents. (That didn't necessarily mean those monarchs were English, however. Henry Tudor, who seized the throne in 1485, was born in Wales of a Welsh dynasty whose founding father was one Owain ap Maredudd ap Tudwr ap Goronwy.)

As the Tudors settled in, however, they anglicized, bringing something like English rule to England throughout the sixteenth century. Then, in 1603, and with Elizabeth childless, English rule came to an end again with the coronation of James I of England. James was Scottish, and was already King James VI of Scotland. It's easy for us now to think of him as British and so not really foreign at all, but this is a hopelessly anachronistic attitude. Scotland was an independent country with its own laws, parliament and religious make-up. James spoke with a broad accent that firmly placed him as being un-English. Indeed, James's inability to deal with the different requirements of his different kingdoms (and his son, Charles's, equal lack of sensitivity) was a major part of what precipitated civil wars in and between England, Scotland and Ireland in the middle of the century.

Those conflicts quietened, but didn't altogether settle until the turbulent year of 1688, when the Dutchman, Willem Hendrik, Prins van Oranje, landed with 40,000 men to contest the crown of England. James II chose to run away. Willem summoned an illegal parliament, surrounded it with troops, and asked those assembled to choose their new king. They chose the Dutchman. But was he King William? William certainly wasn't his name. Just like Guillaume le Bâtard before him, the new king was a foreign conqueror whose name and native language were not English. If one is being strict about these things, England up to this point had had two King Guillaumes and one King Willem. It had never had a King William at all.

In 1707, England united with Scotland. There would never be another foreign invasion. The dynastic line settled down, with no more of the bloody excitement of medieval times, but the monarchs that ruled were still hardly English. On the death of Queen Anne in 1714, it was necessary to find a new monarch. This wasn't quite as simple as it should have been, because the 1701 Act of Settlement excluded any Catholic or anyone married to a Catholic from the throne. Unfortunately, the fifty-seven people closest in line to the throne were all

Catholic. The lucky fifty-eighth was one Georg Ludwig, Duke of Brunswick-Lüneburg. Georg, of course, was as German as *Bratwurst*. He spoke almost no English, and what little he did speak was overlaid with a thick German accent.

Much more astonishing is how German the family stayed. Heirs to the British throne needed to marry those who were both Protestant and of princely blood. Since the best supply of such marital material was to be found in the principalities of Germany and Scandinavia, it came about that every single monarch from George I to Victoria married a German spouse, so that every British monarch from 1714 to 1901 had two German-speaking parents, at least one of whom was also German-born. That icon of high British imperialism, Queen Victoria, preferred speaking German to English and spoke mostly German with her children. In 1901, Edward VII came to the throne (fluent in German, naturally), accompanied by his Danish wife, the magnificently styled Alexandra von Schleswig-Holstein-Sonderburg-Glücksberg. It wasn't until 1910 that Britain, for the first time in its history, would have a British king married to a British queen – and this is true only if we include those who are naturalised British.* The Queen Mother, a Scot, was the first Briton to marry a British royal. The first Englishwoman to come close to the British throne was Princess Diana. Since Camilla will not become queen, there's not a clear contender even now.

What does all this prove? Perhaps not much; or rather it proves two contradictory things: first, how ordinary our

---

* Queen Mary was also Princess von Teck in the kingdom of Württemberg, so that the princely-'n'-Protestant rule was still being obeyed, if only rather notionally by this point.

country used to be; second, how unordinary it became. The story of post-Conquest Britain is one of kings and warlords struggling for power, whether through battle or marriage. For a time England did well, securing a huge chunk of France from the Channel to the Med, before in due course losing the lot. The foreign kings were simply an emblem of the way the country's affairs were being handled: by men whose thoughts, fortunes and hopes for the future often lay elsewhere.

The later long spell of foreign monarchy indicates something quite different. In 1714, the Act of Succession drove parliament to look for a new king fifty-eight places down the pecking order, in Germany. But the choice of a monarch who couldn't speak English wasn't awkward: it was a definite plus. How could a king govern if he couldn't even speak its language? He couldn't – and parliament never wanted him to. A foreign mon-arch was an impotent one: the emblem of the final, decisive shift towards a revolutionary form of government, par-liamentary rule. The monarchy's very survival has depended on its ability to slip into insignificance.

Which brings us back to the question that we started with. If Charles's elder son is crowned king, he will – if we are to be strict about these things – be just the second king to bear the name of William. (There was one other true William, who reigned 1830–37, just preceding Victoria.) Yet though Charles's son may be crowned king, there's a school of thought which argues that he won't be the *rightful* king of anything at all. When Prince Willem seized the English throne in 1688, the deposed monarch, James II, refused to give up the cause. There was sporadic fighting for another half-century, culminating in the disaster of the 1745 Jacobite uprising. But military failure didn't mean the end of the succession. According to modern-day Jacobites, the rightful king of the United Kingdom is alive and poised to take the crown.

His name? None other than the impeccably German Duke of Bavaria, Franz Bonaventura Adalbert Maria von Wittelsbach. Or, as we would certainly insist on calling him, good King Frank.

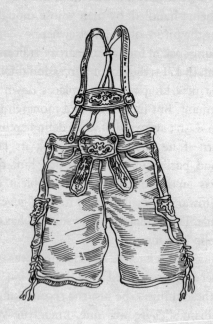

A MOST STRANGE AND WONDERFULL HERRING

In 1477, Wiliam Caxton brought the printing press to England. With the press came some of the finest fruits of the human mind: poetry, chivalric romances, history, the best of classical antiquity; in due course, Bibles, scriptures and theology too.

And rubbish. The more the cost of printing fell, the more it became possible to make a living from printing ephemera – early-modern chip papers. In 1597, for example, one enterprising printer brought out a pamphlet that showed images of 'A most Strange and wonderfull Herring' whose scales displayed 'on the one side the picture of two armed men fighting, and on the other most strange Characters, as in the picture is here expressed.' (After all, a woodcut never lies.)

Sensation and scandal also found a ready market. A 1605 newsbook – an early newspaper, in effect – announced that the 'pittilesse' John Fites, 'thirstie of blood', had killed a man and his wife before turning the sword on himself. 'Proude heart, wilt thou not yielde?' Fites is reported to have said. 'Split, split and in this onely wound die: that I thy owner may not live, to heare the honour of my credite stayned with these odious actes.' The style may be more Shakespeare than *Daily Star*, but the journalist's willingness to make stuff up is eerily modern.

What's more, the market then was as entrepreneurial and inventive as the market now. The illiterate masses, after all, were as thirsty for news as anyone else, so the market found ways to satisfy that thirst and make a groat or two at the same time. News might be put out in the form of plays, or broadside ballads. Here's one such, reporting the destruction of a Suffolk town. (It is the town itself which speaks the lines.)

> But now beholde my great decay,
> Which on a sodaine came;
> My sumptuous buildings burned be
> By force of fires flame:
> A careless wretch, most rude in life,
> His chymney set on fire,
> The instrument, I must confess,
> Of God's most heavie ire.

As poetry goes this is as bad as it gets, but then cash, not posterity, was the aim. Printed ballads were sold, and spoken out loud (or worse still, sung) in markets and meeting places. Enterprising publicans often subscribed to whatever news sources there were going, in order to tempt people in to eat, drink and catch up.

For those wanting a more serious approach to news, there were more upmarket approaches available. One notch up were corantos and newsbooks, both early forms of the newspaper.

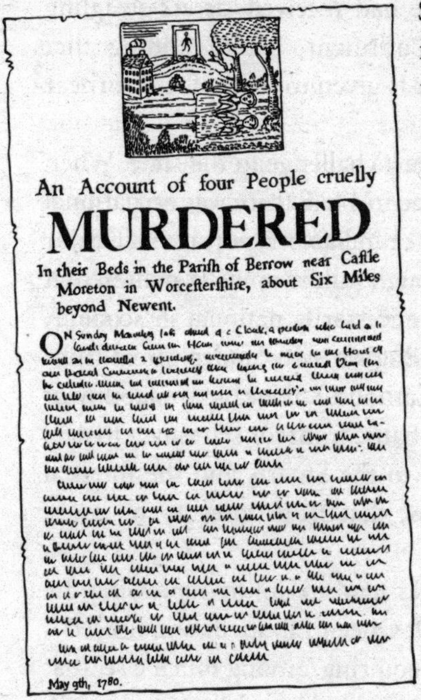
An Account of four People cruelly

MURDERED

In their Beds in the Parish of Berrow near Castle Moreton in Worcestershire, about Six Miles beyond Newent.

May 9th, 1780.

Such productions were widely regarded as having more weight than the populist and mass-market ballads, but contemporaries remained sceptical all the same. In 1632, one wit commented that 'now every one can say, its even as true as a Currantoe, meaning that it's all false'. Yet more positive journalistic ethics were also visible. The better corantos tried to give themselves a reputation for truthfulness, even at the expense of having nothing interesting to say. According to a recent article in *The Economist*, the world's oldest surviving political headline is the splendid 'The new tidings out of Italie are not yet com' – an early precursor of the 1920 BBC's 'Good evening. There is no news tonight.'

The very top end of the news market was occupied by professional news-gatherers who would compile regular newsletters in manuscript form (that is, written longhand) for sending out to paying subscribers. The fees for such a service were by no means cheap – say about £20 a year for a weekly newsletter, which you could multiply at least a hundredfold to get a contemporary equivalent. Anyone paying these sums for news wanted accuracy, not sensation, and on the whole they got it. One professional letter writer,

John Flower, reported that he had received 'divers stragling reports' of events on the Continent, before adding that 'because I perceive noe creditt is given to them, I will forbear the writing of them'.

All of this posed a wholly new challenge to the state. When Henry Tudor came to the throne in 1485, there was no national news market and no instant or reliable reportage of major events, with the result that though public opinion mattered, it was neither volatile nor even necessarily national in scope. A hundred years later, with the English state under threat from without (Spain) and within (Catholics), the easy availability of news formed a dangerous new battle front for statesmen to deal with. As the Tudors gave way to the Stuarts and the internal dissension and pressures grew, that front grew to be more complex, more ominous.

The state responded as states tend to do: by repressing the offending institutions. In 1559, Queen Elizabeth announced a number of royal injunctions, requiring, among much else, that all new works needed to be submitted in advance to herself, one of her half-dozen closest counsellors or a handful of other luminaries. For plays, pamphlets and ballads – mass-market productions whose volume would have swamped the Queen and her counsellors – licensing was to come from one of three London ecclesiastical commissioners. No ballads or suchlike could be printed outside London.

The new rules weren't wholly obeyed, but they weren't wholly disregarded either. If printers wanted to bring out 'strange and wonderfull' news of herrings, or anything equally uncontentious, they generally dared to do so without prior authority. But the people of England weren't going to be satisfied with stories about fish, no matter how remarkable. The pressure of demand continued to boil up, threatening to overload the system of censorship, whose rules were constantly being adjusted in the effort to cope.

Those who did offend the powerful faced draconian punishments. In 1579, for example, a pamphlet appeared, snappily entitled *The Discovrie of a Gaping Gulf whereinto England is like to be swallowed by another French marriage; if the Lord forbid not the banes, by letting her Maiestie see the sin and punishment thereof.* This was dangerous stuff – not simply a discourse on high politics, but an attack on that holy of holies, the Queen's own intentions regarding marriage. The offending author and printer were immediately searched for and found. After failing to get the men hanged for one offence, Elizabeth had them prosecuted for another, conspiracy to excite sedition. This time the men were convicted, and the author, John Stubbe, had his right hand chopped off by way of punishment: press management, Taliban-style.

As time went by, the profusion of printed material continued to grow, state affairs grew, if anything, more delicate, and the censors struggled to cope. On the one hand, they sought to release the pressure of demand by allowing innocent material to see the light of day. On the other hand, the punishments for 'sedition' – very broadly defined – grew more savage and unconstrained by conventional courts. Under the early Stuarts, James and Charles, the tensions increased and, in the end, the challenges overwhelmed the system. As war broke out between king and parliament in the mid-seventeenth century, censorship collapsed completely. Printed matter of every variety proliferated. Views of every conceivable description were aired. Although the mechanisms of prosecution and punishment still existed, the country was in too much chaos to bother with such things. One collection of newsbooks held in the British Museum indicates the huge surge that took place over the period. The collection holds just four newspapers from 1641, 167 from 1642, 402 from 1643, and a monster 722 from 1645. In all this ferment, the poet John Milton published his pamphlet *Areopagitica*, proclaiming the virtues of free debate:

> And though all the winds of doctrine were let loose to play upon the earth, so truth be in the field, we do injuriously by licensing and prohibiting to misdoubt her strength. Let her and falsehood grapple; who ever knew truth put to the worse in a free and open encounter? ... Truth is strong next to the Almighty; she needs no policies, no strategems nor licensings to make her victorious ... [Above all liberties] give me the liberty to know, to utter and to argue freely according to conscience.

This was a stirring trumpet blast for freedom, a revolutionary call addressed to a revolutionary age, one that should have heralded the birth of press freedom in England and the world.

Except that it didn't. No reference to Milton's *Areopagitica* has ever been found in the literature of the time, and it took later generations to rediscover its brilliance. Furthermore, the surge in printed matter proved to be nothing more than a temporary aberration. Under Cromwell's Protectorate, the old repressive rules came back as before, as, indeed, they were always bound to. Nobody in those days conceived of freedom of speech as being the fundamental right we think it today. The concept itself simply hadn't entered political thought. When Milton spoke of 'the liberty to know, to utter and to argue freely', we naturally understand him to mean that *anyone* should be able to say *anything*. He meant no such thing; indeed, he'd have been shocked at the very suggestion. What he meant was that any well-educated Puritan-inclined Protestant should be able to say anything not threatening to the integrity of the state. The idea that riff-raff or women or (whisper it softly) Catholics should be able to pick up their pen and write what they liked would have struck him as both barmy and dangerous. Indeed, it wouldn't be long before Milton himself was working as a censor for the new Puritan regime.

By 1660, with Cromwell dead and a king back on the throne once again, that whole period of revolutionary upheaval would seem to have accomplished nothing as regards broadening the freedom of the press. Press freedom was an issue neither in England nor on the Continent. There was no doctrine or philosophy of free speech, no popular movement in its support. The issue seemed so dead that no one even recognized there was an issue.

Yet the times they were a-changing, all the same. London was the centre of one of Europe's two fastest-growing economic powers (the other was the Netherlands). Commerce, finance, insurance and shipping all relied on a free flow of news, often mediated through the newly fashionable coffee houses. Alongside the purely economic factors, there were the more frivolous ones. People liked their gossip, their scandal, their sense of being in the know. The prevailing mood was expressed in one 1665 poem, in which a coffee drinker says:

> Sirs unto me
> It reason seems that liberty
> Of speech and words should be allow'd
> Where men of differing judgements croud,
> And that's a *Coffee-house*, for where
> *Should men discourse so free as there.*

The poem wonderfully encapsulates the mood of the times, and the forces of change that mattered. It's often lazily said today that 'people died' for our right to freedom of speech. And they didn't. That simply wasn't how it happened. That radical call for 'liberty of speech and words' came not in the ferment of revolution, but in the very ordinary context of the leisured rich demanding their entertainment.

In 1695, the basic tool of state censorship, the Licensing Act, came up for renewal. The old system was widely seen as necessary, but unworkable in its current form, so the decision was made to let the old act lapse, in order that a whole new system could be brought into being. The aim wasn't to give up on censorship, but to invent a whole new, improved system for the coming century. That new system never came. When parliament assembled to look at a version of the proposed new bill, a hundred niggling objections were raised, mostly having to do with small but significant details of implementation. The bill was sent back to committee, and never came out again. The basic mechanism of state censorship had gone for ever. One of the greatest constitutional revolutions in world history had come about because no one could quite figure out a sensible way to hold it back. In the more autocratic regimes of continental Europe, any such niggling technicalities would have been simply shoved aside in the interests of the state. In England – more permissive, more responsive to opinion, more commercially pushy – those technicalities made the difference.

The press in England still wasn't entirely free. It wouldn't be for another hundred years and more. (The prosecution for seditious libel would become the state's favourite new weapon of attack; the Stamp Act, a tax on newspapers among other things, its favourite form of restraint.) Yet the eighteenth-century British press was the freest in the world: scurrilous, lively, satirical, dissenting, abusive, creative, argumentative. Further battles for press freedom were fought and won. By the time the American colonists fought for and won their independence, the central importance of free speech to a free society was widely embedded in political thought. It stands there in the very first amendment to the US constitution, which requires that 'Congress shall make no law … abridging the freedom of speech, or of the press'.

The concept spread from Britain to America, and from those countries to the rest of the free world. No one now doubts the

central, elemental importance of freedom of speech: a freedom
won not at the barricades, but at the coffee houses; a freedom
brought about less by philosophers than by that 'most strange
and wonderfull herring' – a free people's appetite for news.

CLEAN HANDS, DIRTY MONEY

As I write, a police investigation of a possible cash-for-honours scandal creeps ever closer to the walls of Downing Street. An entire cabinet has been interviewed. The honours system has been debased. A prime minister's integrity is in doubt.

There's much to relish in stories such as this, but the joy does not lie in novelty. The dirty connections between money and power are no doubt as old as money itself, and even the form of those connections has altered remarkably little. Take, for instance, the whole business of selling honours. When Queen Elizabeth I died there were just fifty-five peers and around 550 knights, slightly fewer in both cases than the totals at her accession to the throne, implying that honours in late Tudor England formed a fairly stable currency of prestige. The problem with a stable currency, however, is that there are fat profits to be made in debauching it, and Good Queen Bess's successor, James, lost little time in doing just that. He marked his ascent to the English throne (he was already king of Scotland) by knighting some 432 men on a single day, then went on to create knights at the rate of about seventy a year for the rest of his reign. During that time, the number of English peers more than doubled; the number of Irish ones more than quadrupled.

His motivation was simple: cash. Most of James's honours were either sold or given in the expectation of gifts in exchange.

Eager as any young entrepreneur to spot any gap in the market, James even created a brand-new honour, the baronetage, available to punters for the handsome price of £1,095. There were ninety English takers for the honour – a product launch so successful that James rolled out the offering in Ireland and Scotland too, which produced a further forty-four and 132 baronetages respectively. Nor did he stop at flogging off honours. Monopolies, licences and other economic privileges were all available for sale, as were positions in the royal household. (Or rather households, plural. After all, why restrict yourself to just one, if you could create – as James I did, following precedent – separate royal households for yourself, your wife and your three children?) Put like this, the Stuart court seems like some kind of car boot sale, the king himself a regal Del Boy.

There are two conclusions one might draw from this. The first is that all power corrupts, and it hardly matters whether you're talking about the Stuart court or the Blair one. Alternatively, one could draw roughly the opposite conclusion: that autocratic government tends to foster corruption on a major scale; while democratic governments and bolshy voters do at least limit the extent of sleaze. This second line of argument looks like a good one in principle, except that eighteenth-century Britain, an imperfect but real democracy, was itself so deeply enmired in corruption that the phenomenon was regarded as pretty much normal, like mud in autumn.

Parliamentary management of the press offers one of the most glaring instances of that autumnal mud. So little were Britain's first true parliamentary rulers comfortable with the idea of being criticized by mere journalists that they brought in the Stamp Act of 1712. The tax was Kremlinesque in its unabashed directness of purpose, the idea being to tax newspapers off the news-stands and into bankruptcy. Alas, the act contained an unfortunate loophole. For smaller newspapers, the act imposed a tax of one penny 'for *every* printed copy', but for larger ones the tax was to be three shillings 'on *one* printed copy'. The tax came close to destroying the daily newspaper industry, which went into immediate decline, but the larger weekly newspapers, in blatant defiance of the act's intended purpose, claimed that they had to pay their three-shilling tax on the *first* copy of any edition they published – all the others were to be tax free. Worse still, it was the opposition newspapers which jumped on the technicality. Newspapers loyal to the government felt obliged to pay the tax as it was intended, and so started going out of business.

There were plenty of solutions available to the government of the day. They could simply have abolished a tax whose purpose was the repression of free speech, or they could at least have levelled the playing field by closing the loophole. Neither option appealed. Instead, the government took public money and used it to make secret payments to friendly newspapers and editors, thus keeping them in business, and ever more dependent on government favour. At the same time, hostile newspapers were prosecuted or bought off. The whole ugly episode was notable for the government's utter disregard for an independent press, and its willingness to use taxpayers' cash for narrow political advantage.

Debasement of the honours system and underhand methods of controlling the press all have their echoes today, but we do at least feel reasonably secure in the knowledge that those appointed to run the most basic function of government – the defence of the realm – are in their positions on the basis of ability, not connections. That wasn't always the case. In the Georgian navy, recommendations based on 'interest' or influence flew around right, left and centre (or rather, for the purist, starboard, larboard and amidships). These recommendations mattered. Almost to a man, the navy's most senior commanders had obtained their positions through nepotism, influence or the use of aristocratic rank. If we consider just the Seven Years War, then even a short roll-call of senior names would throw up the following connections:

ADMIRAL HAWKE Nephew of a commissioner of trade

ADMIRAL KNOWLES Bastard son of the Earl of Banbury

ADMIRAL TOWNSHEND Half-brother of a viscount

ADMIRAL SMITH Half-brother of Lord Lyttleton and a relative of the prime minister

ADMIRAL POCOCK Nephew of Lord Torrington, a First Lord of the Admiralty

VICE ADMIRAL WATSON Nephew of Sir Charles Wager, another First Lord

VICE ADMIRAL HOLBOURNE Protégé of the Duke of Argyll

VICE ADMIRAL CARNEGIE aka the Earl of Northesk

REAR ADMIRAL COLVILL aka Lord Colvill

This list merely scratches the surface. One could also add the names of the senior men at the Admiralty (Anson, Boscawen, Forbes and West), as well as numerous other admirals or rising captains (Frankland, Hardy, Holmes, Rodney, Keppel, Douglas and Howe). Every single one of these men had significant connections to senior figures in the navy, the House of Lords or the government, and they all made full use of the connections they had.

It's as one surveys facts such as these that one is tempted to draw the obvious conclusion that Britain is just a grubbily corrupt country like any other; that it always has been and always will be; that wherever power or public money exists, there are plenty of Brits ready to thrust their noses into the trough. The conclusion is certainly true *to an extent* – but extent is everything. Before we descend into cynical gloom about our rulers, it's worth reminding ourselves of a fact that receives almost no coverage at all, namely that today's Britain is one of the least corrupt countries of any size, and the least corrupt *large* country in the world.

Transparency International,* Corruptions Perceptions Index 2006

United Kingdom	8.6 out of possible 10.0
Canada	8.5
Germany	8.0
Japan	7.6
France	7.4
USA	7.3
Italy	4.9
Russia	2.5

The only countries that do better than us are mostly either small and Scandinavian (Finland, Iceland, Denmark, Sweden, Norway), or small and a little bit British (New Zealand, Singapore, and Australia, which is smallish in population

* Transparency International is the world's leading anti-corruption pressure group, and its stats have become the international benchmark in the field.

terms, if not geography). If you care to look not at who takes bribes but who is paying them, then you might expect Britain to do badly, given that many of its stronger industries (oil, mining and armaments, for instance) take its corporations into some fairly dodgy territory. All the same, Britain still does better than any of its big-country peers, except that it and Canada switch places at the top.

The simple truth, counter-intuitive as it may seem, is that while Britain isn't quite squeaky clean (you need to be Scandinavian for that), it still does very well indeed by international standards. Nor should this be surprising. When a country's major political scandals revolve around expediting a visa for a nanny (the first Blunkett resignation), or taking a perfectly legitimate loan from a friend (the first Mandelson one), then that country's politics would seem to be in fairly good shape.

So what of the past? Are we a dirty country that's cleaned up its act? Or a clean one that's just got cleaner? It's hard to say. The data available today wasn't around twenty years ago, let alone two or three centuries back. What is clear, though, is that the attitudes of today don't necessarily make sense when imported back into the past. All those honours flogged off by the early Stuarts? This certainly was a kind of corruption, and the Stuart court was compared unfavourably with that of Elizabeth by contemporaries. But in the early Stuart era, the number of 'gentlemen', or better-off middle classes, had vastly increased compared with the start of Elizabeth's reign, and some kind of catch-up was certainly overdue. Furthermore, given that in England it was parliament, not the king, who held the purse strings, then that Stuart entrepreneurship can perhaps better be interpreted as a sign of the onset of constitutional government than as something fundamentally rotten in our make-up.

How about those early eighteenth-century efforts to control the press? Shocking, of course, and it caused a furore at the time, but it needs to be reiterated that the British press of the era was the freest in the world. Historically speaking, it would seem more remarkable that the press was allowed to function at all than that the government was clumsily authoritarian in its response.

Finally, what about all those nepotistic admirals? It's all very well to tut-tut about cronyism, but in the end it makes no sense to judge an eighteenth-century system through purely twenty-first-century eyes. The simple fact is that the list of senior naval officers above includes those responsible for virtually every major British victory over a period of thirty years and more. Not one of those officers obtained his position without thoroughly meriting it. Although it's certainly true that promotion in the Georgian navy depended heavily on 'influence', the recommendations of men of influence formed a highly competitive market of their own, allowing men of talent to thrust their way to the very top. In short, though connections certainly mattered, ability mattered more.

In the end, perhaps the best conclusion is the simplest. Government is a dirty business by nature, but the things most likely to clean it up are representative democracy, a free press and the weight of public opinion. Since Britain has, to a considerable extent, led the way in these respects, it would hardly be surprising if we had also led the way in the basic cleanliness of our public life. If journalists function as the natural killer cells in our political immune system, then stories about sleaze indicate an effective kill. It's fine to enjoy the headlines, but we'd do well to bear in mind the context. Far from being doomed to live in a dirty country, we're lucky enough to live in a clean one.

WARFARE

INVASION

What's the one fact everybody knows about British history? The fact that could decently claim to be *the* central fact about our past?

That's easy, isn't it? We're an island. The last time we were invaded was in 1066. We're protected by our coasts, virtually immune against attack; an island stronghold; or, to quote the Bard, a 'fortress built by Nature for herself / Against infection and the hand of war'. Shakespeare's boast stands to reason, after all. Land transport is as easy as kiss my hand. It's only when we get to the coast that things get more complicated. In the old days of wind and oar, sea transport must have been an immensely complicated and unpredictable way of getting around. No wonder that invading armies preferred to stay away.

Of course, there is one teeny little flaw in this view of our history: namely, that it's completely false. It's not just that Britain *has* been invaded since 1066, it's that we used to be invaded all the time. There have

• 123 •

in fact been nine seaborne invasions which successfully toppled the government of England, and one which saw the Scottish throne change hands. For invasion anoraks, the dates are:

1139 Matilda invades, toppling King Stephen (temporarily, at least).

1153 Henry of Anjou invades, forcing Stephen to acknowledge him as heir.

1326 Isabella and Mortimer invade, deposing Edward II and installing Edward III in his place.

1332 Edward Balliol invades Scotland, defeating the Regent.

1399 Henry Bolingbroke lands to seize the throne, becoming Henry IV.

1460 Warwick invades, captures Henry VI and installs Edward IV.

1470 Warwick invades again, this time putting Henry VI back on the throne.

1471 Edward invades, beats Henry, and it's his turn to be king again.

1485 Henry Tudor invades, defeats Richard III and becomes Henry VII.

1688 William of Orange invades and ascends to the throne.

This list, however, is based on a fairly restrictive definition of invasion. Arguably, a successful invasion is one that succeeds in delivering hostile campaigning forces on to British soil, whether or not those forces go on to win the subsequent land war. If we expand the definition in this way, there were seven further occasions of successful invasion, namely 1069, 1101, 1215, 1405, 1462, 1469, 1487 plus a Scottish one in 1708. That's eighteen invasions so far, and the total excludes countless other seaborne raids and landings; numerous occasions when foreign assistance was sent to local rebellions; any expeditions that failed to put troops ashore; and the count ignores Ireland altogether.

Now of course, most of these invasions were mounted by domestic contenders for the English crown, a sort of bloody medieval version of musical thrones. The abrupt refashioning of the country that took place under William the Conqueror was fortunately never repeated, but that fact shouldn't blind us to the truth that Britain has long been highly vulnerable precisely *because of* the seas around her. This assertion should hardly come as a surprise. Why do we think of the sea as a barrier? Quite simply because it is *to us*. Thanks to the car and (in an earlier age) the railway, we find it extremely easy to move about the country by land. It's only once we get to the edge of it that the going gets tough. But this modern experience inverts an age-old historical reality, namely that land transport has been slow and cumbersome, transport by sea has been fast and easy.

It's hard to exaggerate how bad land transport used to be. Carts were rudimentary, roads basic, horses expensive. Rain and mud were the thieves of speed. Bandits and highwaymen were, well, just thieves. By contrast, the sea was fast, safe and reliable. In his *Wealth of Nations*, Adam Smith claimed that 'six or eight men by the help of water carriage can carry and bring back in the same time the same quantity of goods between London and Edinburgh as 50 broad-wheeled wagons attended by a hundred men and drawn by 400 horses'. Smith probably exaggerated a tad, but his point was sound – and he wrote after decades of private investment in turnpike roads had transformed Britain's previously backward road system.

What's more, if the goods in question were heavy – artillery pieces, for example – then moving them by land was so difficult it could only just be done at all. At the epoch-making Battle of Blenheim in 1704, the entire French army boasted about sixty guns, the allied side about fifty. By naval standards, this kind of firepower was simply piffling. A single ship of the line carried more firepower than an army. A battle fleet carried infinitely more. Nor was Blenheim exceptional. Nelson's flagship *Victory* at Trafalgar would have easily outgunned Wellington's army at Waterloo, and that's not even to consider *Victory*'s infinitely greater rate of fire or the accuracy of her gunners. It wouldn't be until the advent of the railway that armies could begin to compete with the firepower of navies, a transformation in warfare which any infantryman of the First World War would, unfortunately, understand all too well.

Nor did sea transport merely have the edge in terms of speed, brute transportation capacity and reliability; it also offered the killer advantages of surprise and secrecy. Attacks by land came so slowly that the intended target of attack generally knew all about it well in advance. Attacks by sea, on the other hand, came by surprise. Defenders had no way of knowing if an attack was coming – or where – or when – or in what strength. Britain was, in effect, surrounded by an open highway to invasion. There must have been countless Britons who wished the country had had the good fortune to be surrounded by that most effective of barriers: more land, bad roads, a few hills and plenty of mud.

In short, if you want the central fact of British history, perhaps it's this: that the country was highly vulnerable not *despite* its island nature, but *because* of it. For five hundred years after the Battle of Hastings, the country got invaded a lot, and there was damn all its rulers could do about it. But exceptional vulnerability called forth an exceptional response: the navy. In

1588, the men and ships of the Navy Royal (as it was then) defeated the largest invasion force that Spain, the world's richest and most powerful nation, could muster. Within little more than two hundred years, the Royal Navy was more powerful than every other navy in the world *combined*. During the great age of British expansionism, it was the navy which protected our trade, 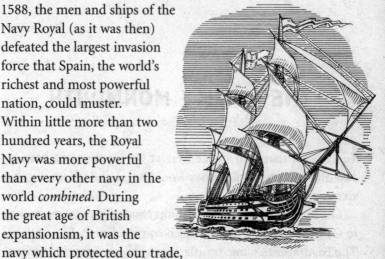 the navy which won our wars, the navy which made empire possible. If you're looking for a central fact, then there it is. An island nation, surrounded by danger, seeking security the only way it could: by learning to master the element that threatened it.

THE MIGHTY MONMOUTH

In 1758, Britain and France were at war, as they had been on and off for sixty years, as they would be on and off for another sixty.

On 28 February, the French ship *Foudroyant* was on its way to Cartagena to relieve the French commodore stationed there. The *Foudroyant*'s name translates roughly as 'lightning-striker', and the ship deserved the boast. It was a brand-new eighty-gun two-decker, one of the finest of its class. The ship was under the command of a senior officer, Admiral Duquesne. She was in all ways a pretty formidable piece of naval hardware.

On that night of the 28th, however, she was intercepted by a British squadron of three ships of the line: the *Monmouth*, 64, *Swiftsure*, 64, and *Hampton Court*, 70. (The numbers after the name of each ship are the standard way of representing her number of guns.) On the face of it, the British squadron was much more powerful, but that night its three ships were widely separated. HMS *Monmouth* encountered *Foudroyant* at about 8 p.m. The other British ships would not be able to join the action until close to midnight. That was four hours of fighting, ship to ship, with the *Monmouth*'s 64 guns against the *Foudroyant*'s 80.

That still sounds like a reasonably equal contest, until one delves a little deeper. The *Monmouth* was not in the first flush of youth. Although ships are female, and therefore normally entitled to a certain privacy in these matters, it seems appropriate to mention that she had been built in 1667, and was, at the time of the action with *Foudroyant*, some ninety years old. What's more, her guns were smaller than those of her enemy. *Monmouth*'s guns could shoot a broadside totalling 504 pounds. *Foudroyant*, the lightning-striker, could fire a massive 1,222 pounds – and those are French pounds, which were 8 per cent heavier. In total, therefore, *Foudroyant* had more than two and a half times the firepower of its enemy. When you combine that with the fact that the British ship had smaller scantlings – that is, a lesser thickness of timber armouring her sides – the contest was profoundly unequal.

The battle began at about eight in the evening. By half-past nine, *Monmouth*'s Captain Gardiner was struck in the head by a piece of flying grapeshot. He was carried below, where he subsequently died. His place was taken by Lieutenant Robert Carkett, and the battle continued. Heavy fire from the *Foudroyant* brought down the *Monmouth*'s mizzenmast, rendering her hard to manoeuvre or sail. But the elderly *Monmouth* continued to fight. Before long, she brought down the mainmast of her enemy, and before long the French ship's fire began to weaken. By midnight it had almost completely ceased. When HMS *Swiftsure* finally arrived on the scene, she poured one broadside into *Foudroyant*, which struck her colours immediately. The honour of taking possession of the defeated vessel would normally have gone to *Monmouth*, except that all her boats had been completely destroyed and she had no way of getting over there. A small, ancient, hopelessly outclassed vessel had defeated one of the newest and best ships in the French fleet.

How come?

The very first point to make is that while *Monmouth*'s action was remarkable, it wasn't exactly unheard of. If we take all the single-ship encounters of the Seven Years War, including those where there was an approximate equality between the two opponents, the results are as follows:

British ship (with number of guns)	Men killed in action	French ship (with number of guns)	Men killed in action
Monmouth, 64	30	*Foudroyant*, 80	134
Bellona, 74	6	*Courageux*, 74	240
Achilles, 60	2	*Comte de St Florentin*, 60	106
Badger, 14	0	*Escorte*, 16	55
Dorsetshire, 70	17	*Raisonnable*, 64	110
Tartar, 28	4	*Duc d'Aiguillon*, 26	60
Boreas, 28	1	*Sirène*, 32	80
Lively, 20	2	*Valeur*, 20	38
Trent, 20	1	*Bien Aimé*, 20	20
Fortune, 18	1	*Marie*, 26	12

What's striking about this table is that the British ships didn't merely overcome their opponents – they overwhelmed them. French casualties were four, ten, even eighty times greater than British losses. The creaking old *Monmouth* killed four and a half enemy men for every one of her own losses. The little *Badger* with her fourteen guns blasted the slightly larger *Escorte* into submission, without losing a single man in the process.

Many of the most easily available explanations for this wild disparity of destructiveness are simply wrong. Were the French cowardly, simply not up for the fight? No. There is no evidence for the accusation, and it was certainly never made by British naval officers of the age, who had every respect for the fighting spirit of their adversary. Were the French ships simply worse built? No. British captains rated the enemy vessels as better built than their own. When the *Foudroyant* was patched up and taken into the Royal Navy, she was regarded as the best two-decker of her day. Or perhaps there were other technological differences to account for the difference? No – and if there had been, they would hardly have been of much benefit to the geriatric *Monmouth*.

The difference appears to come down to simply this: the rate of fire of the two sides. It's hard now to assess exactly how fast and hard each side was firing – presumably the officers of the *Monmouth* had better things to do than stand on deck with a notepad and stopwatch – but the scraps of evidence that we do have suggest that British ships were capable of much faster fire than their opponents. This answer, however, merely pushes the question one level farther down. Firing guns quickly is, to say the least, a rather obvious tactic to deploy. Why were the French so weak at it, the British so strong?

The answer falls into two halves. The first part has to do with training, experience, discipline, leadership and ethos. The Royal Navy of Georgian Britain was not merely the largest organization in the world, it was also one of the most perfect. All the complex interlocking parts of manning, leadership, infrastructure, finance and the rest were as well engineered as it was possible for them to be. The continuing myths about the brutality of life in the Royal Navy are largely nonsense, at least when measured against the brutality of life that was general in those days. In many ways, the navy was the first truly modern organization of the industrial age. Since the purpose of that organization was efficacy in warfare, one shouldn't be surprised that the Royal Navy outclassed its more lumbering opponents.*

But the second part of the answer has to do with something deeper: the nature and purpose of the two rival navies. For the French, the navy was a means to an end. It was there to convey troops, support troops, allow troops to land. The French navy was never an end in itself, always the means to a military end. This outlook, of course, meant that the French navy never had the prestige, and sheer recruiting power, that the British navy enjoyed, but more significant still, it shaped French ideas on tactics too. On the whole, the French sought battle at a distance. Their aim was to fire high into the masts, spars and rigging of the enemy. The point was to disable the enemy, so that the French vessels could choose to avoid close action, manoeuvre or move in for the kill. This made perfect sense if the French purpose was to preserve their ships for the tactical support of the army. It would have made no more sense to jeopardize their ships unnecessarily than it would to have had their Catering Corps suddenly decide to charge the enemy, frying pans in hand.

For the British it was never like that. The fundamental purpose of the Royal Navy was simply this: to prevent invasion. Given that overriding central purpose, then gunnery, tactics and ethos came to be about destroying enemy ships wherever and whenever possible. Every enemy ship destroyed was one less threat to domestic security. Duelling at a distance made no

* Another factor that came to be of great importance was the British strategy of blockading French ports. The result was that British crews – monotonously sailing the waters outside Brest or Toulon – had ample time to learn how to work together as a sailing and fighting unit. The French crews inside the ports came to be desperately short of match practice.

sense, and British captains liked to get in close and personal. At Trafalgar, some British ships had their guns literally *touching* those of the enemy. In such a duel, the advantage naturally went to those who expected this kind of encounter, wanted it, trained for it – and were confident of winning it.

It was this ethos which made the Royal Navy what it was, this ethos which contributed to the construction of empire, the growth of trade, the globalization of industry. The doddering *Monmouth* proved mightier than she knew.

HOW TO BE A SUPERPOWER

Back in the 1970s and 1980s, the United States was merely a superpower, clashing nuclear arsenals with the Soviet Union. Since the demise of the USSR, however, the United States seems to have become something bigger: a hyperpower. It's become a commonplace to say that the military dominance of the United States is greater than that exerted by any country ever; that the world has never seen such a formidable concentration of armed force.

Well, maybe. Back in 1810, nobody talked about hyperpowers or their merely super cousins. All the same, the Sea Lords of the British Admiralty weren't exactly fretting about the opposition. The maths looked like this:

Ships of the line

Britain	152	France	46
		Russia	35
		Spain	28
		Holland	13
		Sweden	13
		Portugal	11
		Denmark	2
		United States	0

Rest of the world total 148

Cruisers

Britain	202	France	31
		Russia	14
		Spain	17
		Holland	5
		Sweden	8
		Portugal	14
		Denmark	0
		United States	9
		Rest of the world total	**98**

Quite simply, Britain had a fleet that was larger than the naval forces of the whole of the rest of the world combined. Of course, there were nations other than those listed which possessed warships of some kind, but the above list includes all nations in possession of a serious modern navy. If Britain had had to fight the rest of the world at sea, Britain would have won.

Those Sea Lords of 1810 couldn't just look at the mathematics of power with some smugness, they could think with equal calm about the qualitative factors too. Whose men were the best trained? Whose officers were the best? Whose ships were most modern, most technologically cutting-edge? Whose ships were (thanks to their copper bottoms) able to spend most time at sea and the least time in port? Which navy had the best infrastructure at home, the strongest political support, the best range of facilities overseas? In every case, the answer was Britain. On sea at least, Britain was the superpower's superpower, a hyperpower before its time.

Yet the fact that Britain then and America now both attained a similar degree of strategic dominance (albeit that the British dominance was naval only) should not be taken to mean that they got there the same way. America's current military strength is based on money. According to recent figures, the United States spends just shy of $500 billion on defence, the rest of the world together just over $700 billion. Of course, such things as technological supremacy make a difference too, but that technical know-how also carries a price tag. The US hyper-power is mighty indeed, but the source of its strength is the American economy, political support – and all those billions of American tax dollars.

In 1810, Britain was in a very different position. Britain's shipyards were formidably productive, but they'd been outbuilt and outspent by France and its Bourbon ally Spain in the long century of warfare that led up to that moment. From 1689 to 1815, the track record looked like this:

	Total ships built Displacement tons
Franco-Spanish Alliance	2,291,000
Britain	1,907,000
French advantage	384,000

Displacement tonnage of 384,000 represents an awful lot of ships – the equivalent of about 110 HMS *Victory*s, or more than three times the entire British fleet at Trafalgar. If amassing the biggest navy was simply a question of building the most ships, then Trafalgar Day would now be celebrated in Paris, not London.

This simple calculation reminds us that there are two routes to superpowerdom: the wallet and the gun. If you can't out-spend the enemy, you can always outfight him. If you succeed in capturing the enemy's ships, then you can patch them up, change the flag and add them to your own fleet – in effect, getting your enemy's shipbuilders to work on your behalf. Both sides played this game, of course, but the British were much, much better at it. Over the same time period as before, the record of ships captured then incorporated into the victorious fleet is as follows:

(Displacement tons)	Ships lost by capture	Ships gained by capture	Balance
Franco-Spanish Alliance	692,000	160,000	−532,000
Britain	160,000	692,000	+532,000
British advantage			1,064,000

British superiority in warfare meant that the French and Spanish lost a net naval tonnage equivalent to 152 HMS *Victory*s, while Britain added the same number of vessels to its own fleet – a total advantage equal to 304 *Victory*s, or much more than ten times the British fleet at Trafalgar. And that's simply to talk about ships *captured*. Yet for every three ships that were captured and added, there were roughly two more that had been burned, blown up, sunk or wrecked in combat. This was a fighting advantage that foreign shipbuilders couldn't even begin to match. When Nelson sailed into action at Trafalgar, he didn't *think* he was going to win, he *knew* he would – just as the French and Spanish commanders knew they'd lose.

Does all this mean that Britain was the first ever superpower? Probably not. Its land army was and would remain puny. But the size of armies matters only if they meet – and the navy was there to make sure that never happened. In 1803, Lord St Vincent addressed the House of Lords, seeking to calm the renewed fears of a French invasion: 'I do not say they cannot come, my Lords,' he declaimed, 'I only say they cannot come by sea.' They were the confident words of a naval hyperpower.

LACKING ELAN

When, at a recent dinner party, I happened to mention that I was writing a book on British exceptionalism, one guest asked me to explain in detail what the book was to be about. When I told him, he leant forward and said emphatically, '*Good!* After all, we've won a lot of wars, haven't we?' It's not only patriotic, Middle England Brits who think this way. Before the 2002 football World Cup in Japan and Korea, the Japanese police commenced intensive training to deal with the expected horde of hooligans from Europe, and most particularly those from England. I recall reading the comment of one Japanese police officer to the effect that the English had 'never lost a war'.

Such assessments are flattering, but hardly accurate. Yes, we've won plenty of wars, but then we've fought so many it would be surprising if we hadn't.* Whereas British naval history, from at least 1588 to the outbreak of the Second World War, is largely a record of mounting success, our purely military record is a thing of fits and starts, remarkable successes and painful failures.

---

* We're not the most bellicose nation, however. According to Niall Ferguson's reworking of statistics first compiled by Jack Levy, of 125 major wars since 1495, France fought 50, Austria 47 and Spain 44. England/Britain lies just outside the medal positions with 43.

That fitful record stretches a long way back. The one story that everyone knows about Anglo-Saxon England is Alfred burning the cakes, then beating the Danes. What's usually omitted from this record of culinary failure and military success is what followed: the Danish resurgence, which would lead to England being ruled by the Danish King Cnut. Although the country that William conquered was certainly under English rule, it could easily have been otherwise.

For the five hundred years following the Conquest, England's military record is easily summarized. In 1174, the king of England's possessions included a huge chunk of France stretching from the Channel to the Med, and from the Atlantic coast almost as far east as Paris. In 1558, Queen Mary died, having just lost Calais, England's last toehold in France. Agincourt may be the only battle we remember from our school history lessons, but the simple truth is that England fought and failed to maintain its possessions. We lost. France won.

The era of civil war and parliamentary rule brought an end to English failure. For the first time, English military leaders really applied themselves to understanding European techniques. That's why so many military words of that era are foreign in origin: *colonel, corporal, culverin, musket, bayonet.* Under Oliver Cromwell – and for the first time ever – the English army came to be as good, in terms of discipline, arms and leadership, as any in Europe. The good times, however, didn't last. With the return of royal rule and parliamentary stinginess, the army became rapidly inconsequential once again.

Through the eighteenth century there were highs (Marlborough) and lows (the loss of America), though the army certainly succeeded in establishing itself as the efficient and bellicose enforcer of a rising imperial state. Napoleon's eruption on to the European scene changed things again. His mobile tactics and search for the crushing victory revolutionized the nature of land warfare. Though the British forces under Wellington were (or became) excellent, they remained a minor factor in the scheme of things. When the Duke of Wellington crossed the Pyrenees into France in 1814, he had with him some 50,000 men. The French army entering Russia two years earlier had numbered almost 700,000.

In the nineteenth century, the British army perfected the art of colonial warfare: adaptable, resourceful and increasingly able to make its technological superiority tell. (Before the nineteenth century, there was often little or no technological gap to be exploited.) When European war broke out again in 1914, the British Expeditionary Force was remarkable for its professionalism and nerve, but neither quality could ever win the day against the mass industrial-age armies of the Continental powers. Though the British army changed into a conscript army like every other, its leaders remained mired in nineteenth-century thinking, nineteenth-century attitudes.

The Second World War was rather the same, fought by decent, reliable but unspectacular soldiers, who performed well or poorly depending on leadership. General Sir David Fraser summed up the army's performance thus:

[At the outset of war] it was starved of resources, incompetently administered and too small. For years British Governments persuaded themselves, and a public ready to hear, that Britain could stand aside from Continental war on land and that the dangers, if they existed, could be dealt with by others …

The British Army did not always behave impeccably, whether in battle or out of it. It was sometimes ponderous and lacking in élan. It rarely showed the 'handiness' in mobile battle which was the hallmark of the Afrika Korps … But it came to know its business. And, without histrionics, it did it.

Those comments could well serve as a verdict on British soldiering in general – and one that, in a book whose purpose is to search for the exceptional, suggests that we might do well to hurry on to more glorious things. If things military are under the microscope, then the Duke of Parma's Spanish troops, or Napoleon's revolutionary ones, or the Panzer-mounted ones of the Wehrmacht, would all deserve closer inspection than anything the British have ever assembled. Yet General Fraser's pithy summary hints at perhaps the British army's most curious – indeed exceptional – characteristic: it performed 'without histrionics'.

From the age of Henry VIII onwards, English, later British, strategy was founded on two axioms: (1) the army would never be capable of defeating a major European power in equal combat, and (2) a powerful navy was the first and surest defence against invasion. Those axioms remained true right through to the build-up to the First World War (and, as Fraser implies, their shadow continued to be felt thereafter too). The navy was the 'Senior Service'; senior in date of formation, but senior in importance too. Nor was the army simply secondary.

For much of its history, it was feared and despised – not by its enemies, but by those it guarded. For almost two centuries, England hung back from the European trend towards perm-anent standing armies. When a standing army was finally called into being under the pressure of civil war, it seemed to stand for everything that the English most loathed: high taxes, rapacious billeting, food shortages, disorderly behaviour.

When Charles II was restored to the throne, parliament cut him the following deal: it would control and pay for a standing navy; Charles could have an army, but only if he paid for it himself. One particularly curious consequence of the arrangement was that parliamentary statute law didn't even recognize the army's existence. The army's code of discipline therefore had no legal standing, which meant that the army had almost no power to punish such things as desertion or insubordination, except by such strikingly unfrightening punishments as stoppages of pay or dismissal. Furthermore, since soldiers' pay came from the royal pocket, the men were paid badly, and consequently recruited from the worst sections of society – those parts best calculated to exhibit the true English love for boozing and brawling. Of course, those impressed for the navy were hardly likely to be teetotal Sunday school types either – but they were hidden away on ships; the soldiers were in yer face and down yer high street. Time and reform were to change these stereotypes, yet their anti-militarist after-image would remain, right up to the First World War.

Secondary and unloved, the army was also small. In 1715, the British army – spread between Britain, Ireland, North America, India, the West Indies and the Mediterranean – was about the same size as the king of Sardinia's. By the end of the nineteenth century, when Britain's empire was by far the largest the world had ever seen, the country's army was about the same size as Switzerland's. Outside Britain and India, the army numbered just 41,000 men. The Roman army had deployed more legionnaires than that in England alone.

Sharply restricted in terms of its European capabilities, the British army's psyche was deeply shaped by that restriction. With the huge success of German conscript armies in 1866 and 1870, all leading European states, barring Britain, followed suit: conscripting men, training them, drilling them. 'The effect', wrote leading military historian John Keegan, 'was to maintain inside European civil society a second, submerged and normally invisible military society, millions strong, of men who had shouldered a rifle, marched in step, borne the lash of a sergeant's tongue and learnt to obey orders.' Such armies militarized society, their status endowing them with a strut, a martial arrogance, not given to their humbler British cousins.

It's this lack of strut, of 'histrionics', which is most genuinely remarkable about the British army. We should bear in mind that armies are seeking to do something almost impossible. They are there to dispense extreme violence to other human beings when called upon to do so, yet are asked to form an orderly part of normal civilized society at all other times. This is a big ask. In most places, most of the time, the warrior class has taken great care to distinguish itself, to call attention to its exalted status, all clashing boot-heels and swooshing testosterone. The British army has some of this, of course,* but on

---

* No country has a greater degree of regimentalism than the UK. Elsewhere regiments are often not much more than a way to organize troop numbers. British regiments, by contrast, jealously guard their own culture and traditions, busbies, bearskins and all. The importance of such traditions is exactly what you'd expect, given the context. After all, if the society doesn't properly honour its army, then the army had better find ways to honour itself.

the whole its army affects something almost self-deprecatory. Officer cadets at Sandhurst are expected to change into 'civvies' when not on active duty; officers in the mess call each other by their first names, as the mess dissolves all rank below the level of colonel. That civilian aspiration has even been visible in the uniforms worn: according to John Keegan again, British field marshals of the First World War 'in their whipcord breeches and glittering riding boots' resembled nothing so much as 'masters of foxhounds'. Rather than the army lending its character to the society, the British army has emphatically been moulded by the society that formed it.

This curious reticence is reflected in our national literature. The Napoleonic Wars were celebrated by Frenchman Victor Hugo in *Les Misérables*; the Russian contribution was famously honoured by Tolstoy in *War and Peace*. Yet in victorious Britain, the most famous literary monument is Thackeray's comic and bathetic rendition of Waterloo in *Vanity Fair*. Two generations later comes the next major British war, and its most famous literary landmark would be Tennyson's *Charge of the Light Brigade*, which celebrated martial valour for sure, but only in the context of a major-league and costly balls-up. The First World War would in turn generate a huge literature, and often a deeply patriotic one, yet that literature was again almost entirely devoid of bloodlust.

In short, British ambivalence about the army's very nature and existence has bred a military culture with less arrogance than most, more humanity than many. Of course, a successful army is not usually a pretty sight, and Britain's has had its share of ugly episodes. Yet even in its moments of brutality, the British army has often not been without some kind of countervailing pressure too: a revulsion against that brutalilty;

a protest, even. An ancedote related by Niall Ferguson makes the point. In the aftermath of the Indian Mutiny, British reprisals were savage: war crimes, as we'd rightly call them today. Following the relief of Lucknow, a young boy, supporting an elderly man, threw himself on the mercy and protection of a British officer. That officer put a gun to the child's head. He pulled the trigger once. The gun misfired. He tried again. The gun misfired. He tried a third time, with the same result. Then he had one further go. This time the weapon worked. The boy fell down dead. To quote Niall Ferguson:

> To read this story is to be reminded of the way SS officers behaved towards Jews during the Second World War. Yet there is one difference. The British soldiers who witnessed this murder loudly condemned the officer's action, at first crying 'shame' and giving vent to 'indignation and outcries' when the gun went off. It was seldom, if ever, that German soldiers in a similar situation openly criticized a superior.

There perhaps is the point. Armies aren't humane organizations, in any normal sense of the term. They can't be. Violence is their purpose. But, in the extraordinary and desperate circumstances of war, we can at least ask that the army's culture uphold the better values of the culture that surrounds it. The British army – small, professional, underloved, unhistrionic – has managed that challenge better than most.

PRESIDENT MONROE'S TROUSERS

At Trafalgar in 1805, the British fleet defeated not one navy but two. The French fleet was battered, the Spanish one all but destroyed.

For Spain, that was only the start of the bad news. Three years later, in 1808, Napoleon invaded the country, deposed the king and placed his own brother on the throne. Spain's colonial possessions in Latin America were immediately under threat. Not only had they been weakened by the unfavourable contrast between Spain's authoritarian colonialism and Britain's own more liberal version, it was now pretty clear that the ruling regime in Madrid lacked any real legitimacy of its own. A slew of independence movements sprang up all across the region. Argentina declared its allegiance to the deposed king in 1810. Chile declared independence the same year. Paraguay, Venezuela, Bolivia and Colombia all followed soon after. Without a fleet to convey an army or threaten action, Spain had no way of responding.

Time passed. Napoleon was defeated. A restored monarchy in Spain did what it could to recover the lost territory. The other principal powers of the age, including Britain and the United States, didn't approve of Spanish action, but did nothing decisive to prevent it.

Then, in 1823, President Monroe of the United States waded in. On 2 December, in a message to Congress, he declared:

> that we should consider any attempt on [the part of Spain or Portugal] to extend their system to any portion of this hemisphere as dangerous to our peace and safety. With the existing colonies or dependencies of any European power we have not interfered and shall not interfere. But with the Governments who have declared their independence and maintained it ... we could not view any interposition for the purpose of oppressing them, or controlling in any other manner their destiny, by any European power in any other light than as the manifestation of an unfriendly disposition toward the United States.

By the standards of the age, this was blunt speaking indeed. President Monroe was telling Spain and Portugal to butt out of the Americas or face the armed wrath of the USA. History recalls this declaration as the Monroe Doctrine. It's a phrase that most of us will have heard. The confidently threatening declaration seems to foreshadow the mighty impact that the USA would come to have on world history in the twentieth century.

Only – and here's the thing – President Monroe was all mouth and no trouser. Monroe's United States had no navy to speak of and not much of an army either. If Spain had chosen to stamp her control over her former colonies, there wasn't a whole bunch the United States would have been able to do about it, short of building up some armed forces pretty much from scratch.

If the US was toothless, Britain was anything but. British liberals strongly sympathized with the Latin American nationalists, while British capitalists welcomed the commercial opportunities that would flow from a more open trading environment. Ideology and commerce being thus neatly aligned, Britain warned Spain against re-establishing her rule. The warning, backed by overwhelming naval force, proved decisive. Without access to the sea, Spain was powerless to act and her Latin American possessions became ex-colonies, colonies that had ceased to be.

So much for Spain. With Portugal, long a British ally, things were not vastly more subtle. In 1825, with the Portuguese wavering about their future colonial policy, the British issued a stern warning – and, just in case the warning wasn't clear enough, they parked a substantial war fleet outside Lisbon to back it up. The Portuguese got the message and Brazil too got its independence.

The history here is interesting enough, but the really intriguing bit is this. Britain liberated half a continent from colonial rule, and virtually nobody knows it. It's an episode almost expunged from our collective memory. Even historians neglect the fact. The (generally outstanding) *Oxford History of the Royal Navy*, for example, doesn't give the entire business so much as a sentence. Indeed, the one element of the entire story that's percolated through to the national consciousness is President Monroe's ringing – but trouserless – declaration.

What's going on? Two things, I think, one specific to this story, one not. The non-specific part is simply that we are wonderfully forgetful about our own past. It was a Briton who invented the electronic computer – but not one in fifty of us could put a name to the inventor. We believe that Britain has suffered no successful foreign invasion since 1066 – and somehow we manage to blot the torrent of other invasions, successful and unsuccessful, from our consciousness. Compared with forgetting about a dozen or more invasions of our own country, forgetting about our role in Latin America seems rather simple.

At the risk of (temporarily) diminishing our capacity for happy oblivion, there's one specific issue from the Latin American episode that seems worth highlighting. These days, we tend to view the British Empire as a simple tale of land-grab, exploitation and hopelessly asymmetric warfare. Our armed forces, including the navy, can come to seem simply like the jackboot on the end of the violent, imperial foot. There's plenty of truth in this picture, of course, but the story of empire contains much else besides, and it would be quite wrong of us simply to retain in our memory all the elements that fit our simple picture (the massacre at Amritsar, for example) and to expunge all those that don't. Our role in freeing Latin America would be one such example, but there are plenty of others too. Would you care to speculate as to which major naval power did much to secure Greek victory in their war of independence? Or hazard a guess as to whose ships cleared Borneo of slavery and piracy? Or conjecture who might have made their extraordinarily accurate naval charts available free of charge to the shipping of the entire world? Yep, that's right. President Monroe it wasn't.

SCIENCE

THE FIRST SCIENTIST

Who was the first ever scientist?

There are some ancient Greek claimants to the title, also perhaps some Indian and Arab ones, but on the whole early advances in scientific knowledge were either mathematical in nature or mixed observation and wild theory in a way that could hardly be described as scientific. And in Europe, at least, for more than a thousand years after the decline

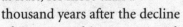

of Greece, nothing even vaguely resembling science was being pursued: the Dark Ages, indeed.

Then came the *annus mirabilis* of 1543. In that same year, two of the most important documents in scientific history were published. The first was *De Humani Corporis Fabrica* ('On the Structure of the Human Body'), written by one Andreas Vesalius.* The book was closely based on the teachings of the Greek physician Galen. It's hard to overemphasize how influential Galen had been. Lectures in anatomy were

* A Belgian – a famous Belgian!

often based less on the dissection of human or animal corpses, and more on a close *textual* analysis of what Galen had written. Anatomy professors tended to stand at a good distance from the corpse, while a barber-surgeon did the messy stuff.

Vesalius changed all that. In part, he did it by correcting some of Galen's errors, and making a big song and dance about so doing. Often enough, though, Vesalius simply repeated Galen's mistakes, propagating them for a whole new generation. Yet his book was revolutionary. New printing technology made it affordable to reproduce beautifully engraved woodcuts to illustrate the text. In a sense, it didn't matter too much what Vesalius *said*, when his pictures spoke so much louder than any words. No one who had turned the wonderfully illustrated pages could any longer think that anatomy was something to be studied with a dictionary. The new anatomy was all about *seeing*: observing nature, not reading about it.

It was a huge change, a revolutionary change, a change that marked the start of the scientific revolution, but Vesalius couldn't truly be considered the first complete scientist. He began the process of correcting flawed observations, but no new theory was born. No experiments had been conducted, no new laws identified. Perhaps a better claimant for the title was Copernicus. In 1543, the same year that the young Vesalius launched into print, Copernicus – old and close to death – published the book that would immortalize his name. His work, *De revolutionibus orbium coelestium* ('On the Revolutions of the Heavenly Spheres'), postulated that the earth revolved around the sun, not vice versa. Although similar ideas had been formulated in ancient Greece, India and the Arab world, Copernicus's ideas were certainly the most comprehensive and detailed. He didn't simply figure out that the earth revolved round the sun, he worked out the motion of other planets, the order of those planets, and he understood that the earth's axis must be tilted, thus creating seasons. What Copernicus produced, in fact, was a comprehensive new *theory* of celestial motion – systematic, comprehensive and mathematically elegant.

If Vesalius lacked the theoretical scope to be called the first complete scientist, then Copernicus was lacking on the empirical side. He made no observations to prove his theory. Indeed, the first preface to the book (which Copernicus himself had nothing to do with) said, in effect, 'this book contains a convenient mathematical shortcut for working out the movement of the planets, but don't for a moment think that this model is actually intended to be *true*'. The preface was a travesty of what Copernicus himself actually thought. (Indeed, as if in protest, the old man died of a cerebral haemorrhage shortly after receiving the first printed copy of his work.) But the fact that the preface could even have been written points up the limitations of what Copernicus had done. It was a vast achievement – a turning point in intellectual history – but its essence was theoretical, not empirical.

Modern science still has its Copernicuses. Stephen Hawking is a modern-day example: a theoretician who has never needed to mess around in a laboratory or squint starwards through giant telescopes. Contemporary science also has its Vesaliuses: field biologists who go out collecting, anatomizing and categorizing, but without aiming to prove any great new general theories of anything. In between these two ends of the spectrum, however, there are countless scientists who observe nature, perform experiments and build theories. It is this activity, performed in a systematic, disciplined way, which is the heart and soul of the scientific enterprise.

And the first man to understand that enterprise – and not just understand it, but actually do it? Enter the Englishman William Gilbert. Born in 1544, Gilbert went to Cambridge and trained as a doctor. Then, most likely in the early 1570s, he began the series of experiments that were the first truly modern example of scientific endeavour.

Back in those days, there was a lot of interest in electrical charge and magnetism, which were thought to be mani-festations of the same thing. Amber rubbed with fur would attract small bits of straw and suchlike. A magnet would attract iron and might attract or repel other magnets, depending on which face was presented. But none of these observations had been put into any coherent theoretical order, and even the observations were liable to be ludicrously exaggerated.

Gilbert sorted through all this. His first task was to tackle electric charge. Amber was thought to gain its charge from the warming effect of rubbing. Gilbert exposed this as nonsense, warming the amber by other means and demonstrating the lack of attraction. He found that electric charge could be carried in a number of other materials, not only amber. He showed that whereas magnetic attraction seemed to carry effortlessly through solid objects, electrical charge did not. He theorized that when a body was electrified through friction, a 'humour' was removed, leaving an 'effluvium' or atmosphere around the body. If we update the language and substitute 'charge' for 'humour' and 'electric field' for 'effluvium', then Gilbert's theory is essentially identical with modern concepts. It was Gilbert who coined the Latin word *electricum*, from which *electricity* is derived.

Turning his attention to magnets, Gilbert performed the same work of detailed experimentation and cautious, accurate theorization. He understood that the earth was a giant magnet. He understood that a magnet needle dips below the horizontal, and that the angle of the dip was dependent on latitude. He worked out the directions of internal magnetic fields, the polarity of a cut magnet, and explored the processes of magnetization and demagnetization. His work on what we'd now call magnetostatics was so complete that in 1859 the physicist William Whewell would write, 'Gilbert's work contains all the fundamental facts of the science, so fully examined, indeed, that even at this day we have little to add to them.'

Gilbert's work was an instant success. Future work on magnetism and electricity all recognized its debt to Gilbert, but his importance went far beyond simply reform of those two disciplines. For the first time in history, Gilbert was performing modern, experimental science – and he knew it. In the preface to *De Magnete*, he wrote:

> To you alone, true philosophers, … who not only in books but in things themselves look for knowledge, have I dedicated these foundations of magnetic science – a new style of philosophising. But if any see fit not to agree with the opinions here expressed and not to accept certain of my paradoxes, still let them note the great multitude of experiments and discoveries – these it is chiefly that cause all philosophy to flourish … Let whosoever would make the same experiments handle the bodies carefully, skilfully, and deftly, not heedlessly and bunglingly; when an experiment fails, let him not in his ignorance condemn our discoveries, for there is naught that has not been investigated again and again, done and repeated under

our eyes. Many things in our reasonings and our hypotheses will perhaps seem hard to accept being at variance with the general opinion; but I have no doubt that they will win authoritativeness from the demonstrations themselves.

Gilbert is a marginal figure now. He didn't possess the glamour of Galileo, the influence of Bacon, the genius of Newton, the precedence of Vesalius and Copernicus. Yet there, in his *De Magnete*, you can hear the authentic voice of modern science, spoken by the world's first scientist, who sought his knowledge 'not only in books but in things themselves'.

EX UNGUE LEONEM

In June 1696, the Swiss mathematician Johann Bernoulli published a letter to the mathematicians of Europe, challenging them to solve two problems that he had himself developed and solved, and proposing a six-month time limit for the solutions.*
By Christmas of that year, nobody had come up with the answers, so Bernoulli extended the time limit by another year. On 29 January 1697, the challenge first came to the attention of Isaac Newton, then in his fifties and with his most productive years long behind him. Newton solved both problems overnight and, just for the hell of it, invented a more complex version of the second problem and solved that too. In all Bernoulli received four solutions to his challenge, including an anonymous one, authored by Newton. The lack of a signature didn't deceive Bernoulli for a moment. He recognized the proof as Newton's, '*tanquam ex ungue leonem*', telling the lion by its claw.

The lion had been born in 1642, almost exactly a century after the Scientific Revolution had been launched by the twin

* The first problem was this: if you want to roll a ball from point A to a point B that is lower than and at some distance from A, then what shape of curved track will get that ball from A to B the fastest? You might think that such a problem could hardly be further removed from popular culture, but not so. In *Spider Man 2*, Peter Parker exclaims: 'Did Bernoulli sleep before he found the curves of quickest descent?' Not quite $E = mc^2$ admittedly.

efforts of Copernicus and Vesalius. A century on, and scientists were increasingly getting the hang of their new occupation: experimental, observational, mathematical. The Italian Accademia del Cimento, the English Royal Society and the French Académie des Sciences all set up shop between 1657 and 1666, just as the teenaged Newton was emerging into adulthood – the young man and the scientific community sharing the same coming of age.

Newton was an introverted child, with few close ties. His father, a minor landowner in the Lincolnshire hamlet of Woolsthorpe, died before he was born. Three years later, his mother remarried, taking as husband a prosperous rector twice her age. The new husband knew what he wanted – an attractive young wife, yes; an awkward stepson, no thanks – so the boy was palmed off on to a grandmother, who brought him up for the next seven years. At that point, the new husband had the good grace to drop dead, allowing his suddenly wealthy widow to return, three new kids in tow. (What Isaac thought about all this is, alas, not known.)

Locally schooled, the young lad was little suited to the rural life. He was fined for allowing his pigs to trespass, fined again for letting his fences fall into disrepair. At his uncle's instigation, Newton was sent away to Cambridge in 1661, which, far from being as it is now a hotbed of the latest scientific thinking, was wedded to a Latin- and Greek-based curriculum that had changed little for aeons. All the same, Cambridge had books and Newton had time to read them. He read, thought, studied, asked questions, made notes. In 1665 the plague came to Cambridge. The university closed down. Newton went home, aged just twenty-three.

Back in Woolsthorpe, the pigs still no doubt ran riot, the fences still no doubt gaped with holes, yet Newton wasn't completely useless. As he recalled later: 'In November [1665, I] had the direct method of fluxions and the next year in January had the theory of colours and in May following I had entrance into ye inverse method of fluxions.' 'Fluxions' was Newton's term for the differential calculus, and the 'inverse method' his term for the integral calculus, which together form one of the most essential tools in mathematics.

> And the same year I began to think of gravity extending to the orb of the Moon, and ... I deduced that the forces which keep the Planets in their Orbs must be reciprocally as the squares of their distances from the centres about wch they revolve: and thereby compared the force requisite to keep the Moon in her Orb with the force of gravity at the surface of the earth, and found them answer pretty nearly. All this was in the plague years of 1665 and 1666. For in those days, I was in the prime of my age for invention and minded Mathematicks and Philosophy [that is, science] more than at any time since.

Newton hadn't yet cracked the theory of gravitation, but he'd made the first emphatic breakthrough in thinking about it. More than that: he'd developed the mathematical tools he required for the mature theory to emerge. His account, just quoted, doesn't mention his work on infinite series and the binomial theorem during those plague years, but his work in either field would have secured him a permanent place in the mathematical history books.

If you or I had just spent a couple of years producing the most important series of mathematical breakthroughs in the history of humankind, we'd probably want to tell someone about it. Not so Newton. He got back to Cambridge, became elected a Fellow of Trinity, and went on working (on cubic equations this time). He told nobody what he'd done. Fortunately, however, though Newton was reclusive and uncommunicative, he was also touchy. In 1668, one Nicholas Mercator published a book, *Logarithmotechnia*, which presented a few results in the study of infinite series. Newton – way ahead of the game, but hating others being given the credit – started to let his results and findings leak out, though often anonymously. His fame spread. Other mathematicians called on Newton for help. Teasingly, partially and unpredictably, he responded, so that while European mathematicians started to become aware of his powers, they were still very much in the dark as to what he had actually achieved.

In 1669 Newton was appointed Lucasian Professor of Mathematics at Cambridge, and quickly turned his attention to optics, another area he'd studied during those plague years in Woolsthorpe. Fresh from mathematics, Newton now turned his hand to the experimental. In the words of Rupert Hall, author of the classic text *The Revolution in Science*:

> Spread over a series of years from 1664, perhaps ten years, Newton effected the greatest experimental investigation in all seventeenth-century physical science – indeed one of the greatest of all time ... Newton created completely novel standards of scientific method both with regard to the accuracy and detail of an investigation, and of the closeness of relationships with experiments and theory.

For the crucial experiment, he darkened his room at Trinity College, allowing sunlight to enter only through a small round hole. That sunbeam was allowed to strike a glass prism, which split the beam into all colours of the spectrum. Thus far, he was in well-known territory – 'a pleasing divertisement' but nothing more. What Newton noticed, however, was a phenomenon that no one else had taken interest in. The prism didn't simply split the light beam, it elongated it, just as it would if different sorts of light were being differentially refracted by the prism – a testable hypothesis. Having separated white light into all seven colours through one prism, Newton used a second prism to refract the blue light that had emerged from the first. This blue light was once again refracted, but it was no longer elongated as abruptly, or split into colours. After a series of accurate and minutely observed experiments, he drew the only possible conclusion: 'Light itself is a heterogenous mixture of differently refrangible rays.' The final proof was simply this: 'all the Colours of the Prisme being made to converge … reproduced light, intirely and perfectly white'.

To a world that believed that white light was the ultimate symbol of purity – of God's love, even – such a conclusion, which cast white light as nothing but the mongrel amalgam of everything going, was deeply shocking. Or rather: it would have been shocking if Newton had bothered to tell anyone. Characteristically, he did not. Instead, he was now hot on the trail of another goal. If light was a mixture, then the focal depth of blue light would be different from the focal depth of red light, and so on. One consequence of this fact was that no glass lens could focus without generating annoying coloured fringes around the image. Newton realized that light could be focused instead by reflection, 'provided [that] a reflecting substance could be found, which would polish as finely as Glass, and reflect as much light as glass transmits, and the art of communicating to it a Parabolick figure be also attained'.

That was hardly a minor ask, but Newton knew just the man for the job: himself. The mathematician-turned-experimenter now turned technician. In his own furnace, Newton developed a tin-and-copper alloy which he used to cast his curved reflecting lens. He then ground that lens himself, using all his strength to bring the surface to a perfect reflective pitch. The result, finally, was a reflecting telescope just six inches long but as good as the best telescopes in London and Italy.

Did he tell anyone? Of course not. This was Newton. For two years, the new device remained virtually unknown. Then, one day, he lent the telescope to his Trinity colleague Isaac Barrow, who took it to the Royal Society in London. Fame suddenly broke over Newton's head: welcome and unwelcome, intrusive and gratifying. For the first time in his life, Newton got ready to disclose something of consequence: 'the oddest if not the most considerable detection which hath hitherto been made in the operations of Nature'.

His optical discoveries, published in 1672 in the *Philosophical Transactions* of the Royal Society, caused a storm. Newton loved the praise, but detested the inevitable arguments. When the great Robert Hooke had the cheek to refer to Newton's conclusions as a mere 'hypothesis', Newton brooded over the supposed insult for several months, then wrote a rancorous and bitter reply, attacking Hooke personally and deliberately and needlessly widening the realm of disagreement.

For the rest of that decade, Newton remained largely withdrawn from public attention. His vendetta with Hooke ended, unreconciled, in 1676.* He passed his time in alchemical and

---

* It was in his final letter on the subject that Newton used the famous sentence 'if I have seen further it is by standing on the shoulders of Giants'. He never meant it, though. He was the giant, and by goodness he knew it.

scriptural researches. In both activities, Newton's drive towards investigative completeness was as total as his drive in his other, more 'modern' pursuits. Newton didn't simply read the Bible. He read it in English, Latin, Greek, Hebrew and French, and supplemented his biblical readings by consulting the writings of the early Church leaders, Athanasius, Arius, Origen, Eusebius, and many more besides. Newton's writings on scripture would amount to millions of words, dozens of times the length of this book, far more than he ever wrote on maths or physics. In alchemy, the same thing. He built furnaces, which he used to melt, burn, distil, sublime and calcine. He poisoned himself with mercury. He was, though almost unknown, the greatest alchemist in Europe.

Newton might well have stayed with his furnaces and scriptures. When Hooke wrote to Newton in 1679 asking his opinion as to whether planetary orbits might be caused by some central attractive force, Newton replied, saying that he had 'for some years past been endeavouring to bend my self from Philosophy … I am almost as little concerned about it as … a country man about learning'. Hooke persisted and soon managed to provoke Newton into a second quarrel, this time over how a body might fall to earth. Quarrelling, vendettas and claims of academic priority had always been the best way to get Newton to divulge his knowledge. This time, however, Newton kept his silence, though not before an exchange of letters had brought into sharp focus the problem of reconciling planetary motions, falling bodies and the mathematics of an attractive force. Never before had the problem been so accurately specified. Science stood waiting for an answer.

For four years – nothing. Among members of the London Royal Society, however, debate was escalating. There were a few ingredients in the pot already: Kepler's rule of periods, an inverse square law of attraction, the elliptical movement of planets. Debate, ingredients, but no resolution. Then, in August 1684, the astronomer and scientist Edmond Halley made a trip to Cambridge, where he asked Newton the million-dollar question. If planets were reacting to a central attractive force, what shape would their orbits be? Casually, Newton replied that the shape would be an ellipse; that he could prove it; that he'd known it for years; that he'd dig out the proof and send it on. Halley was flabbergasted. Newton, in effect, was saying that he'd solved the central scientific question of the age and had told no one.

From that point on, no one was going to let Newton keep his silence any longer. His first paper on the topic, a short piece of just nine pages, caused a storm of excitement. Under the pressure of excitement, outward and inner, he began to drive himself to systematize his own only partially formed insights. The recluse became ever more reclusive. He left aside his alchemy and his scripture. He ate standing up. If he went outside, he looked lost, distracted, and soon returned indoors. He wrote obsessively. The result, delivered to Halley in April 1686, was quite simply the greatest intellectual achievement in human history: Book 1 of the *Philosophiae Naturalis Principia Mathematica*. Book 2 was already mostly complete, and Book 3 wouldn't be far behind (once Newton had got another quarrel with Hooke out of the way, that is).

What did the completed *Principia Mathematica* achieve? It achieved everything. It gave precise definitions to concepts such as weight, mass, force: terms that had never before had exact expression. It defined the laws of motion. It contained the law of gravity. It proved the key postulates of gravitational theory, such as the elliptical movement of planets, or the way that a massive spherical object, such as the earth, was mathematically equivalent to a single point of equal mass located at the centre. It explained phenomena: the tides, the passage of comets, the motion of the moon. It made predictions: that the earth was not a true sphere, but a flattened one; that comets could return, in a slingshot action, past the sun. It contained massively detailed computations: reconciling observations of the moons of Jupiter with the mathematics of their orbital periods and distances from the planet. Ditto for Mercury, Venus, Mars, Jupiter, Saturn and the moon. It calculated the density of the planets, explained the precession or movement of the earth's axis. It was also a how-to book: how to locate a body travelling a given parabola at a given time; how to find the velocity of waves; how to determine an orbit without knowing a focus. If the book had done half of what it actually did – a third, a tenth – it would still have been the greatest work of science in history. As it was, it introduced the modern age of mathematical, physical and scientific knowledge as emphatically and decisively as it was possible to conceive. What the Glorious Revolution was to do for English and British politics, the *Principia* did for knowledge itself.

That's not to say it was all correct. It wasn't. Book 2 of the *Principia* may have inaugurated an entirely new field (rational fluid mechanics), and it may have demolished for ever the old Cartesian view of planets swimming in some invisible ether, yet the book was riddled with errors, albeit ones so abstruse that it would take more than a century to sort them out. Nor was the book entirely straight with its reader. Having calculated the speed of falling bodies on earth, Newton wanted to demonstrate that his predictions were borne out by reality.

Since no sufficiently accurate measurements existed, Newton simply used those he had available and pretended to greater accuracy than really existed. Modernity also arrived dressed in curious clothes. While Newton's argument was entirely modern in its reliance on infinitesimals and calculus-based modes of thought, it was defiantly classical in its use of Euclidian-style geometrical proofs and magisterial Latin prose.

Newton went on to live a long life. He became rich. He pursued his intellectual vendettas with a wholly needless intensity. (When Leibniz independently invented calculus, Newton savaged him and pursued him for years. English mathematics was deeply harmed by the feud.) He became not just the head of the Royal Society, but its Hooke-hating, Flamsteed-belittling autocrat. He became Warden, later Master, of the Royal Mint. On his deathbed, in 1727 at the great age of eighty-four, he refused the sacrament of the Church, his heretical, anti-Trinitarian views finally obtaining their full expression.

So immense is Newton, so much greater was he than those who stood around him, it's easy to miss one final point. Newton was a genius, one of the greatest ever, but he was not an isolated one. Although the scientific revolution had been born in Italy, it didn't long stay there, migrating north, passing through France and coming to rest in England. The oddness of this is easy to overlook. The English scientific community wasn't simply the largest in Europe, it was *by far* the largest. Even if you discount the idle, useless or dilettante members of the Royal Society, its core of serious scientists was by a distance the largest such community in the world. Yet England was then a small country, with a population less than half that of Italy, about a third the size of France or Germany. Though the country was becoming more prosperous, it was coming from some way behind. The Netherlands was still by far the wealthiest country in Europe per head. Britain ranked about the same as Italy; somewhat better than France and Germany. Whatever was going on can't be accounted for by either wealth or population.

England's scientific community wasn't simply the largest, it was also the best. Of the scientific ideas that poured out during the Scientific Revolution, a wholly disproportionate number came from England. These things are hard to measure with any objectivity, but some approximate indications are possible. For example, Professor Hatch, an American historian of science with, presumably, no nationalist axe to grind, has compiled a list of the greatest thinkers of the Scientific Revolution. Of his top sixteen names, five are English (Harvey, Bacon, Hobbes, Boyle and Newton). Of his 'second sixteen', four are English (Horrocks, Flamsteed, Halley, Hooke) and one a German (Henry Oldenburg) who came to live in London, where all his most significant work was carried out. In short, almost one third of all the most important endeavour in Western science was carried out in England, a country far smaller than Italy, Germany or France; a country that was not and had never been of much international consequence; a country that had long stood on the outer edge of Europe's cultural mainstream. Newton's own massive work was prompted, niggled and nudged out of his recalcitrant hands by the ferment of intellectual activity led by Hooke, Halley, Wren, Flamsteed and others.

From the point of view of British exceptionalism, Newton's legacy is simply too important to ignore. Yet, from this perspective, the more important point has less to do with one man's genius than with the national culture that nurtured him. No sober historian could write even a two-page summary of British history that ignored, say, the empire or the Industrial Revolution. Yet sober historians – indeed, the best historians of our age – have been able to write entire histories of Britain that make no mention of the Scientific Revolution, none of Newton, none of the most important development in all human thought. Such an exclusion is, frankly, bananas.

Why was Britain special? Why did the Scientific Revolution centre itself there and not in one of the more obvious candidates, France, Italy, Germany? The answer is complex and not fully understood. Yet the kernel of any answer must surely be a simple one. Britons were free to think what they liked. The contrasts are there wherever you look. In 1633, Galileo was tried as a heretic. In the 1680s, Newton was fêted as a genius. In 1553, the Spaniard Michael Servetus was burned at the stake for, among other things, his controversial views on the biology the human heart. William Harvey's much more extensive views on the topic were gathered together in a book with a respectful (nay, fawning) inscription to the king. The first recognizable scientific society was the Italian 'Academy of the Secrets of Nature', which had a cool name but a short life: the Pope didn't like it, and closed it down. The Royal Society, by contrast, so little threatened the state or the Church that Charles II liked to refer to the scientists as 'mes fous', my jesters. Ridicule may be bad, but it's better than the barbecue.

For Newton himself, two epitaphs best summarize the man and his work. Leibniz, so shamefully treated by his rival, told the queen of Prussia that all mathematics could be divided into two halves, Newton's half and everything else; and that of the two, Newton's was the better. The second epitaph came in a foreword written to a twentieth-century reissue of Newton's *Opticks*:

Nature was to him an open book, whose letters he could read without effort ... In one person, he combined with experimenter, the theorist, the mechanic and, not least, the artist in exposition. He stands before us strong, certain and alone; his joy in creation and his minute precision are evident in every word and every figure.

The author of that foreword: Albert Einstein.

THE LAST SCIENTIST

For the last half-century and more, the world of physics has been harbouring a dark secret. On the one hand, Einstein's theory of general relativity seemed to explain the world of the very large: planets, stars, galaxies and the rest. On the other hand, quantum theory seemed to explain the world of the very small: electrons, quarks, muons and the rest. Yet although both theories have made repeated, detailed and accurate predictions about their respective spheres, they are nevertheless in flat contradiction to one another. Where Einstein's universe is smoothly curved, the quantum universe is anything but. The result has been a physics rather like a car with only two gears: an ultra-low one for steep hill climbs in snow, and an ultra-high one for bowling along the motorway at a hundred miles an hour. The two gears work just fine when they're left to do what they're designed to do, but woe betide anyone who tries to shift from one to the other. Instead of a nice smooth shifting of gears, all you'll get is an ugly crunching sound and the smell of (highly mathematical) smoke.

The problem arises because the two theories are handling different things. There are just four fundamental forces of nature: gravity, electromagnetism, the weak force and the strong force. Einstein's relativity handles gravity. Quantum mechanics deals with the other three. And what's needed, of course, is a theory that combines all four forces in a single set of equations: a Theory of Everything, in fact.

The first hint that such a theory might be available came from a young Italian researcher at the CERN particle accelerator in Switzerland. The researcher, Gabriele Veneziano, discovered to his surprise that a two-hundred-year-old mathematical formula seemed to capture perfectly much of the data being generated by all that atom-smashing. A flurry of research ensued, aimed at using the formula to model the strong force in quantum mechanics. It was discovered that if elementary particles were thought of as tiny vibrating strings, then their nuclear interactions would be correctly described by the formula. So far, so exciting. Then it all went wrong. More powerful atom-smashers produced data that flatly contradicted the early predictions of string theory. Other theories were developed which seemed to cope much better. By the late 1970s, string theory seemed like just one of those things: a promising idea that had turned out to be a bust.

Not everyone, however, had given up. Physicists and mathematicians are driven by a sense of beauty – almost impossible to explain to a non-mathematician, but central nevertheless – and there at the heart of string theory lay a formula at once vastly simple and vastly rich in insight.* The American string theorist John Schwarz said, 'the mathematical structure of string theory was so beautiful and had so many miraculous properties that it had to be pointing towards something deep'. So he, and a handful of other string theorists, persisted with

---

* The formula, should you care to admire it, looks like this:

$$B(x,y) = \int_0^1 t^{x-1}(1-t)^{y-1}dt$$

their unfashionable work. Chief among the problems with which they wrestled was what appeared to be some apparently lethal inconsistencies. It was as though one part of the theory predicted that X = 1, while somewhere else in the theory it was predicting that X = 2. A self-contradictory theory was no theory at all; either the anomalies, or the theory itself, would have to go.

Of the true believers, two of the truest were the American Schwarz and a Briton, Michael Green. Both men were mildly fanatical, starting from a position that a theory so beautiful simply had to be true – and that if that were the case, then those mathematical anomalies couldn't really exist, however much it might look as if they did. For five years, they battled. Then, one summer's night in Colorado in 1984, they were ready for the final showdown. The whole thing – the future of string theory – came down to one single monster equation. On one side of the blackboard the equation solved out to 496. If the number on the other side was the same, then string theory was saved. It the number was anything else – even 497 or 496.00001 – then string theory would vanish in a puff of contradiction. In Green's words:

> I do remember a particular moment, when John Schwarz and I were talking at the blackboard and working out these numbers which had to fit, and they just had to match exactly. I remember joking with John Schwarz at that moment, because there was thunder and lightning – there was a big mountain storm in Aspen at that moment – and I remember saying something like, you know, 'We must be getting pretty close, because the gods are trying to prevent us completing this calculation.'

But complete it they did: 496 on the left-hand side of the blackboard, 496 on the right. What was more, in the course of all their work Schwarz and Green had given the theory enough demonstrable power to unite all four forces of nature – strong, weak, electromagnetic and gravitational – all in one theory. A revolution was born.

In no time at all, string theory was all the rage. At its core, it might be beautiful, but its beauty was wondrous strange. According to the theory, the fundamental units of nature are tiny vibrating strings of energy so small that, if you were to expand an atom to the size of the solar system, one string would be about the size of a tree. And that's not even the strange bit. According to the theory, there are three regular dimensions of space, a fourth one of time, then six further spatial dimensions: teeny-weeny ones, curled up on themselves so tightly that we never get a chance to see them. These tiny extra dimensions were enough to do the trick. Einstein's universe could now shake hands with its quantum twin. The car of modern physics suddenly found a full range of gears. String theory certainly isn't proven or anything like it, yet it's the first wholly plausible model of what a Theory of Everything might look like. Just three hundred years after Newton's *Principia* launched the quest for the deep mathematical truths behind the structure of the universe, physicists may have come to a credible final solution – first glimpsed on a stormy Colorado night as the gods thundered their disapproval.

The story is a nice one, adding a touch of drama to what is not exactly the most dramatic of human activities, yet it carries some broader lessons too. Three hundred years earlier, back at the birth of physics, Newton's *Principia* arose not simply from one man's genius, but also from the creative energy of the

world's leading scientific nation. Three hundred years on, and
that energy has spread across continents. Those responsible for
the creation of string theory include, to name just a few,
Gabriele Veneziano (an Italian), Yoichiro Nambu (a Japanese-
born American), Holger Nielsen (a Dane), Leonard Susskind,
John Schwarz and Ed Witten (all Americans), Joel Scherk
(a Frenchman) and Michael Green (a Briton). Yet even in our
more international age, scientific brilliance is not evenly
distributed. The easiest way to measure that brilliance comes to
us courtesy of Alfred Nobel.*

The first Nobel Prizes were awarded in 1901 and they have
been awarded almost every year since (the war years being
partial exceptions). Because multiple awards are often made,
there have now been slightly more than five hundred awards
made for scientific achievement. Unsurprisingly, it is the United
States which heads the medal table, with more than two-
fifths of scientific Nobels having been awarded to American
scientists. Britain comes second in the table with seventy-four
prizes, followed by Germany, France and Sweden. To lie second
in this table is a pretty decent achievement by any standard. The
United States has a population of 300 million, about five times
that of Britain. Since the Americans have won just three
times the number of Nobel Prizes then, on a size-for-size basis,
Britain has done at least as well, or rather better.

---

* Nobel was a manufacturer of explosives, dynamite his most famous
product. In April 1888, he woke up to find his own obituary splashed across
his morning newspaper, under the headline 'Le Marchand de mort est mort' –
the merchant of death is dead. The obituaries were a cock-up, of course: it was
not Alfred but his brother, Ludwig, who had died. All the same, the incident
is thought to have made Alfred reflect on the way the public perceived him;
his lavishly endowed prizes being the happy result.

Yet the scale of the British scientific achievement is obscured by comparing us to the American powerhouse. It's when you look at how we do in comparison with other countries that the British achievement really leaps out. Britain has won as many Nobel Prizes in science as France, Russia, Italy, Spain, Japan, Canada, Australia, China, India, Africa and Latin America *combined*. Only Germany, with its sixty-five prizes, comes even close to matching the British haul. British success has been shared reasonably evenly both across the disciplines (physics, chemistry and medicine) and over the decades. If you take Anglo-American science as a whole, then it has accounted for an eye-popping 70 per cent of all prizes awarded over the last four decades.*

This is an extraordinary record. It's easy enough to understand why Britain wins more than its share of prizes compared with the poorer countries of China, India, Africa and Latin America. In a way, it's unfair even to make the comparison. But what about France, Spain, Italy, Japan, Canada, Australia, Russia? The Royal Society of Newton's era puzzles us with the degree of its success, relative to its home country's size and influence. The same puzzle occurs in relation to the twentieth century. If anything, indeed, this later puzzle is still more baffling. In Newton's time, scientists were still learning how to do science. It was hardly surprising that the new, innovative ways of thought weren't equally dispersed across Europe. Somewhere, in short, was likely to be in the lead, and the country that was least likely to griddle scientists (for disagreeing with the Pope) or stop their mouths (for disagreeing

* To take a somewhat broader measure, British scientists produce about 12% of all papers cited in peer-reviewed journals – an impressive feat.

with the king) – or indeed the country that had moved farthest from witch-burning and belief in magic – was the one most likely to take that leading position.

In the twentieth century, no such easy explanation offers itself. The scientific outlook was common to all of Europe, North America and beyond. Popes no longer impeded science; kings no longer mattered; witches were no longer the stuff of bonfires. To be sure, Britain was a bit richer than some of its neighbours, some of the time, but British scientific excellence persisted well after its neighbours' economies had caught and surpassed its own. Likewise, it's true that British political liberties have provided a generally benign climate for scientific research; *die Hitlerzeit* in Germany did much to wreck that country's extraordinary scientific prowess. Yet this explanation too falls far short of what it is called upon to explain. German liberty and economic might returned speedily after the war, with Konrad Adenauer and the *Wirtschaftswunder*, yet German scientific achievement has (by its own high standards) been anaemic ever since 1933. Democratic France and Italy have been less impressive still. The elite British universities have probably been more effective at nurturing talent than their more state-directed Continental cousins, yet it's hard to avoid the feeling that, as with the British literary achievement, there's something about Britishness and science that makes them go happily together. The empirical spirit, so precocious in Newton's England, so notable in the British philosophical tradition, seems alive and well today, and that Nobel medal table seems to prove it.

There's probably truth in this conclusion, yet satisfaction in the past should not breed complacency as to the future. Increasingly, British Nobel Prize winners are likely to be based not here, but in the USA. Increasing wealth is likely to be on the brink of unlocking the huge creative energies of China and India: the latter country today produces more mathematicians than the whole of the EU. Meanwhile, the number of those studying physics in British schools has dropped by some 40 per cent over the last decade and a half. This section is entitled 'The Last Scientist' because Michael Green may just possibly have played a pivotal role in concluding the intellectual quest launched by Newton some three hundred years ago; but it's called this for another reason too. Britain may have had a great track record in science, but in a competitive world you need to compete: that means physics teachers in schools, plenty of cash for universities. No political party has yet sought to address these challenges with the urgency they deserve. Will the next generation of policy-makers do any better? Maybe. Maybe not. The future of British science depends on the answer.

A PAINFUL ADMISSION

Alfred Nobel never endowed a prize in mathematics. Some people maintain that he refused to do so because his mistress once had an affair with the Swedish mathematician Gösta Mittag-Leffler, but then again, some people maintain that the CIA killed President Kennedy and has an underground bunker in Nevada full of aliens in cages. There's not much evidence for any of these hypotheses and, most likely, Nobel ignored the subject because his bent was more practical, and because there were already some well-run maths prizes around at the time.

This book, however, sets out to track down British exceptionalism in every area, every age. It seemed to me that, if British science has been exceptional, it was perfectly likely that British maths has been too. Slave to my readers that I am, I made it my job to find out. But find out how? Although I know which end of a calculator is up, my knowledge of holomorphic dynamics, functional analysis and homological approaches to field theory is, I freely admit it, a little rusty. Luckily for me, a Canadian mathematician, John Charles Fields, did in 1936 what Alfred Nobel had failed to do, and established a prize that has come to be the gold standard award in the subject. The prize is awarded every four years, with multiple awards commonplace. Though only mathematicians under forty are eligible, most of the best work in mathematics is done by relative youngsters in any case, so that the awards are reasonably representative. The prize has been running for long enough that, as with the Nobels, it's possible to put together some kind of international medal table.

The results are by no means disappointing. There have been six British winners of the medal, plus, in 1998, a silver plaque in lieu of the medal itself was awarded to the forty-one-year-old Andrew Wiles, for his extraordinary proof of the most famous conjecture in mathematics, Fermat's last theorem. So: six winners, or, cheating only marginally, seven. Not bad at all. The United States has had thirteen winners in total, but since the US population has been between three and five times as large, Britain has certainly exceeded it on a per capita basis. By the same argument, we can also hold our heads high in comparison with the Russians and their eight medal winners. As for our old scientific rival, Germany, the country has produced just one medal-winner during the seventy years of the prize.

Unfortunately, there is a but. It's hard to know how to put it. Readers of a sensitive or nervous disposition may prefer to skip the rest of this chapter and scurry forward to safer things. Anyone else … well, you've been warned. You read on at your peril. The ugly truth is simply this: the French have beaten us, with nine medallists to our six or (cheating) seven. No excuses spring to mind. In twentieth-century mathematics, the French have simply been better.

Perhaps at this point, it's worth coming completely clean. It would be easy to make the mental leap from Isaac Newton at the dawn of serious mathematics to British excellence in the twentieth century and assume that everything in between has been rosy. Easy and wrong. British mathematics after Newton was not quite a desert, but it came close. All the maths that mattered was being done elsewhere. In the eighteenth century, the best mathematicians were largely French. During the nineteenth century, when the foundations for modern mathematics were being laid, the most important contributors came from Germany (Gauss, Cantor, Rieman, Hilbert and others), from France (Cauchy, Galois and Poincaré, for example), and elsewhere in Europe (Lobachevsky). If all British mathematicians working during the era had had their working papers stolen by the CIA and locked away in that alien-infested Nevada bunker, the history of modern mathematics wouldn't be so very different. The inauguration of the Fields medal more or less coincided with the renaissance (or, more accurately, just the plain old naissance) of maths in Britain.

Since it's confession time, we may as well make a clean breast of things. The problem with a book like this one is that it's all too easy to end up sounding like the father in *My Big Fat Greek Wedding*, who claimed every good thing as Greek, no matter how contrived his reasoning. So let's be clear. This book explores the numerous ways in which Britain has been exceptional, and simply leaves aside the ways in which we've been nothing special, or even a bit rubbish. In science, we've had a good twentieth century, and before that made groundbreaking contributions to such things as biology, geology and physics, but our overall record in those earlier centuries was patchy. We contributed little to the early development of chemistry. During the nineteenth century, Britain made numerous practical advances in medicine, but our contributions to medical theory fell far short of the work being done in France and Germany. We lost leadership in the electrical and chemical industries because our engineers couldn't keep pace with Germany's.

And why stop at science? We aren't the world's most musical country. It's no coincidence that our most notable composers include the less-than-entirely-English-sounding Georg Friedrich Händel and Gustav von Holst. Our most famous operas are those written by Gilbert and Sullivan. Our track record in the visual arts has been solid, but no more. We've had some good architects, but Paris is a prettier city than London, as are (feel free to make up your own list) Prague, Amsterdam, Rome and Stockholm. Our development of consultative government was precocious and of huge significance, but we were nowhere close to leading the next crucial movement towards one-person-one-vote democracy. We haven't been a very feminist country. We do badly by our children. We lack the social egalitarianism of northern Europe, without enjoying the economic dynamism of North America. By American standards, our entrepreneurs are feeble. By German standards, our manufacturing is laughable. By French standards, our record of state intervention in the economy is simply awful. Our education has mostly been worse than that of our neighbours, our technical education vastly worse. Our elite universities have, over the centuries, had a record that is sometimes wonderful, but often hopeless. We aren't a spiritual nation. There have been some British contemplatives and mystics, but almost none of us could name one. Our principal religious denomination, Anglicanism, is notable mostly for its very English aversion to anything too religious. (At a famous Oxford college, a former chaplain used to remark, 'I can't be doing with all this Jesus worship.') When it comes to abstract philosophy, we're good at producing a particular brand of empiricism, but have almost nobody to compare with Sartre, Hegel, Heidegger or the rest. Though we've excelled at naval warfare, fighting on land has seldom been our forte. Our army has mostly been an ordinary little army, which has chiefly excelled at winning minor colonial wars against hopelessly inferior opposition. We've had some good generals, but many more lousy ones. Even by sea, there was nothing remarkable about the British naval record from AD 400 to almost 1600. Our kings and queens have generally been poor, usually foreign, and have included a generous quotient of dolts, thugs, rogues and lunatics. Our sports teams nearly always lose. Our food is rubbish. Our fashion sense has generally been derivative or just plain bad. Throughout the 1,200 years since the Romans left these shores, the British Isles were remote, poor and mattered little to anyone except those living there. And if it's mathematicians you're after, then you'll need to learn French.

TECHNOLOGY

RAISING WATER BY FIRE

In Monty Python's *Life of Brian*, Reg (played by John Cleese) demands: 'What have the Romans ever done for us?' Getting more answers than he's bargained for, he adjusts his question:

> **REG:** All right, but apart from the sanitation, medicine, education, wine, public order, irrigation, roads, the fresh water system and public health, what have the Romans ever done for us?
>
> **ATTENDEE:** Brought peace?
>
> **REG:** Oh peace – shut up!

That interchange encapsulates much of how we view the Roman and post-Roman era. The Romans got things sorted. The Dark Ages were, well, dark. It's striking, however, that not one of the items on Reg's list represents new technology. Those masterpieces of Roman engineering – roads, irrigation, aqueducts and the rest – were largely dependent on the effective implementation of existing technology. (The most notable exception: a much-improved cement.) The Roman Empire was largely powered by men and animals, while use of inanimate power sources was rare. Exceptional builders the Romans may have been; good technologists they were not.

Conversely, two or three centuries after the collapse of the Roman Empire, Dark Ages Europe began fizzing with creativity. The seven centuries from AD 700 to 1400 were vastly more productive than those seven Roman centuries from 300 BC to AD 400. Along came the heavy plough, capable of working the heavier clay soils prevalent north of the Alps. Along came the three-field agricultural system. Along came three-masted ships, better navigational tools and carvel-type construction.

And power. Despite the empire's dependence on ox- and horsepower, Roman harnesses were bizarrely hopeless, involving a neck strap that pulled directly against the animal's windpipe and jugular. If you've ever wondered why the chariots in *Ben Hur* were so flimsy, part of the answer is that the horses pulling them were half choking as it was; heavier chariots might have finished them off completely. Medieval Europeans sorted out a proper harness, first a breast strap, then the shoulder collar. When those later animals pulled, they didn't have to stop because they were nearly dying.

Water and wind power played their part too. By the end of the tenth century, waterwheels had been vastly improved and widely disseminated. We don't know where most such inventions and innovations originated – the records simply don't exist – but we do know that the English were, at the very least, enthusiastic adopters of such techniques. In 1086, the Domesday Book listed an amazing 5,624 watermills in England south of the Severn, or one for every fifty households. As a rainy country, England is, of course, ideally suited to such technology, but not more so than Ireland, where waterwheels were comparatively scarce. It's significant too that the first windmills whose dates can be accurately documented sprang up in

Yorkshire in 1185. England, and other technologically enthusiastic European nations, were the first societies in the world to make wide-scale use of inanimate power; not animals, not slaves.

With the Renaissance, the technological clock began to beat faster. The old distinction between thinkers and makers disappeared. It wasn't science as such which pushed technology forwards – science-based invention would play little part in things till 1850 or later – but it became normal for thinking men to become interested in the mechanical, to mess around with lenses, pumps, clocks, navigation, and the rest. Inventors became a protected species – literally, with the world's first patent law arising in Venice in 1460 and numerous copies across Europe thereafter. England's own 1624 Statute of Monopolies was the most effective such law anywhere.

For all these advances, however, the Renaissance was a time of incremental improvement only. The great medieval revolutions – the watermill, the heavy plough, the stirrup, the printing press – had no counterpart in the quarter of a millennium from 1500. The horse, wind and water power of Norman England had not been superseded. Machines were scarce. The use of raw materials was restricted. Production was small-scale. By 1900, none of that was any longer true. From a purely technological point of view, the Europe of 1750 would have been less awe inspiring to a time traveller arriving from 300 BC than the Britain of 1900 would be to one arriving from 1750. In each of these crucial dimensions – power, the factory, machines and the exploitation of raw materials – Britain would lead the way. That leadership wouldn't last, of course. By 1900, Britain was no longer pre-eminent in any of these areas, but there's no doubt at all who got the party started. Of all these revolutions, the most central was power. Without power, machines were useless. Without machines, factories were just big buildings. Without machines and factories, those raw materials were never going to get cooked. Power lay at the very heart of things.

In the economically sophisticated climate of the eighteenth century, it was fairly obvious where that new source of power might come from. Back in the first century AD, Hero of Alexandria had made steam-driven toys. A French Huguenot refugee in London, Denis Papin, had invented a simple 'steam digester'. More significantly, in 1698, Thomas Savery patented an engine 'for raising water by fire', which Thomas Newcomen would come to refine. In Newcomen's engine, steam was injected into a piston, forcing it to rise. Cold water was then injected into the cylinder, causing the temperature to drop, the steam to condense and a vacuum to be created. Atmospheric pressure then drove the piston back down the cylinder, and the downward action was converted by a see-saw type beam into an upward action, used to pump water. These engines worked and were widely used. For the first time in history, the energy in a lump of coal was being converted into economically useful motion.

It was a crucial start, but not yet a revolutionary one. Newcomen's engines were wasteful. Because steam was both injected and condensed in the same cylinder, the cylinder itself went through a continual cycle of heating and cooling. In other words, coal was burned both to bring water to boiling point *and* continually to reheat a huge metal cylinder. The process was so wasteful that it only made commercial sense where coal was cheap (as in coal mines themselves) or where the potential rewards were so large that wasting coal didn't matter (as in the Cornish tin mines). For revolution to happen, steam power didn't just need to work, it needed to be cheap.

Enter James Watt. As a youth, Watt had his own space in his father's large and well-equipped workshop, building intricate working models of cranes, capstans and other devices. Equally significantly, perhaps, the family was Scots Presbyterian, with the true Scots Presbyterian horror of idleness and waste. Watt became an instrument maker, working closely with Glasgow College, then seething with talent.

One day, in 1760, Watt was asked by the college to fix a toy-sized model of a Newcomen engine, a demonstration model used in lectures. In due course, as his aptitudes were better known, he was asked not simply to fix it, but to make it work better. At that stage, no one had any idea of doing anything more than turning an unreliable toy into a more dependable one, but Watt was intrigued. Early on, he came to understand the challenge as one of waste: wasting steam, wasting coal.

Although Watt was no scientist, his mode of thinking was

utterly scientific in approach, in tune with the rationalism and empiricism of the age. Watt conducted experiments to see how far water expanded when converted into steam. He investigated the issue of latent heat and heat capacity. He tested out different materials for the cylinder. He came to understand and deal with the fact that the condensation point of steam (normally 100°C) was altered by the ever-changing pressures inside the cylinder. He applied all these findings to the task in hand and in the process his mission changed. No longer was he interested in that classroom model. He was interested in Newcomen's engines themselves, and how to perfect them. In 1765 came the masterstroke. In Watt's own words:

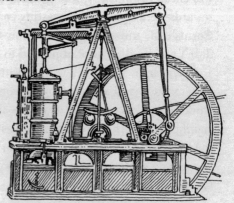

I was thinking upon the engine at the time and had gone as far as the Herd's house when the idea came into my mind, that as steam was an elastic body it would rush into a vacuum, and if communication was made between the cylinder and an exhausted vessel, it would rush into it, and might there be condensed without cooling the cylinder … I had not walked further than the Golf-house when the whole thing was arranged in my mind.

That separate condenser was a stroke of genius, the stroke of genius on which the Industrial Revolution would depend. Rather than cooling the cylinder, the engine that Watt envisioned would simply allow steam to rush out of the hot cylinder into a separate condensing chamber. There, the steam could be condensed and a vacuum created without the constant need to cool and reheat a huge chunk of metal.

Yet to say that the 'whole thing was arranged' was just a tad premature. Building an engine of commercial scale proved deeply challenging. Just to pick one example, Newcomen's pistons had been kept airtight by leather packing with a pool of water sitting on top. Watt's engines, which would eventually use cylinders some six feet in diameter, would need something better than that, and it was only when cannon-boring technology was applied to the problem that it really gave way. (A notable example of the way in which the proto-industrial navy helped spark industry itself into life.) With every problem, every part of his machine, Watt sought to innovate. Some of those innovations never worked. Others became standard.

In 1776 – the year in which the first shots of America's War of Independence were being fired – an almost equally revolutionary moment took place on the other side of the Atlantic. Watt's steam engine went into commercial production. Where Newcomen's engine had used 30 pounds of coal per horsepower-hour,* Watt's used just 7.5. It was the birth of cheap energy, the birth of energy that could be used when, where and how humans wanted.

Watt's place in history was already assured, but he wasn't done. He had the temperament of the true inventor, constantly seeking to refine and improve. Watt didn't merely invent the first commercially efficient steam engine, he invented its

---

* It was Watt who first defined and christened the unit of horsepower as a marketing gimmick to advertise his engines.

second-generation replacement too: the double-acting engine, which used steam to pull as well as push. He invented the centrifugal governor, by which the engine regulated its own speed. Perhaps most crucial of all, he realized that factories wanted power not just in the thump-pause-thump-pause mode of Newcomen's pumps, they wanted constant rotary power too. Through a brilliant sun-and-planet gearing system, Watt provided just that. He hadn't simply invented the world's best source of industrial power, he'd invented its crucial gearing mechanism as well.

The importance of Watt's engine also lies in the extent to which it released a flood of innovation by others. In 1802, Richard Trevithick built the first high-pressure steam engine, working at 10 atmospheres, rather than Watt's 1.5. Other innovations followed. By 1850, the best steam engines burned just 2.5 pounds of coal per horsepower-hour, a threefold improvement on Watt.

Watt's innovations may have been born of his own technical genius, but if so they were midwifed by the culture that nourished him. It's significant that virtually every major technical development in steam power, from Papin to Trevithick, took place in Britain. Watt's own development was nourished by at least three critical influences: his childhood access to a well-equipped, technically advanced and commercially bustling workshop;* his access as an adult to the brains and scientific thought of Glasgow University; and the huge economic fires that lay just waiting to be kindled in the only just pre-industrial Britain. The first two of these

---

* The link between the navy, commerce and industry pops up here too: Watt's father's business was fed by Glasgow's shipping trade.

influences, the technical and the scientific, were to be found in plenty of other locations in Europe, yet they were to be found more densely in Britain than elsewhere. As for the third, British industrial readiness made a difference at every stage of the process. The British readiness to make wide-scale commercial use of power did much to encourage investment in the development process – profits, not necessity, being the mother of invention.

The basic friendliness to invention of Britain in this period can hardly be overstated. From about 1770 to about 1850, Britain's inventors were rampant, hyper-productive, world dominant. The key technologies to emerge in the cotton spinning and weaving industries were British. The key power technologies, ditto.* The key innovations in iron-making, ditto. The most important innovations in machine tools, ditto. At the Great Exhibition in London in 1851, British exhibitors and technologies were dominant. Extraordinary as it seems to us now, the American exhibitors weren't even able to fill their allocated space.

The splendour of British invention in this period shouldn't trick us into drawing any false conclusions. Above all, it needs to be remembered that for Britain to be noted for its inventiveness was a quite new phenomenon. As late as 1766, a Swiss textile printer commented that the English 'cannot boast of many inventions but only of having perfected the inventions of others … for a thing to be perfected it must be invented in France and worked out in England'. That wasn't Gallic solidarity speaking. The British themselves said much the same thing.

---

* The one exception: Watt's effective patent protection drove some invention overseas.

Furthermore, Britain's inventors led the field during a time when there really wasn't much of a field at all. Industrialization on the Continent was held back by decades of war and social turmoil. The United States was still, overwhelmingly, a country of farmers and small towns, and its industrial sector was still in its infancy.* As a result, if it wasn't always British brains which came up with the key ideas of the Industrial Revolution, it was in the furnace of British industry that those ideas were most likely to take shape in iron, wood and steam. These were the glory years, the period in which modernity itself was forged in the factories, workshops and satanic mills of William Blake's Britain.

Watt's invention was *the* central technology of that golden age, the invention that most called our modern age of technical advancement into being. What's more, the age of steam has lasted much longer than we're inclined to think. Steam locomotives weren't phased out in Britain until the 1960s. When I travelled in India as a student in the 1980s, steam trains there were still commonplace. Even today, fossil-fuel power stations work by turning water into steam, and using that expansionary force to drive turbines. Though Watt never dreamed of trains or power stations, he remains their presiding genius all the same. Joel Mokyr, a leading historian of technology, sums it up when he writes: 'In short, in the history of power technology, Watt is comparable to, say, Pasteur in biology, Newton in physics, or Beethoven in music. Some individuals did matter.' Watt was one of them.

---

* A precocious infant, mind you. Productivity per head in American manufacturing exceeded British productivity as early as 1820 – a remarkable statistic.

THE HORSE, THE CAR, THE POGO STICK

Jeremy Clarkson – journalist, broadcaster and all-round motormouth – is wont to claim that 'the British invented everything', a view that has settled rather lazily into the popular consciousness. Even with a Clarksonian view of the world, however, the claim is hard to support.

Take, for instance, the area of transport technology. It's pretty clear that the pogo stick is not a British invention. Originating in Germany, the modern all-metal, enclosed-spring pogo was developed and patented in the United States by an Illinois toy designer, George Hansburg, in 1919. The device proved a big hit. Hansburg taught the girls at the Ziegfeld Follies how to pogo, and in 1920 the world's first pogo wedding was celebrated. There are other modes of transport that the British have not invented. Neither the car nor the internal combustion engine was a British invention. Equally, not even the most patriotic British historian has suggested that the horse was first perfected on these shores. In the history of transport technology, therefore, the British record does admit some fairly gaping exceptions.

TRANSPORT

Things invented by the British	Things not invented by the British
Macadam roads	Horse
Steam locomotive	Car
Iron-hulled, screw-driven ships	Pogo stick
Aeroplane	
Steam traction engine	
Underground trains	
Chain-driven bicycle	
Pneumatic tyre	
Jet engine	
Jet-engined passenger aeroplane	
Hovercraft	
Supersonic passenger jet	

A small number of readers may be inclined to query the notion that the aeroplane was a British invention. It's certainly true that the Wright brothers were the first to achieve flight that was controlled, powered and manned. But what actually did the Wright brothers *invent*? Gliders had been around for decades before the Wright brothers. So had internal combustion engines. So had airscrews or, as we'd now call them, propellers. The basic design of the aeroplane had been settled long before. The achievement of the Wright brothers was twofold. First, they were brilliant development engineers – tinkerers of genius. They took existing designs and made them better. Second, as bicycle men, they figured out that planes needed to bank like a bicycle, not steer like a ship. Their particular device for achieving this – 'wing-warping', or deforming the wings to alter the attitude of flight – was rapidly superseded by the wing and tail controls still in use today, but that same basic insight has lasted the course. That's why (centripetal force aside) your drink spills in a turning aeroplane, but doesn't in a turning ship.

The actual invention of the aeroplane occurred half a century or more earlier, thanks to one Sir George Cayley, a Yorkshire baronet. Cayley's genius was to forget all about birds and hot-air balloons, and to divide the problem into its component parts. An aeroplane needs lift to keep the thing airborne, thrust to keep it moving, and control to stop it killing everyone on board. Lift, thrust and control were and are the central problems of flight, and it was Cayley who both defined the problems and took the first serious steps in solving them. He developed and tested the concept of the aerofoil-shaped wing. He tested different designs for airscrews. He worked out that dihedrally set wings (high at their tips, lower at their base) improved lateral stability in flight. He built and tested numerous working models. He laid out the basic design of the aeroplane, including the long body, the non-moving wings and the tail section. His 1810 treatise 'On Aerial Navigation' effectively inaugurated the field of aeronautics.

If Cayley had stopped there, he'd certainly have been the father of flight, but he went one better and built the world's first aeroplane. The plane was a glider, perforce, since the only sources of power available to Cayley were steam engines (too heavy) or horses (prone to airsickness). Having built his glider, Cayley did what baronets do and ordered his coachman into the contraption for the world's maiden aeroplane flight. The glider flew five hundred yards across a Yorkshire valley and came to an awkward but not life-endangering halt. (The coachman, alas, resigned anyway.) If the Wright brothers and Cayley had ever come to slug out rights to the component parts of the aeroplane in a patent court, Cayley would have won on virtually every fundamental count.

In Clarkson-world, therefore, while the British record on transport isn't quite spotless, it's hardly bad either. In power technology, for example, a similar list of British achievements would include at least the following.

POWER

Things invented by the British

Steam engine

Gas lighting

Self-contained electrical generator

Transformer

Light bulb

Fossil-fuel power station

Commercial nuclear power

James Watt's steam engine, which for the first time allowed humanity to convert chemical energy into usable power, must rank among the most significant technological achievements anywhere, ever. What's less well known is that Britain played a significant role in every other major evolution in power technology. The first commercial use of gas lighting took place in Westminster in 1816. Many of the bits and pieces needed to turn electrical power into something of practical use were invented here. (They were sometimes independently invented elsewhere as well, the electric light bulb being one of the best known examples.) The world's first fossil-fuel power station of commercial scale was built in Deptford in 1889. Much more remarkable, however, is that while both the Americans and the

Russians had made significant breakthroughs in nuclear power generation, it was Britain's Calder Hall which, in 1956, became the first commercial nuclear power station to go online anywhere in the world. In the new field of eco-friendly power technology, Britain lost out to Denmark in wind power, but is currently making a credible bid to lead the way in wave power: Britannia's last-gasp attempt to rule the waves, perhaps.

Arguably more impressive still, however, is British achievement in the sphere of communications and IT.

COMMUNICATIONS & INFORMATION TECHNOLOGY

Things invented by the British

Steam-cylinder printing

Electric telegraph

Penny post

Fax machine

Undersea telegraph

Dry-plate, multiple-print photography

Telephone

Radio

Television

Fibre-optics

Radar

Electronic computer

World Wide Web

Steam-cylinder printing sounds a bit too technical to be geniunely revolutionary but, by mechanizing the actual print process, it represented the most important development in print technology since Gutenberg's invention of the printing press. Likewise, the invention of the penny post may seem slightly out of place in a basically technological survey, but the cheap standard rate and the 'sender pays' model inaugurated the era of a mass postal system, which still remains one of our most basic communications media today.

In terms of electronic communications, telegraphy inaugurated the modern era. It had long been recognized that pulses of static electricity could be sent down a wire for the purposes of communications. A Spanish inventor, Salva, had even suggested that the signals could be read at the far end of the line by an operator receiving small electrical shocks through his fingertips. Brilliant as this solution may have been, it was through the collaboration of two Britons, Crooke and Wheatstone, that the first useful telegraph system emerged. The system was deployed in 1838, and received vast publicity a few years later when a suspected murderer was seen to board a London-bound train at Slough. The news was telegraphed to Paddington, where the murderer was arrested, charged and later hanged – mid-century electronics on this occasion beating the transport technology of a couple of decades earlier. Less well known is the fact that a Briton, Scotsman Alexander Bain, also invented the first fax machine in – I kid you not – 1843: the key element of the invention being a means of converting electrical impulses into print.

British contributions to the phone, radio and television are all fairly familiar. Alexander Graham Bell made his crucial breakthrough in the United States, but had not yet taken US citizenship, so certainly counts as a British inventor.* In radio,

* Though Bell's most famous invention may have triumphed, he failed on another significant count: it was Edison's 'Hello!' not Bell's rousing 'Ahoy!' which won the battle of the telephone greeting – more's the pity.

the key advance was made by Marconi, an Italian working in England, but vital contributions were made also by Oliver Lodge (who developed the first radio receivers) and Ambrose Fleming (who developed the thermionic valve – don't ask, but it mattered). In the world of television, John Logie Baird didn't simply offer the world the first demonstration of black-and-white TV, he also helped pioneer colour TV, transatlantic TV, video recording, fibre-optics, radar and the forerunner to Ceefax/Teletext. In the computer industry, many of the key first steps were taken by British engineers, although the industry quickly migrated to America, where it has largely stayed. The Briton Tim Berners-Lee made one of the nost notable inventions of the century by pioneering the World Wide Web* – and, in a strikingly altruistic decision, made it available to the world for free, on the basis that the technology was too important to have a price attached.

Alas, this cheering roll-call of British achievement is all rather deceptive. The true story is all rather different. To break the recent history of technology into three roughly equal-sized chunks, it would be more accurate to say that from 1770 to 1850, Britain was by far the world's most technologically fertile nation. Then, from 1850 to the First World War, Britain was still able to count herself as being in the first rank of nations for invention, albeit that in industry after industry other nations – most notably Germany and the United States – were catching

---

* A current advertisement put out by UK Trade & Investment, a government agency, claims that a Briton invented the Internet. Not so. The Internet is a computer networking technology that was invented decades ago in the USA. The World Wide Web, which piggybacks off the Internet, consists of a set of standards regarding addresses, transfer protocols and the content and structure of hypertext documents.

and then surpassing her. In the final period, after the first war, Britain's contribution has been fitful at best: sporadically important, generally not.

Take, for instance, that oh-so-impressive-looking list of communications and IT inventions. The first five items on the list (steam-cylinder printing, the electric telegraph, the penny post, the fax machine and the undersea telegraph) were all crucial inventions, dating respectively from 1810–14, 1838, 1840, 1843 and 1851. In each case, it's more fair than not to say that the key developments were essentially British, albeit that steam-cylinder printing was developed by a German immigrant to Britain, and that there was plenty of American experimentation with undersea cables too.

Beyond that point, however, the British ownership of the list becomes increasingly contestable, or downright misleading. The key development in photography was Eastman Kodak's invention of celluloid film. The telephone was invented in the USA, by a British émigré who soon became a US citizen. In radio, TV and fibre-optics, the most important contributions to the development process were made by overseas inventors, not British ones – a fact wholly forgotten when we laud the (amazing, but rather isolated) achievements of Baird and others. When we push still farther into the twentieth century, it becomes ever harder to muster a credible roll-call of British achievement. True, the first electronic computers were built here, but virtually every innovation since that point has come from the fertile minds of the United States. True, Tim Berners-Lee gave the world the Web, but again virtually every other notable software development arose elsewhere. To claim things such as the computer and the Web as British inventions may be justifiable in some narrow sense, but entirely false if taken to imply wider leadership.

The same pattern holds wherever else you look. In transport, those early inventions (the train, the screw-driven iron ship, macadam roads and, yes, George Cayley's glider) do indicate something genuine about Britain's technological lead at the time. The farther down you look, however, the more misleading the list is likely to get. The jet engine was first developed by a Briton, true enough; but in a three-way race between Britain, Germany and the USA, it was Germany who first put a jet aircraft into the air. The first passenger jet was indeed British, but it had the slightly bothersome habit of falling apart in mid-air and was withdrawn from service. The hovercraft was genuinely British, but of minor consequence. The supersonic passenger jet was amazing, but a commercial dead end. The same basic pattern holds true in power technologies. It holds true pretty much everywhere else too.

In short, the Clarksonian view of the world just isn't tenable. Of course, the scale of that early technological lead was never going to last for ever. That Britain's relative position slipped was inevitable, but the problem ran deeper than a mere increase in competition. Inventors don't invent in a vacuum. They need to have an intimate relationship with manufacturing industry. Without competent manufacturers to turn ideas into products then money, no invention will clamber far from the drawing board. The dawning twentieth century was one in which British brains would fall foul of British manufacturing ineptitude. That sorry tale is the theme of the next chapter.

COLOSSUS

At the outbreak of the First World War, British companies owned around 80 per cent of the world's international cable network, the information superhighway of the age. As a result, the international traffic of enemy combatants, including Germany, was easily intercepted by the British, whose own traffic was entirely secure. The Admiralty's code-breaking team, known simply as Room 40, deciphered some 40,000 messages during the course of the war, of which one altered its course completely. In January 1917, a cable was intercepted which offered Mexico military assistance from Germany in recapturing 'her lost territory in Texas, Arizona and New Mexico'. Much as Woodrow Wilson hated the war, he could no longer resist the pressure to join on the Allied side. German hopes of winning the war were effectively ended by that single interception. On both sides, the lesson was learned: codes mattered.

When world war broke out for a second time, both sides were well prepared. The Germans made extensive use of a mechanized encoding device, the Enigma, whose plugboards and rotors generated a theoretical 22,000,000,000,000 possible encodings. That was the bad news. The good news was that early on in the war Polish sources had let the British code-breakers at Bletchley Park know what they were up against, and an electromechanical device – Alan Turing's famous 'Bombe' – was constructed to help mechanize the code-breaking process. These Bombes had a single very specific role. Let's say that a message was intercepted from a particular unit. The message would quite likely begin with some preset formula, OBERKOMMANDO5WEHRMACHT, for example. If Bletchley's code-breakers thought they could guess even a portion of the underlying text in the intercepted message, they could get the Bombe to test which of those 22,000,000,000,000 encodings might generate the appropriate bit of text. The power of geometric progression meant that the number of possible encodings might fall to a few hundred only, easily enough to be tested out by hand. It was a huge breakthrough, one that made an important contribution to the Battle of Britain, and a crucial one to the Atlantic war, yet the breakthrough was a partial one, all the same.

Such has been the mystique around Enigma that few people realize how limited its function was. It was hand not machine operated, which made it slow and labour intensive, capable of a maximum transmission of just five hundred characters. Although it was used extensively by Germany's navy and air force, the army high command made little use of the device, preferring instead the non-Morse-based *Geheimschreiber*, or 'secret writer'. The *Geheimschreiber* was completely automated, permitting messages of any length to be sent. Unlike Enigma, where British intelligence knew the physical make-up of the machine, the *Geheimschreiber* was a completely unknown quantity. The only route into it was the enciphered intercepts themselves.

For a long time, frustratingly little progress was made. Then, in August 1941, two signals were received both beginning with the same twelve-letter indicator, HQIBPEXEZMUG. This moment of slackness on the part of some German signaller provided the crucial breakthrough that the British had been needing: the opportunity to crack open the code for the first time. It wasn't that the signals contained useful military intelligence – they didn't – but some brilliant detective work by Bletchley's finest finally laid open the the logical structure of the *Geheimschreiber* itself. In effect, they used the nature of the encoding to work out the physical design of the machine that had generated it. They had figured out what they were up against. The next task was to beat it.

Easier said than done. Bletchley now knew that their opponent was a far more complex beast than Enigma. Enigma, poor dear, had managed only a few thousand billion combinations. The *Geheimschreiber* used a few thousand *million* billion. Against this monster, the old Bombe technology was of no help. There continued to be a trickle of decrypts, which came about largely because of human error on the German side. As the Germans continued to tighten their communications security, Bletchley Park risked losing even the limited gains it had made so far.

A new approach was called for. That approach relied on the oldest trick in the cryptanalyst's book, the statistical analysis of letter frequency. In English, E is the most common letter, followed by T, A, O, and so forth. In the particular language of Germany military transmissions, *following decryption*, the most common characters were 9, E, N, 5 and 8. (The numbers in this sequence all had specific meaning: 9 representing the space key, for example.) The trouble was that in the encrypted text these very marked variations were all evened out. There was random variation in the encrypted text; nothing more. The actual insight that led to beating the *Geheimschreiber* for good is so complex that it's (thankfully!) well beyond the scope of this book to describe it.* In shorthand, though, Bletchley Park came to understand that the final random-looking stream of characters was created from the combination of two non-random streams. If a moment of enemy sloppiness allowed the British to get a handle on the pin settings that generated one of those streams, then a brute-force statistical analysis might well be able to do the rest.

But just how brutish would that force need to be? Even half cracked, the *Geheimschreiber* was reluctant to give up its secrets. A two-thousand-character message might need a total of 17.8 million operations to crack it. Each message would need to be separately decrypted. Plainly enough, the task called for mechanization – but mechanization how?

Two approaches were mooted. The first – the Robinson, later renamed the Heath Robinson – involved a hybrid electro-mechanical device involving punched paper tape. The second, an all-electronic device, was advocated by Tommy Flowers, a senior engineer at the Post Office. Flowers' proposal, involving as it did a massive use of electronic valves, was thought unlikely to be reliable. The decision was therefore taken to go with the Heath Robinson, which was duly built. The Heath Robinson (looking rather like two bedsteads festooned with toilet roll) worked, but it was slow, temperamental and acutely vulnerable to human error. More was needed.

---

* It's almost beyond the wit of man to do so. Paul Gannon's *Colossus* is an admirably clear and readable history, but even so it's forced into using sentences like: 'The delta stream of an enciphered text stream is the same as that which would be produced by creating the delta of the plain, the delta of the Chi and the delta of the extended-Psi and then combining them.' Got that?

Fortunately for all concerned, Tommy Flowers was as stubborn as he was creative. He commented, 'They [Bletchley Park] didn't commission me [to build a computer, but] they said if you feel like it, that's up to you. So we said, we'll do it.' And do it they did. The Post Office gave Flowers authority, manpower, cash and freedom.* Work started (at Dollis Hill of all places) in February 1943. The first prototype was ready in December of that year. The first machine was delivered in January 1944. By February, it was already largely responsible for cracking the enemy codes. This machine, Colossus, was the world's first electronic computer. In its first version it could handle an astonishing 5,000 characters *per second* – and it was only constrained to this speed because the paper tape ripped apart if they ran it any faster. The second Colossus ramped its speed up to 25,000 characters per second. The paper still had the same tearing speed, but the computer got around that with parallel processing and wider paper.

This was an extraordinary degree of computing power. The German security apparatus never conceived of facing such an adversary. The *Geheimschreiber*, with its 160 thousand million billion combinations, was undone. What's more, the Colossus and its successors were no mere one-trick ponies. From the start, Flowers had built logical flexibility into the design of the machine. If German code-setting procedures altered (as they did), the Colossus could simply adapt to deal with them. The machine proved perfectly reliable, just as Flowers had predicted. The D-Day landings and the subsequent war in Europe were conducted with an unprecedented understanding of the

---

* Not unlimited cash, though. Flowers often paid for essential parts out of his own pocket.

enemy's intentions, an advantage of immense strategic value to the Allies.

The war over, the British were understandably reluctant to reveal their secrets. Colossus was dismantled. Those who knew about it were sworn to secrecy. As far as anyone knew, Colossus had never existed at all.* All the same, all technologies have their moment, and the post-war world was clearly ripe, scientifically and technically, for computing. In America, large and well-funded research projects began to grind systematically towards the rediscovery of the computer. Remarkably, however, their ill-funded, make-do-and-mend British counterparts were at least as well advanced, and probably more so. The first serious work on computer programming? British. The first stored program computer? British. The first genuinely flexible programmable computer? British. The first computers to be built and delivered by commercial manufacturers? British. The first office computer? British. The American historian Kenneth Flamm summarized this fertile period, saying simply, 'The first modern electronic computers, by any definition, were built in Britain.'

All this comes as heartening confirmation of the resource-fulness and creativity of the British boffin. Yet it will not have escaped the reader's notice that twenty-first-century Britain is not exactly well endowed with computer companies. The great hardware manufacturers – IBM, Compaq, Dell, HP, Apple – have all been American. The two principal processor manu-facturers – Intel and AMD – are both American. The most

---

* One by-product of which is that Tommy Flowers has never obtained due recognition. Since he built the first computer and won the Second World War (with a bit of help from his friends), isn't it time that changed?

important software companies – Microsoft, Lotus, Sun, Oracle – have all been American, as have the major providers of IT services – IBM, EDS and Accenture. The most important dot.commers – Google, Amazon, Yahoo!, eBay – are as British as pumpkin pie, cheerleaders and drive-by shootings.

The truth is that the great age of British invention ran for two centuries from 1750 to 1950. In the first half of that time, British invention was effervescent, rampant, world-beating. Increasingly thereafter it became stymied, not by any lack of brains or creativity, but by the inadequacy of the British companies that should have nourished it. It was probably inevitable that computing's centre of gravity should shift to the United States. After the war, the American commercial lead was so immense that American buyers would form by far the most important market for all the fancy new equipment being built. Britain's make-do-and-mend computers of the early electronic era were masterpieces of innovation, but they didn't necessarily form the most obvious basis for lasting commercial success. But, to paraphrase Oscar Wilde, to lose leadership in one technological sphere may be regarded as a misfortune, to lose leadership almost everywhere looks like carelessness. There are still technological areas in which Britain has (or rather shares) world leadership. We're top notch in pharmaceuticals, and certain military and aerospace areas. We're strong in some niche areas such as Formula One racing cars. But in any field that requires mass manufacturing, we're nowhere. How could it be otherwise, when we have no mass manufacturers left? From 1850 onwards, invention and innovation had less and less to do with eccentric geniuses cobbling something together in a garden shed. Success in modern technology required organization, discipline and the *industrialization* of research. When invention left the potting shed and entered the research lab, British inventors were doomed to be left behind.*

An investment banking friend of mine once heard a senior executive from the German company Mannesmann talking about their recent acquisition of a British maker of forklift trucks – the last such independent manufacturer in Britain. The Mannesmann executive said that every single one of the major innovations to have been made in the forklift industry since the war had been made in Britain, but went on to comment that 'follow-through is lousy'. That epitaph should be carved in stone, and placed over the gates of every failing, failed or extinct British manufacturer.

British inventors have often been among the best in the world. British manufacturing, alas, has been a forking disaster.

---

* Of course, there's more to creativity than just inventing things. While Britain's commitment to R&D is notoriously poor, its creative industries (design, publishing, broadcasting etc) are almost twice as large in relation to national income as those of its nearest competitor.

ECONOMY

WHOSE LAND?

If you were to sneak out on to the tarmac at Heathrow airport and look around at the vast agglomeration of stuff that lies all around – planes, terminal buildings, runways, baggage trucks, boarding ramps, catering units, engineering works and the rest – you wouldn't be able to find a single object that wasn't *owned*. Every blade of grass has an owner, every rivet, every gallon of fuel. What's more, those assets exist in an invisible web of legal relationships. The airline leases a plane, pays for landing rights, sells tickets, and so on. If any of these rights – whether of ownership or contract – are breached, then the injured party can go to court and get compensation.

Because this system is all we've ever known, it seems as natural as the air we breathe, but of course it's no more natural than the jet engine or the airline meal. I was reminded of this most starkly myself when (during my dark past as an investment banker) I worked on the privatization of CSA, the Czech national airline, not long after the fall of communist rule. To privatize a company, you have to know what you're selling. In Prague, this was no simple matter. Take a really basic asset: the runway. Who owned it? Did it belong to the airline? Or the airport? Or the civil aviation authority? Or the transport ministry? Or central government itself? In Britain, these questions would have had a precise answer. In Prague, it made no difference whom you asked; the standard answer took the form of a shrug followed by that all-encompassing communist answer, 'the state'. Getting the airline ready to be sold involved a massive allocation of assets and rights – in essence, inventing ownership from scratch. The final inventory of assets was a computer print-out so massive it took two hands to lift it.

That experience was a salutary reminder of the importance of property rights to any capitalist system. If you want to go into business, you have to be pretty damn sure that you've got a right to the assets you're using. If not, you'll work hard, take risks, accumulate profit – then stand to have the whole lot taken away from you. The first and most important building block of any capitalist system is that invisible network of legal rights, in particular the *right to own*.

It isn't just ex-communist societies that have no firm idea of individual property rights. Take a classic peasant society – tsarist Russia, for example, or pre-communist China. One family would typically farm a piece of land from generation to generation. Those generations tended to live and work together, labourers on a common project. Such a system was almost completely insulated from the market. Labour came from family members, not hired hands. The bulk of all production was consumed at home. In such a system, money did feature, but not much. It wasn't central.

Unsurprisingly, such systems didn't think of ownership the way we do. The 'head of the household' – a man, nearly always – would be the notional owner. But suppose that man was a drunkard? Or bone idle? Or terminally stupid? In Russia, such a man could, in effect, be fired and replaced by a more competent brother or son. The head of the household wasn't really an owner at all; he was more like the custodian of an asset owned in some eternal and elemental way by the family itself.

If someone wanted to sell the land or leave it in a will to someone outside the family, he couldn't do it – or at least his ability to do so was very heavily restricted.

Pretty obviously, the system had its advantages. Drunken fathers couldn't drink their children into landlessness. But it had disadvantages too. The system resisted acquisitiveness. It resisted innovation. It was anti-capitalist.

In eastern Europe, the system lasted into the nineteenth century. In western Europe, the system was less sharply defined and faded sooner, but it was present nonetheless. And England? Pretty obviously the country made a transition at some point from a subsistence farming culture to a capitalist one – but when and how?

Fifty years ago, the standard view went a bit like this. At the time of the Norman Conquest, England was a peasant society, much like tsarist Russia. Some time around the late Tudor/early Stuart period our peasants began to flirt with capitalist modes of production. A couple of hundred years later and – boom! – proper capitalist farming emerged and with it the Industrial Revolution, technology and, in due course, the jet engine and the airline meal. On this view, property rights developed much as you'd expect them to: very important later on; not nearly so much so earlier.

Then historians began to chip away at the evidence, and the pesky thing about evidence is that it has a nasty habit of overturning even the neatest of ideas. Luckily for researchers, England is exceptional in the wealth of its archive sources. Perhaps only Japan has archives as rich and continuous as our own,* and those archives began to reveal some curious things.

---

* We owe our archives to a combination of bureaucracy, literacy, peace and a climate that doesn't destroy paper.

One historian looked at the pattern of land transfer in Leighton Buzzard from 1464 to 1508. On the traditional view, you'd have expected a sluggish land market, with not many transfers, nearly all of which would have been within the family. That traditional view was simply wrong. Not only was the land market exceptionally active – over nine hundred transfers within a forty-four-year period – but three-quarters of land transfers did *not* involve family members. Just 10 per cent of all transfers involved an owner passing goods on to his family when he died.

Further studies were done, the historical telescope focusing on the ever more distant past. The same thing emerged: an unending flow of property transactions, a large core of which had nothing to do with family. Further surprises surfaced. Classic peasant societies are structured round the extended family, yet this wasn't the case in England as far back as the late Middle Ages, and quite possibly earlier still. Not only were English families largely nuclear, but sons and daughters went out to work from a young age. The surprise here isn't that kids were put to work (it would have been a miracle if they hadn't), the surprise is that they worked in the labour market *for cash*, rather than simply contributing their labour to the family farm. Kids weren't simply kids, they were economic agents. Perhaps more strikingly, even unmarried women – virtually invisible in most traditional systems – were perfectly capable of buying, selling and bequeathing assets. Courts registered transactions. Money changed hands. As far back as 1200, England seems to have been a small but perfectly formed capitalist society. (Perfectly formed, that is, with the not-so-small proviso that feudal obligations severely restricted the freedom of many labourers to seek work beyond the manor.

Those capitalist energies would really start to get full expression only with the upheaval in the labour market that followed the Black Death.)

Although the historical record simply falls silent before 1200 or so, there's no reason to think that this date marked any kind of turning point – indeed, rather the reverse. The Anglo-Saxon system arrived in England from Germany. As the French writer Montesquieu commented, 'In perusing the admirable treatise of Tacitus [a Roman historian] *On the Manners of the Germans* we find it is from that nation that the English have borrowed their idea of political government' – and, he went on to add, their laws of property and inheritance – 'This beautiful system was invented first in the woods.' As far as we know, Montesquieu had it pretty much spot on.

There's lots one could say about all this, but a few points stand out.

First, it's easy for us to think of the British as really becoming exceptional only during the rapid thrust towards modernity – say in the hundred years before the Industrial Revolution and the hundred years after. That view is simply wrong. There's no doubt that the most obvious fruits of our exceptionalism emerged then, but the soil had been prepared long, long before. Why did Britain become the first industrial society in the world? In part, because it had long been the world's truest capitalist society: the one with the most developed labour and product markets; the one with the most developed system of property rights.

Second, there's lots about Britain that makes sense when we understand where we've come from. Our property obsession, for instance, seems to be part of our historical DNA, but there's more to it than that. Modern Britain leads Europe in the gloomy statistics of divorce, teenage pregnancy, absent fathers and single mothers. This may be sad – but is it surprising? Other European societies all come from a past in which families were more tightly bound than ours. The family structures we have today are not so very different from those present in 1250. Being the world's über-capitalists brought us all kinds of good things, but the strong extended family was never one of them.

Third, it's become an *idée reçue* that England has long been stultified by a rigid class structure. Really? Was there any society in Europe that has allowed more social mobility than ours has done over the last thousand years or so? All those property-dealing small farmers were aiming to better themselves. Local archives are full of just such success stories: subsistence farmers who did well, whose kids became yeomen, whose grandkids became gentry.* This was an English phenomenon much more than it was a European one.

And last, consider this. This piece began by mentioning two societies – communist Czechoslovakia and tsarist Russia – which lacked fully developed property rights. Those same societies were oppressive, undemocratic and unfree. That's no coincidence. On the whole, as a vast generalization across time and place, the more developed a society's property rights, the more free that society has been. If the courts and legal system defend a person's right to own something, then the political system tends to value that right too. The last word† goes to John Aylmer, a well-travelled Englishman writing in 1559:

---

* Not to mention the inverse: gentry whose grandkids became peasants.
† Not an unbiased one, it has to be said: this is the man who wrote 'God is English'.

Oh England, England, thou knowest not thine own wealth: because thou seest not other countries penury. Oh if thou sawest the peasants of France, how they are scraped to the bones, and what extremities they suffer: thou wouldest think thy self blessed ... The husbandman, all that he hath gotten in his whole life, loseth it upon one day. For when so ever they have war (as they are never without it) the kings soldiers enter into the poor mans house, eateth and drinketh up all that he ever hath ... Now compare them with thee: and thou shalt see how happy thou art. They eat herbs: and thou Beef and Mutton. They roots: and thou butter, cheese and eggs. They drink commonly water: and thou good ale and beer.

Meat, beer and an aversion to veg. Who knows? Perhaps those ancient property rights go some way towards explaining our diet too.

THE MONSTER WITH 10,000 EYES

In the late 1680s, Europe stood braced for war. An expansionist France sought to secure its own borders by dominating the lands that lay immediately beyond, most notably the Dutch Republic. In the past, England had been Holland's firm (and Protestant) ally against the French – but now that England had, in James II, a Catholic king with a Catholic heir, that alliance looked shaky at best. The precarious balance couldn't last for long, and didn't. On 27 September 1688, French troops attacked across the Rhine. Fearing its imminent destruction, the Dutch Republic, gambling heavily, put together an invasion fleet and set sail for England. If the English wouldn't support the Dutch of their own accord, then Willem, the Prince of Orange, planned to force them.

These manoeuvres were the opening gambits in what was effectively the first world war: a long century of conflict that would stretch from Lisbon to Moscow within Europe, and from India to North America beyond. It was a war that would sow the seeds for violence right up to the present day, notably in Ireland. It was a war of global domination, fought between Britain and France. To the victor, everything: imperial, naval, commercial, financial, industrial and technological superiority. To the loser, revolution, regicide, invasion, bankruptcy and defeat.

Because we know the outcome of this contest, it's easy to ascribe a kind of inevitability to the way things played out.

ECONOMY

Britain's invincible navy protected her commerce, won overseas territories and gave the country the financial strength to subsidize the constant Continental wars that so drained the French state. There's truth in that picture, of course, yet one only has to shift perspective very slightly to give events an entirely different complexion. Britain was a small country, France a big one. Since France was allied to Spain through most of that long century of struggle, the resources ranged against British success seemed almost insuperable.

	Britain	France	Brit as % of France	France + Spain	Brit as % of France and Spain
Population, million					
1700	8.6	21.5	40%	30.2	28%
1820	21.2	31.3	68%	43.5	49%
National income, billion 1990 dollars					
1700	10.7	19.5	55%	27.0	40%
1820	36.2	35.5	102%	47.8	75%

In population terms, Britain was hopelessly inferior to France; in economic terms less so, but still at a decisive disadvantage to the combined House of Bourbon.

These resources would matter. The 'long eighteenth century' would see a series of major wars.* In each case, the British state

* Namely: the Nine Years War (1689–97), the War of the Spanish Succession (1702–13), the War of Jenkins' Ear, which merged with the War of the Austrian Succession (1739–48), the Seven Years War (1756–63), the American War of Independence (1775–83), the French Revolutionary War (1793–1801) and finally the Napoleonic Wars (1803–15).

ended up spending at least 85 per cent of its resources on the army, the navy, or in servicing the debts that military spending had generated. In the final three wars of the era, that figure rose to well over 90 per cent. Even in peacetime, it was rare for the state's ordinary civil expenditure to come to more than one fifth of the total. In short, the Georgian British state was a war machine, gathering resources to fight wars or, in peacetime, paying down the debts from the last war and maintaining armed readiness for the next one. Money alone wins nothing, but simple maths would have argued that Britain was playing against impossible odds.

To make matters worse, seventeenth-century England had possessed no more than the most rudimentary methods of public finance. English kings had long been obliged to live off their own royal estates and the occasional grudging subvention from parliament. When all this wasn't enough, monarchs had grabbed any other means available: borrowing short term, looting monasteries, selling offices.* Though English tax collection had improved, public finance was still in the Dark Ages.

Fortunately for the country's future, in 1688 it enjoyed the excellent good fortune to be invaded by the ever-competent Dutch. The Dutch not only brought a new king, they brought the first truly modern system of state finance: long-term borrowing, no forced loans, repayments out of general

---

* The variable standard of kingly behaviour meant that those lending money were taking something of a punt, to put it mildly. When Edward I expelled the Jews, it was no coincidence that he was expelling his major group of creditors. The Jews, however, were luckier than the French Templars. When Philip IV's debts to the Knights Templar became too onerous, he dissolved the organization and, for good measure, had a good many of its members tortured for heresy.

taxation, and the whole thing monitored by a representative assembly. It was this system that William brought to England in 1688. The first long-term loan in English history dates from 1693. In 1694, the Bank of England was created. Further reforms followed, and bore fruit. In 1690, the English government had borrowed at rates of around 11 per cent. By the 1720s, borrowing rates had dropped to just 3 per cent, only a whisker above the rates enjoyed by the Dutch themselves. With an effective finance system in place, the British used it with gusto. From the Glorious Revolution in 1688 to the Battle of Waterloo in 1815, the gross national debt increased about seven times over, more than doubling as a share of national income.

Borrowing is all very well, of course, but debts have to be repaid. As the scale of war and borrowing ratcheted up, so too did taxes – to the extent that almost everything had some kind of tax slapped on it. To quote Sydney Smith, writing in 1820, Britons were obliged to pay:

> Taxes upon everything which it is pleasant to see, hear, feel, smell, or taste. Taxes upon warmth, light, and locomotion. Taxes on everything on earth or under the earth, on everything that comes from abroad or is grown at home. Taxes on the raw material, taxes on every fresh value that is added to it by the industry of man. Taxes on the sauce which pampers man's appetite, and the drug which restores him to health; on the ermine which decorates the judge, and the rope which hangs the criminal; on the poor man's salt and the rich man's spice; on the brass nails of the coffin, and the ribbons of the bride; at bed or board; couchant or levant, we must pay ... the dying Englishman, pouring his medicine, which has paid 7 per cent.,

into a spoon that has paid 15 per cent., flings himself back upon his chintz bed, which has paid 22 per cent., and expires in the arms of an apothecary who has paid a licence of a hundred pounds for the privilege of putting him to death … His virtues are handed down to posterity on taxed marble, and he will then be gathered to his fathers, to be taxed no more.

Smith's rant didn't even mention the land tax and (horror of un-British horrors) the short-lived income tax. Because Britain spent more per capita on war than any of her Continental rivals, she also paid more to finance it, becoming the most highly taxed nation on earth, with a per capita tax take that far exceeded French levels.

Highly taxed, hugely indebted, spending lavishly on war –

Georgian Britain might appear as if disaster was inevitable. Yet when disaster fell, it struck France, not Britain. The French problem was threefold.

First off, the French king in effect contracted out a huge swath of tax collection to private 'tax farmers', who had the right to levy the land tax, or *taille*, in exchange for a fixed payment to the king. The system could hardly have been better designed to incentivize venality and exploitation in the 'farmers' – and bitterness and resentment in the 'farmed'. By contrast, the British system relied on the first truly modern tax collection bureaucracy. Though that bureaucracy was nick-named the 'monster with 10,000 eyes', at least those eyes were largely impartial, largely uncorrupt and watched everyone.

Second, the French system was blatant, where the British one was subtle. Although Britons knew they were taxed, those taxes blended invisibly with the cost of goods they were purchasing (a Georgian stealth tax, in fact). What was more, regressive though the system often was, luxury items from carriages to hair powder bore rates of tax that were sharply higher than the rates imposed on simple necessities. In France, excise taxes fell heavily on a much narrower range of commodities, including basics such as salt. The *taille* itself was collected by intrusive central officers, who formed an obvious target for dislike.

Finally, taxes levied by a parliament carried more legitimacy than those imposed by a king. It's easily forgotten that, in 1715, almost one quarter of all adult males in England and Wales had the right to vote. (The share fell thereafter.) This wasn't democracy as we know it, but it certainly beat anything available across the Channel. Nobody loves being taxed, but the ability to vote out those taxing you certainly eases the pain.

In the war of resources, Britain won. The British government never once defaulted on its debts, the French monarchy did so repeatedly. The result of those French defaults was permanently higher interest rates. In the aftermath of the 1770 default, French interest rates were over 10 per cent, when British rates were barely more than 3 per cent. All that interest needed to be paid. Where British taxation went directly to fund war, French taxation was often simply paying off past financial mismanagement.

Furthermore, as any investment banker knows, financial distress isn't simply about paying more for your money, it's also about being vastly more limited in your ability to access it at all. Military theorists sometimes speak of a 'strategic reserve', referring to troops deliberately withheld from battle so that they can be deployed when and where they'll do most good. Likewise, the concept of 'strategic depth' refers to the distance of the front-line troops from the industrial heartland of the combatants, and the ease with which any attacking thrust can be absorbed by those distances – Russia being notably well endowed in that respect. The financial flexibility afforded by a decent credit rating offers something strategically akin to both reserve and depth. If more resources are needed to tip the course of a war, a strong borrower can find them. If an attacking thrust cuts deeper than anticipated, a strong borrower can muster the men, ships, guns and cash needed to repair the damage and recommit to combat.

Britain always had that flexibility; France, when it mattered most, did not. Just as the United States is said to have won the cold war by engaging in an arms race that the Soviet Union could not afford, so too did British financial competition end up pushing the French monarchy into tax increases that the country wouldn't bear. When, in 1788, French fiscal problems came to crisis point, the king's attempts to solve them ended up triggering revolution and, in due course, the loss of the royal head to Madame Guillotine. That same royal head probably had other things to contemplate as it lay beneath the shadow of the blade, but its fate had been determined not merely by the *citoyens* and *citoyennes* of Revolution, but by the bankers of Threadneedle Street and the taxmen of Whitehall too.

WHEAT WITHOUT DOONG

Five million years ago, apes clambered down from the trees. A hundred and fifty thousand years ago, those early hominids had spawned a line that was recognizably human: *Homo sapiens*. Some ten thousand years back, humans began to develop agriculture. The old upper limit to the size of human societies was swept away. Civilization became possible.

And then? Well, progress. Crops were improved. Ploughs were invented and refined. Farmer-power was supplemented by horse- and ox-power. Agricultural yields increased. But not much. In 1600, English agriculture was pretty typical of the rest of Europe – the same basic methods, the same range of crops, the same approximate level of productivity – and that productivity wasn't much to boast of. Approximately 70 per cent of the entire population worked the land and produced just enough food to keep the country fed. Put another way, each agricultural worker produced only enough food to feed himself (and any non-working dependants) plus about half the food needed to feed a non-agricultural worker (and his non-working dependants). Everything else in human society – religion, commerce, government, science, industry and the rest – had to fit into the narrow surplus generated by those farmers.

Nor was that surplus particularly elastic. If the population grew, there was less food to go around. Less food meant higher death rates. At least three times in history (during Roman times, in the thirteenth century and in the sixteenth century), the English population grew to around 5.5 million, then hit its limit and fell back again, often hard and far. Economic historians have even been able to map the way the price mechanism regulated population size. When population growth was strong, inflation, representing mostly agricultural products, rose. When population growth was weak or negative, inflation was weak or negative. These days, inflation is a mere inconvenience. Back then, it meant that the price of food rose to the point where the poor could no longer buy enough to feed themselves adequately; in those days, inflation killed.

The problem, in a word, was nitrogen. Plants (and the animals that feed off them) need three basic elements for growth: potassium, phosphorus and nitrogen. All three elements are depleted by farming, but the one that proved to be the limiting factor to output was nitrogen. Even with every attention paid to manuring fields, fallow seasons and all the rest of it, traditional farming practices had caused nitrate levels in the soil to fall to some two-thirds of what they would otherwise have been. Other problems existed, but the nitrogen problem was central.

The predicament seemed eternal, unchangeable. In 1798, an Anglican parson, Thomas Malthus, called attention to it, declaring in his famous *Essay on the Principle of Population*:

> The power of population is so superior to the power of the earth to produce subsistence for man, that premature death must in some shape or other visit the human race ... sickly seasons, epidemics, pestilence, and plague advance in terrific array, and sweep off their thousands and tens of thousands.

Should success be still incomplete, gigantic inevitable famine stalks in the rear, and with one mighty blow levels the population.

It seemed fair comment; a bleak but accurate summary of human history so far.

But Malthus was wrong, his words already seventeen years out of date. Because in 1781, something strange began to happen. The ancient relationship between population and prices began to fail. The late eighteenth century was a time of rapid population growth. True to past form, from 1751 onwards, rising population pressure had run hand in hand with higher prices. In 1781, population growth and inflation had both reached their highest levels since at least 1540. The old savage limits on how far a country could grow seemed all set to reimpose themselves.

Only this time, they didn't. As the 1780s progressed, population growth *increased*, while inflation inched down. In the 1790s, the rate of population growth increased yet again to unprecedented heights, while inflation actually turned *negative*. The old chains had finally been broken. The nineteenth century would see continued population growth and continuing gains in agricultural productivity. For the first time since the invention of agriculture, the growth and development of human society were no longer radically curtailed by its ability to grow food.

It was one of the most profound revolutions in human history – profound, and British. Agricultural productivity can be measured in a number of ways, but one of the simplest is this: take the total calories produced and divide by the number of agricultural workers (usually just male workers, as women split their time between farm and household chores). In 1800, farming performance in Europe was as follows:

Calories per male worker
(Britain 1800 = 100)

Britain	100
Netherlands	51
Belgium	40
France	37
Germany	37
Austria-Hungary	28
Italy	28
Sweden	24
Spain	24

Britain wasn't simply out in the lead, it was almost twice as productive as the nearest rival, three times more productive than France or Germany, four times more productive than the sluggards on the periphery. It would take an extraordinary amount of time for Britain's rivals to catch up with the extent of her industrialization. In 1850, slightly over one fifth of Britain's population was still working the land. In France and Germany, this proportion wouldn't be reached until the 1950s.

So what happened? And why did it happen here?

The answer to the first question is both complex and simple. There were a host of causes: land reclamation, increased specialization, new crops, new rotational techniques, better pest control, improved breeds of animal, and more. That's the complex answer. The simple one is that the age-old problem of nitrate deficiency was largely solved. Leguminous plants, including the pea family and clover, have the capacity to take nitrogen from the air and bind it into the soil in the form of nitrate salts. By using clover as fodder for sheep, farmers bene-fited from a double whammy: animals fed on a rich clover diet, while their fields self-fertilized through the magic of plant power. The insight became formalized in a new system of crop rotation, the 'Norfolk four-course', which rotated wheat, barley, clover and turnips. The new technique could as much as double farm out-put, and it caught on like wildfire. (An agricultural version of wildfire, that is: down on the farm, nothing changes *that* fast.) In the five hundred years up to 1750, the pattern of agricultural produce in Norfolk had been virtually static. In the hundred years after 1750, the Norfolk four-course ran riot, with turnips and clover accounting for over two-fifths of all crops grown.

Although accurate as far as it goes, this kind of answer is a little deceptive. After all, farmers had known for centuries about the magical properties of leguminous plants. In 1573, Thomas Tusser's rhyming guide for farmers had included the memorable couplet:

> Where peason [peas] ye had and a fallow thereon,
> Sowe wheat ye may well without doong thereupon.

'Wheat without doong' was the trick at the heart of the Norfolk four-course, yet for centuries farmers had made little systematic use of the knowledge. What changed?

The answer was capitalism. The agricultural revolution took place in Britain (and not, say, France or Belgium or Holland or Germany) because British farming was by far the most capitalist. That capitalism was expressed in every aspect of British agriculture, notably the development of a genuine national market for food. Back in medieval times, markets had been largely local, so that there might be gluts in Gloucestershire at just the same time as there was dearth in Durham. As time went by, markets became regional, then national. Farmers could specialize in the crops that best suited their fields, ironing out inefficiencies and building up the extent of local knowledge and expertise. The result was that localized famines were essentially unknown in eighteenth-century Britain, in an age when they still ravaged the Continent.

Just as important was the long-drawn-out process of enclosure. Medieval farming had mostly operated under a common-field system. Though land was owned by individuals, a great deal of farming was conducted cooperatively, and common rights (such as the right to take firewood) extended over much of the land. Such a system had many merits, but it certainly made it harder for farmers to innovate, specialize or reap benefits from investment. So, little by little, the old open common fields were enclosed, with hedges, walls, fences and ditches. Almost half of English land had been enclosed by 1550, almost three-quarters by 1750. This great upheaval came about by largely legal means. If landlords wanted to remove any common rights over a bit of land, they generally had to pay for the privilege. If matters went to court, magistrates increasingly took the side of tenants, not landlords. Enclosure gave landowners full control over their land, with the result that capitalist investment and innovation became not just possible, but highly profitable.

Fanning these flames of change was demand that was both buoyant and challenging. By 1700, London consumed 200,000 tons of grain annually, requiring sophisticated supply networks to meet the demand. More challenging yet was the Royal Navy. The navy didn't just need a lot of prime-quality food, it laid down strict standards of quality, quantity, packaging, preparation, delivery schedules and more. These were industrial demands, and they called forth an industrial response.

There, in a nutshell, is the answer to the question 'What happened?' Human history had long been pinned back by an inability to move much beyond subsistence living. Then along comes capitalist agriculture, and history can finally get to grips with industrialization, science, technology and all those other good things. But why Britain? It's all very well to say that our farmers were the most capitalist, but why? French and German farmers were hardly less interested in profit. What made money here would, suitably modified for soil and climate, have made money there too. In short, capitalism may explain the *mechanism* of change; it can't, on its own, explain the *location*.

The fundamental answer has to be that the shift away from medieval farming structures was a deeply challenging one. Although the rewards to society, taken as a whole, were huge, the individual losers (smaller farmers and beneficiaries of common rights) were more numerous than the principal winners (larger landowners). In Britain, the system had enough flexibility and fundamental fairness to permit change, as witnessed by all those magistrates who took the side of the tenant when the landlord wasn't behaving himself. In France, by contrast, the social and legal system inhibited change. What was more, in Britain it was pretty clear that if you grew more, you'd get to profit from your extra output. In states that were less protective of the individual and of property rights, small farmers may have worried that the state or local lord would simply appropriate any excess. The English, and later British, model – consultative government, concern for the individual, and the rule of law – allowed change to happen and, to a reasonable extent, ensured that it happened equitably. This combination of fairness on the one hand and commercial freedom on the other lay at the heart of British agricultural success. It has lain at the heart of much else in Britain's distinctive history too.

A WAVE OF GADGETS

We tend to think of history as being about progress. There are setbacks and fallow periods, of course, but on the whole, things get better. Inventions get invented, then refined and disseminated. Bad forms of government compete with good forms of government and are forced to give way. Economic progress, in the end, will always triumph over economic backwardness.

To be sure, it's never hard to find evidence for such views, but at the same time it's easy to be overly impressed by the local and the partial: Venetian glassmaking prowess, say; English watermills or Chinese gunpowder. The simple fact is that if one's viewpoint is sufficiently global, sufficiently long term, then the most striking fact about human history is how *little* the human condition altered over a timescale of millennia. The graph on the next page comes from one of the most audacious exercises in historical enquiry, the attempt to plot human output per capita since the dawn of history.*

For a thousand years since the birth of Christ, nothing changed. Gains in one location were extinguished by losses in another. World population grew, but not much. For the next five hundred years, there was the first whisper of sustained

* The scholar in question is the Scotsman Angus Maddison. His fellow Scot, Adam Smith, would have been proud.

growth, but still only at the rate of one twentieth of one per cent per year. Since the average per capita income in AD 1000 was still only $436 (at 1990 prices), that twentieth of one per cent still left untold millions in grinding, awful, frequently lethal poverty.

The next three hundred years, to 1820, were the same: incremental change, but not nearly enough. World GDP per person was $667 in 1820. Even in western Europe and its off-shoots (notably the USA), average living standards were still little more than $1,200 per person, or just three-fifths of Indian living standards today. In short, even in the world's wealthiest countries, poverty was still grinding, still awful, still killing. In less than two centuries since that time, the world has changed out of all recognition. To be sure, there are areas of the world where poverty is still hideously prevalent. But even in Africa, life is far better now than it was: African GDP per capita is currently around $1,500, or higher than any country managed in 1820, with the sole exceptions of Britain and the

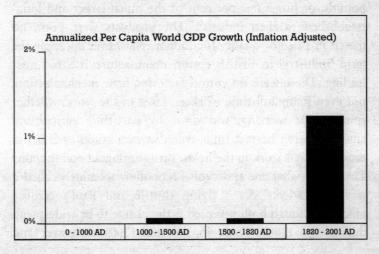

Annualized Per Capita World GDP Growth (Inflation Adjusted)

Netherlands. Just as much to the point, the huge, populous and once terribly poor nations of India and China are growing fast, and helping many millions out of poverty as they do so. Industrialization may have given rise to many challenging side effects, but that shouldn't blind us to its astonishing success: it has plucked humanity from millennia of atrocious living standards; it has done so with astonishing speed; and it is (increasingly) doing so on a genuinely global scale.

Maddison's data make it clear why the Industrial Revolution mattered; they shift attention away from the intricacies of cotton processing and focus it firmly on the main issue, namely the coming alive of humanity, the extraordinary, unprecedented release of human potential. Yet beginnings matter too. The Industrial Revolution had a time and place of origin. The time was around 1770, the place Great Britain.

The chronology of those early changes can be speedily dealt with. In the 1760s, Britain had a cotton industry, but it was no big deal. Exports totalled just a couple of hundred thousand pounds, or just a few per cent of the much larger and long-established woollen industry. The products were poor, no match in price or quality for Indian rivals. Even to apply the term 'industry' to British cotton manufacture is a tad misleading. There were no cotton factories, little mechanization, not even many full-time workers. Most of the work, whether spinning or weaving, was done by part-time agricultural labour. During harvest time, when women could earn better money for less work in the fields, yarn shortages became acute. Then came what one apocryphal schoolboy accurately called 'a wave of gadgets'. Kay's flying shuttle and Paul's carding machine, though both invented earlier, came to be widespread during the 1760s. Then, in the mid-1760s, a weaver and

carpenter named James Hargreaves came up with the crucial breakthrough: the spinning jenny, a machine whereby turning one wheel could spin eight threads not one. From one to eight: the factor of productivity change was already huge, but it didn't stop there. Hargreaves' 1770 patent called for sixteen spindles. By 1800, 120 spindles were common. The innovation heralded a wave of synergistic innovations: Arkwright's water frame (which produced a stronger thread), Crompton's mule (which combined the best of Arkwright and Hargreaves), and the use of steam to power the new machines.* The consequences were

---

* I've followed tradition in crediting Hargreaves and Arkwright, but most historians would now credit Highs as the prime mover of the jenny, and Highs and Kay for the water frame. It was Arkwright who patented the latter, however, helping himself to the profit as well as the kudos.

transformative. By 1812, the cotton industry accounted for 7 or 8 per cent of national income, and almost two-fifths of exports. More than that, something new had been invented: the notion of the factory, where workers looked after a range of machines driven by a central power source. The very concept of work had begun to shift.

As all this was going on, mostly in Lancashire, a second industry – iron – was undergoing radical change. Iron had long been made in Britain, but it was an industry in difficulty. To make iron, you need a source of carbon in order to reduce the metallic oxides thereby transforming the ore into a pure metal. In Britain, charcoal acted as both fuel and carbon source, and the resultant demand for charcoal was vast. Blast furnaces would be set up in areas of woodland, then often move on once those woodlands were depleted. For large-scale industry to develop, it needed to be able to stay put and grow big. An alternative solution was to replace charcoal by coke (charcoal made from coal). The first coke-based ironworks to produce a commercially viable product seems to have been Abraham Darby's plant at Coalbrookdale, as far back as 1709. The local coal was, however, particularly well suited to this kind of process, and though coke-based iron smelting gradually increased, a breakthrough hadn't happened. Then, in 1775, Watt's steam engine was put to work driving the bellows of the blast furnaces – the first time it had done anything but pump water. The new power made all the difference. Coke smelting could now be made to work reliably and efficiently. Cheap cast iron was now within reach, which was the good news. The bad news was that cast iron isn't all that useful. It's brittle and difficult to draw into rods or wire. For many eighteenth-century purposes – ploughshares, hoes, cutlery, tools – cast iron was simply useless. Then, in 1784, Henry Cort patented a process for puddling (iron-speak for stirring) and rolling the molten metal. The process eliminated the carbon impurities of cast iron, producing a top-quality wrought iron. Unfortunately for Henry Cort and fortunately for everybody else, he was ruined by the bankruptcy and suicide of one of his creditors, and was consequently unable to protect his patent. Without the monopoly effect of patent protection, Cort's process spread like wildfire. From the 1760s to the late 1780s, iron production doubled. In the two sub-sequent decades, it quadrupled.

If cotton produced the first factories, it was iron which produced the first industrial giants. John Wilkinson's conglomerate comprised collieries, tin mines, iron foundries, forges and logistics infrastructure. The cotton industry may

have mechanized, but its machinery was often wood-built and water-powered. The new ironworks were recognizably modern in their insatiable need for fossil-fuelled power, their scale and their use of iron machinery, such as Wilkinson's 1782 steam hammer, which could strike 150 blows a minute.

Iron was also significant in another respect. The cotton industry was (and would remain) almost entirely unconnected to the rest of the economy. The raw materials came from abroad. The products often went abroad. Woven cotton was not a raw material in any industrial process. The industry was amazing, but isolated. Not so with iron, which lay at the very heart of things. Growth in iron drove backwards into the related industries of coal mining, steam engines, canal building and (before long) railways. It drove forwards into entirely new industries: machine tools, railways and all those other industries that access to new iron machinery made possible. Cheap, reliable metal made it possible for engineers to dream in iron, the way once they'd been forced to dream in wood. Tolerances and specifications began to become exact, not approximate. The new iron age was the dawn of the machine age proper.

So much for *what* happened. The next obvious question is why? Why Britain? Why the 1770s? Why not some other place, some other time? These questions, or versions of them, feature in virtually every book about the Industrial Revolution, yet they're rather odd questions to ask; akin to wondering why Google is an American company. The point about Google is that *of course* it's American, just as eBay, and Amazon, and Yahoo!, and Oracle, and Intel, and Microsoft, and Apple, and Dell, and IBM, and a gazillion others are American too. Google *could* have sprung up somewhere else, but it's not surprising that it didn't. America is the rule, anywhere else the exception. Something similar is true of Georgian Britain. Why did it host the Industrial Revolution? Because, on every major count, Britain was the country most likely to do so. Of hundreds of possible answers, here are my personal top ten.

One: Britain was already the wealthiest country in the world (barring Holland), and the most strongly growing. (The Netherlands was in decline through the eighteenth century.) If you were seeking a sudden step-change in the frontier of economic possibility, you'd expect it to come from the country that was already farthest out on that frontier, and pushing ahead fastest.

Two: Britain had by far the most capitalist, productive and fast-changing agriculture in the world. Since, prior to industrialization, agriculture was by far the biggest industry everywhere, it would almost be simpler to say that Britain was way ahead of the game in the one industry that really mattered. The habits nurtured in agriculture – experiment, investment, profit-seeking, genuinely capitalist deployment of labour and capital – were precisely those needed for successful industrialization. What's more (to sneak a further reason into my top ten), Britain's aristocratic rulers were as keen on the agro-capitalist game as anyone else. In other countries, noblemen would have thought the intricacies of cattle breeding or turnip-based crop rotations as being preoccupations fit for a peasant. In Georgian Britain, noblemen got cow muck on their riding boots and could talk turnips with the best of them.

Three: Britain had the largest proto-capitalist class of any nation in the world. The term needs a little explanation. In pre-industrial Europe, most manufacture was carried out by rural residents, making stuff at home, and being paid on a piece-rate basis for their efforts – genuine cottage industry, in fact. Merchants supplied the raw materials and picked up the finished goods. Different areas specialized in different trades: Birmingham in buttons and fittings, Oxfordshire in blankets, Leicestershire in stockings, Norwich in woollens, and so on. In 1500, England was typical of most of Europe in its distribution of labour. It had three-quarters of its population working the land, just under a fifth in this rural non-agricultural labour, and a small fraction (7 per cent) living in cities. Fast-forward to 1800 and the picture was transformed. England's populace was divided in approximate thirds between city, agriculture and rural non-agricultural. No other country had such a low proportion of agricultural workers; no other country, conversely, had such a large pool of mini-manufacturers, ready and waiting for a new way to organize things.*

Four: Britain had by far the largest and most diversified commerce of any nation. On the eve of the French Revolution, British trade was roughly 25 per cent larger than the trade of large and populous France. Britain's trade was also much more international, much more varied by product and region. In the ensuing decades, war and the Royal Navy ensured that the disparity went from substantial to enormous. In the aftermath of Waterloo, Britain's trade was four to five times greater than France's. That flood of goods into and out of the country

---

* The partial exception here, as with most other factors mentioned in this section, is the Netherlands, the 'Little Britain' of the age. Or rather, given that British success really took off following a Dutch invasion, perhaps Britain should be referred to as 'Big Holland'. Either way, if the Industrial Revolution hadn't happened in Britain, it would probably be known to history as *De Industriële Revolutie*.

produced profits, employment and capital accumulation, of course. It also meant that Britain could meaningfully address a world market. British cotton cloth could sell to India; British iron goods to Latin America. If British manufacturers needed a raw material not available domestically, then the chances were it was already surging through the ports of London and Liverpool, Bristol and Glasgow.

Five: British transport was better. In part, this was down to simple luck. Britain is a long, thin country, with plenty of natural waterways, and no inland area is far from the sea. In an age when waterborne transport was cheapest and best, this certainly gave Britain a lead. But successful countries make their own luck. British roads (often privately built) were the best in the world. British stagecoaches (built for speed, not comfort, unlike their European counterparts) offered the densest, most frequent, most competitive road transport anywhere. Of about two thousand miles of navigable waterway in England in 1800, just one third was entirely natural, the remaining two-thirds was the work of engineers. The canal boom of 1760-1800 alone accounted for about one third of those two thousand miles, in a classic example of private sector infrastructure investment encouraging a step-change in industrial performance.

Six: the British population was growing like Topsy. Everywhere in Europe grew through the eighteenth century. Between 1700 and 1820, the population of France grew by 46 per cent, that of Italy by 52 per cent, that of Germany by 66 per cent – but British population growth, at a staggering 148 per cent, dwarfed such increases. A hugely growing population meant huge domestic demand, plenty of labour, plenty of optimism to fuel investment.

Seven: Britain had London (Europe's largest city) and the

navy (its largest proto-industrial organization). Both London and the navy acted not simply as major sources of demand, but sources of sophisticated demand: for luxuries in the case of London; for industrial quantities of goods, priced, delivered and packaged according to strict industrial standards, in the case of the navy. Both London and the navy acted as enormous bellows fanning the flames of capitalist growth.

Eight: Britain enjoyed domestic security. Though invasion scares were (and would remain) commonplace, the country was never invaded again after 1688. The navy's 'wooden walls' became an ever more reliable bulwark against outside threats. British capitalists, unlike their brethren elsewhere, could invest with confidence.

Nine: Britain had the most sophisticated financial system anywhere. State finance was well managed, interest rates were low, the network of banks, financiers and insurers was second to none.

Ten (and here I admit to stuffing in as many reasons as one single heading can possibly fit): Britons were politically, economically and intellectually free; they enjoyed stable and legitimate political institutions; the courts upheld rights to personal security, private property and contract enforcement; crimes of violence were limited; government was responsive; political standards of honesty and efficiency were as good as they were anywhere; scientific and technological enquiry had long been open, free, highly regarded and successful; barriers to geographical and social mobility were fairly low; and the religious nonconformity so prevalent in Manchester and other centres of revolution provided an ideology strongly supportive of the new industrial doctrine of self-improvement. Furthermore, Britain had been leading the way on most of these counts for centuries. Georgian Britons weren't simply enjoying a spell of fine weather; their climate was good and they knew it.

So, again, why did the Industrial Revolution happen here? The answer is simply that, short of some quite surprising vagaries of chance and circumstance, it was far more likely to happen here than anywhere else. If you still want proof, then here it is. There wasn't one Industrial Revolution, there were two: in cotton and in iron. Two industries. Two different technologies, product types, capital intensities, geographical centres, and labour dynamics. But both British.

We didn't just invent the Industrial Revolution. We invented it twice.

THE FOOD OF THE PEOPLE

The notion of globalization is pretty unfashionable these days. Youths with radical hairstyles picket oil companies and smash up McDonald's. The World Trade Organization has replaced the international Jewish conspiracy as the sinister puppet-master *de nos jours*. Global warming, genetically modified food, the Doha trade round, American brand names, Big Oil, the Iraq war, Third World debt, the gun lobby, offshoring and various clusters of acronyms (the IMF, WTO, IBRD, IFC, G8, OECD, NAFTA, GATS, MAI) all swim around in a kind of undifferentiated soup of iniquity.

It probably won't surprise readers too much to know that I don't wholly subscribe to the soup-of-iniquity theory. There's plenty of bad stuff going on in the world, but plenty of good stuff too. Contemporary globalization brings with it some profoundly serious challenges – challenges that policy-makers are not yet sufficiently addressing – but huge numbers of people in the developing world are being lifted from poverty, in part as a result of the opening of markets, most notably in India and China.

But, if we can, let's leave aside these twenty-first century debates. Whatever your personal take on contemporary globalization, the issues now are evidently different from the issues in the age of Pax Britannica. Back then, a new magic –

industrialization – emerged genie-like from a rainswept corner of northern Europe. The magic spread, but not uniformly, and not always quickly. The divergence between the world's richest and poorest parts grew very sharply. Some divergence was inevitable. It had taken seven hundred years since the Norman invasion to produce in Britain the conditions that would give birth to industrialization. In the rest of Europe and North America, those same conditions were not far from being achieved. In most of the rest of the world, with its sharply different histories and cultures, those conditions were very far indeed from pertaining. In the eighteen centuries from the birth of Christ to 1820, per capita incomes in Asia outside Japan had grown by around 28 per cent. It would take the Britons of 1820 just twenty-seven years to achieve a similar gain. Nor was Asia, even remotely, the slowest grower. At least incomes had generally risen over those eighteen centuries. In Africa, if anything, they'd declined.

Divergence, then, was a given. What would matter more to the populations of the poorest countries was whether rich-world policies would tend to deepen and extend that divergence, or whether they would minimize and shorten it. (These days poor-world policies matter at least as much, but in a colonial age the poor world didn't get much chance to make policy.) Given that Britain was not simply the world's leading industrial power but also, and by far, its dominant commercial, naval and imperial one, then Britain's role in determining the fates of others would be absolutely critical.

So how did she do?

Let's start with trade. One of the central, and most legitimate, complaints of the modern anti-globalizer is that the rich world raises tariff barriers against imports from the poor world. When tariff barriers are lowered, it is only as part of a tit-for-tat arrangement: mighty America will permit competition from tiny Guatemala only if tiny Guatemala permits competition from mighty America. The arrangement may be carefully reciprocal, but it's hard not to feel that it's a wee bit unbalanced all the same. Any industries (notably agriculture) that the rich world chooses to protect are protected, and hang the consequences for anyone else.

For most of its rise to power, Britain was every bit as protectionist and mercantilist as anyone else. Navigation Acts protected British shipping. Excise duties built a cottage industry from smuggling. In 1815, the price of grain was kept high by Corn Laws, aimed at keeping cheap foreign wheat from undercutting British farmers. By the mid-nineteenth century, however, the old philosophy was under attack from two fronts. First of all, the British classical economists, notably Adam Smith and David Ricardo, built a comprehensive new theory of economics which blew apart the traditional justifications for protectionism. If these theories provided the intellectual weaponry, then the rise of the manufacturing interest in Britain provided the troops. Why, these manufacturers asked, should agricultural interests keep the price of grain high, when the urban poor so obviously suffered as a result? (If that sounds like a surprisingly tender attitude for a Victorian manufacturer, it shouldn't. The same people reasoned that if the urban poor paid less for bread, they could also be paid less for their labour.)

In 1846, the campaigners got their way. The Corn Laws fell, and with them British mercantilism. By 1875, Britain had pretty much shed every last vestige of its protectionist past. How unusual this was – and is – can be seen from the table below.

Average tariffs on imported manufactures, per cent

	1875	1913	Today
Britain	0	0	–
France	12–15	20	–
Germany	4–6	17	–
Italy	8–10	18	–
European Union	–	–	3.6
United States	40–50	44	3.0

It wasn't just manufactured imports which came into the country duty free, it was almost everything else besides. Furthermore, the policy wasn't adopted as a result of some endless series of tit-for-tat tariff negotiations. With one or two exceptions, the tariff reductions were passed unilaterally. Britain would drop its own barriers. If other countries wanted to follow suit, then so much the better; but if they didn't, Britain's policy would remain just the same.*

Even by modern standards, this was a shockingly radical approach. It is not the policy of the European Union now, nor that of the United States, nor that of anyone else at all. British policy was certainly founded on self-interest. The Smith-, Ricardo- and Cobden-inspired Brits believed that free trade brought benefits even if other countries didn't have the good grace to reciprocate. (Most economists today would broadly agree.) Self-interested or not, the policy had huge consequences

---

* The policy would later cause some perplexity in Whitehall. When policy-makers wanted to pressurize foreign rivals into lowering tariff barriers, they found that they'd already given up all the weapons in their arsenal. So instead, they tried invoking moral arguments, and an appeal to equity. You can guess how much effect that had.

for the rest of the world. Emerging economies could flog their goods to the well-heeled British consumer, with no rich-world bureaucrat seeking to trip them up. If the rich world today adopted a comparable policy, the benefits for the poor world would be stupendous.

The British reverence for free trade didn't stop at dismantling tariffs. Practicalities mattered too. Moving goods around the world requires security, and the Royal Navy was there to guard the sealanes of the world from warfare and piracy. The navy also made its own navigation charts available to the entire world, and for free: a quite remarkable sacrifice of strategically and commercially valuable knowledge. Not every policy decision was quite so praiseworthy, of course. British policy-makers were so addicted to trade that they found themselves deeply perplexed by countries that claimed they didn't want to engage in it. The solution to such curious behaviour was simple and Victorian: send in the gunboats. When China had the temerity to sink some of those gunboats in 1859,* Britain went back the next year, captured Peking and destroyed the Summer Palace. The problem resolved, British traders went happily back to work.

As a direct result of all these policies, trade boomed. The world had never seen anything remotely like it. Nor should it be thought that some ineluctable force of economics simply makes trade happen. On the contrary, public policy is of profound consequence. With the end of the First World War, the abrupt decline of British influence, and protectionist thinking firmly installed in the United States, trade collapsed.

* Fact for trivia buffs: this action, at the mouth of the Peiho river, was Britain's only significant naval defeat of the nineteenth century.

Global trade would not recover its nineteenth-century levels (measured as a proportion of total income) until the 1970s. Only in the 1990s would trade emphatically exceed the levels reached by our much-bewhiskered Victorian forefathers.* These are astonishing facts, and their importance is simply this: *trade spreads wealth.* The magic genie that James Watt and Richard Arkwright and Henry Cort let out of the bottle in Britain in the 1770s was soon clambering on board ships and journeying to every corner of the globe.

Even genies need cash, however, and Britain was quick to supply that too. Increasingly, over the Victorian and Edwardian eras, cash poured out of Britain on a huge scale.

Capital invested overseas, 1914
($ million, 1990 equivalents)

	British investments	Rest of world investments	Britain as % of total
Europe	1,129	12,315	8.4%
Western offshoots	8,254	2,919	73.8%
Latin America	3,682	4,708	43.9%
Asia	2,873	3,227	47.1%
Africa	2,373	2,291	50.9%
Total	18,311	25,459	41.8%

Over 40 per cent of all global investment overseas was made by British capitalists, yet even that figure understates Britain's global role. Almost half of all overseas investments made by

* To be sure, there are plenty of reasons for thinking that the extent of global integration is much greater now: trade figures aren't everything.

countries other than Britain went to the already prosperous countries of Europe. All fine and dandy, of course, but hardly a way to help poor countries catch up. British capitalists eschewed prosperous Europe almost completely, preferring instead to plunge their money into the wild frontiers of America and Australia, Latin America, Asia and Africa. British money flowed to the places where it was most needed, not where it was best protected.

Once again, the contrast with today is striking. In the first place, that torrent of Victorian money was remarkable in its scale. Only in 1980 did the world regain the levels of overseas investment (measured as a ratio of national incomes) that it had known back in 1914. Yet the comparison is misleading. Rich countries may now invest billions overseas, yet few of those billions ever creep beyond the rich world itself. Although the opening of China and India is starting to change the arithmetic, for most of the post-war period the poor world has been given aid (grudgingly), loans (irresponsibly), armaments (lavishly) and productive investment almost not at all. Back in Victorian days, no one would have dreamed of taxing Britons to give handouts to poorer countries. Instead, they did something arguably one step better still: they placed their own cash at the disposal of wealth-creating and infrastructure projects in parts of the world that could best make use of it. In the most successful cases, notably Argentina, the effect was enough to help underdeveloped countries catch up with European living standards in the space of one human lifetime.

The example of Victorian Britain should give us pause today, not least when it comes to rethinking the issues involved in globalization. As those radically haircutted protesters smash their burger-bar windows ('McDonald's munchers, spew up your lunches!'), they might do better to revert to the slogans of an earlier age. As the leading free trade campaigner, Richard Cobden, put it in the House of Commons:

> 'How far, how just, how honest, and how expedient [is it] to have any tax whatever laid upon the food of the people? That is the question to be decided.'

It was then. It is now. In the seventy years following Cobden's triumph, food (and all other) exports from the developing world entered Britain tax free, simultaneously helping British consumers and overseas farmers. These days, those same exports are taxed in a bid to keep European food prices high, and European farmers comfortable. The losers are domestic consumers and those farmers of the developing world who are being denied an outlet for their produce. In the century and a half after Cobden, our answers to his question have got worse, not better.

EMPIRE

AND LIKE A TORRENT RUSH

Britain is a nation of contradictions, of which one of the more central has to do with her very identity. The country is the oldest continuously functioning state in the world, with national institutions that date back at least to Alfred the Great. Nor has that state exactly lacked prominence in global affairs, having once been the centre of the world's largest empire. Yet, at the same time, our country seems wildly lacking in even the basic elements of national identity. There's the whole question of names, for one thing. The terms Great Britain, the British Isles, the United Kingdom, Britannia, Albion and England have all been deployed at one time or another. Yet none of these is what you'll actually see on your passport, which says, rather, 'The United Kingdom of Great Britain and Northern Ireland'. Ouch! The name is so unwieldy, it sounds like something concocted by a UN peace commission, or the name given to one of the splinter territories that once made up the Republic Formerly Known As Yugoslavia. You'd think that in the dozen or so centuries since Alfred the Great, we'd have come up with something a wee bit tidier.

The confusion over names points to a deeper truth. Our ancient, once vastly powerful state is a hotchpotch, a bodge job, a thing of shreds and patches. In the Olympic Games, when the country is on show to the rest of the world, we compete as Great Britain. But in the Commonwealth Games, when we're among family, we relax into the groupings we're more comfortable with: England, Scotland, Wales and Northern Ireland, of course, but also the crown dependencies of the Isle of Man and the bailiwicks of Jersey and Guernsey. These islands are not part of the United Kingdom or the European Union, though the Crown is sovereign over them and their citizens carry British passports. (And although little Sark is joined with Guernsey, it possesses its own feudal government, operated according to laws dating back to the rule of Queen Elizabeth I, according to which there is no freehold land – because it all belongs to the seigneur – and the only pigeons or unspayed female dogs permitted on the island are those belonging to that same lucky eminence.) Britain, however, is more than just this cluster of islands. The residue of empire comprises fourteen overseas territories* whose citizens carry British passports, and are therefore just as British as everyone else, though, naturally enough, each sends a separate team to the Commonwealth Games, assuming, that is, that they have any athletes.

This patchwork of nationality, law, government and geography is reflected in that most basic of national emblems, the national anthem. The anthem comprises just two short verses, sixty-four words in total. Yet almost no one knows it. Most of us can stumble through the first verse, but it's a rare person who is confident on the second. When the song is to be sung in a location where the Queen will be close to those singing it, courtiers will warn those seated close by to bone up

* Anguilla, Bermuda, British Antarctic Territory, British Indian Ocean Territory, British Virgin Islands, Cayman Islands, Falkland Islands, Gibraltar, Montserrat, Pitcairn Islands, Saint Helena including Ascension and Tristan da Cunha, South Georgia and the Sandwich Islands, Sovereign Base Areas of Akrotiri and Dhekelia, plus the Turks and Caicos Islands.

on the second verse beforehand, as the Queen hates to see people forced to rely on a printed hymn sheet. So, just to refresh your memory, here is that anthem in full.

> God save our gracious Queen,
> Long live our noble Queen,
> God save the Queen!
> Send her victorious,
> Happy and glorious,
> Long to reign over us;
> God save the Queen!
>
> Thy choicest gifts in store
> On her be pleased to pour;
> Long may she reign;
> May she defend our laws,
> And ever give us cause
> To sing with heart and voice,
> God save the Queen!

Sung by enough voices with a few trumpets in the background, the song can sound all right, but it has to be confessed that it's fairly lamentable stuff. The first stanza sounds like something developed by the Year 4s at the local primary school. Whoever thought of rhyming 'queen' with itself four times over was clearly having a bad verse day, and rhyming 'cause' with 'voice' in the second stanza suggests that the day didn't improve much as it went on.

But the song's problems go well beyond just being a bit rubbish. The two verses of the official anthem are extracted from a longer piece that includes the following:

> Lord grant that Marshal Wade
> May by thy mighty aid
> Victory bring.
> May he sedition hush,
> And like a torrent rush,
> Rebellious Scots to crush.
> God save the Queen!*

Given that Scotland has been part of the Union for three centuries now, this verse is a wee bit embarrassing – or would be, if the Scots national anthem weren't even worse. 'Flower of Scotland' has four stanzas, all of which celebrate the slaughter of English soldiers. The first one, below, is typical:

> O Flower of Scotland,
> When will we see your like again
> That fought and died for
> Your wee bit hill and glen.
> And stood against him,
> Proud Edward's army,
> And sent him homeward
> Tae think again.†

The Welsh anthem, though rather less bloodthirsty, is equally clear about the identity of the enemy:

---

* Wade was a British soldier tasked to make the Highlands secure against a possible Jacobite uprising.
† The Edward in question was Edward II, the battle Bannockburn, the date some seven centuries ago.

> My country though crushed by a hostile array,
> The language of Cambria lives on to this day;
> The muse has eluded the traitors' foul knives,
> The harp of my country survives.

It's not simply that the national anthems of the 'home nations' are all about murdering each other. Because of Britain's imperial past, our national anthem is hardly even ours. 'God Save the Queen' was the Canadian national anthem until 1980, the Australian national anthem until 1984, and still remains one of two official New Zealand anthems today.

The mish-mash of songs, states, laws, flags and identities may be bizarre, but it is certainly British. The contradiction we started with – an ancient state on the one hand, a thing of shreds and patches on the other – is actually no contradiction at all. Why is the British state so old? In large part, because it has managed to *absorb* without seeking to *submerge*. The 1707 union with Scotland left that country with its own laws, its own educational system, its own identity. When Sark joined Guernsey, nobody thought it necessary to tell Sark to stop being so feudal. When Guernsey became a crown dependency, no one told her to grow up and join the United Kingdom like everyone else. It is that quality of tolerance, that acceptance of localism – including a localism in which the Scots sing about slaughtering the English and vice versa – which makes us what we are.

Extending the point a bit, one could argue that it was precisely that tolerance of difference which enabled the empire to hold together as long as it did. The American War of Independence came about because the British state in London failed to understand and flex to the demands of its British-

American subjects. Generally speaking, the lessons of history are no sooner delivered than forgotten, but this one was learned and learned well. In Australia, New Zealand, Canada and elsewhere, the British state showed remarkable tact, exerting control where control was needed, flexibility where something softer was required. Admittedly, one consequence of this policy was that Britain ended up with a number of 'colonies' that could only be ordered to do things that they quite wanted to do anyway – which slightly calls into question the extent to which they were really colonies at all. Yet the result, here in the twenty-first century, was to produce a group of nations that genuinely do feel like extended family, with all the familial virtues and vices: affection and rivalry, banter and bitchiness.

As for the nuclear family of Great Britain itself, now celebrating the three hundredth wedding anniversary between England and Scotland, surely it's time to find a national anthem that avoids insulting any one of its component parts. Many suggestions have been put forward, but none has met with universal acclaim. 'Rule Britannia' is stirring but imperialist. 'Land of Hope and Glory' is noble but Tory. 'Jerusalem' is wonderful but weird. 'I Vow to Thee My Country' is just too public school. The Sex Pistols' 'God save the Queen / The fascist regime' sold a lot of records, but the song might find it hard to secure the royal blessing.

So how about a national anthem that is wonderfully stirring, honours British ideals of courage and liberty, is extremely well known, has universal acceptance as a national anthem, and actually succeeds in commemorating a British war against a non-British enemy, and along the way tosses in a reference to British technological and naval supremacy? Sounds good, huh? Such an anthem already exists. It's the American 'The Star-spangled Banner', which commemorates the British shelling of Fort McHenry in 1814. The 'rockets' red glare' is a reference to the world-leading rocket technology developed by the British inventor William Congreve. The 'foe's haughty host in dread silence reposes' alludes to the invincible strength of the Royal Navy. Although the incident in question was a setback for the British, the war as a whole was a score-draw at worst, a points victory at best. (We burned Washington, but they didn't get Canada.) Obviously a few words would need to be switched around, but surely the 'land of the free and the home of the brave' is something that we could all get behind – English, Welsh, Scots, Northern Irish, Manx, Channel Islanders, Gibraltarians, Falkland Islanders and the rest.

THE GATES OF MERCY

Early in the seventeenth century, an English trader, one Richard Jobson, found himself off the Gambian coast. He discovered that the locals were greatly afraid of him, as well they might be, given that their compatriots had been 'many times by several nations surprized, taken and carried away'. Offered slaves himself, Jobson refused, saying, 'we were a people who did not deal in such commodities, neither did we buy or sell one another, or any that had our own shapes'.

Jobson spoke too much, too early. At the time, it was true that the European market for African slaves was dominated by Spain and Portugal. Whereas northern Europe had been free of slavery for centuries, the institution had existed across the Mediterranean world since Roman times and before. Moors took Christian captives, Christians took Moors. (Plenty of Britons, indeed, were captured and enslaved by corsairs operating from North African ports, the most famous of them being the fictional Robinson Crusoe.) With the rise of their empires in the Americas, the Iberian powers found it natural to extend old ways to new shores. Since wind and currents placed Africa squarely en route for either the outward or return leg of the journey to the New World, the Atlantic slave trade was born.

The commerce didn't seem to bother anyone's conscience all that much. A pope prohibited the enslavement of Christians, but since no Christians were being enslaved anyway the ban was meaningless. European monarchs invested quite happily in the trade. There was a general convenient view that it was easier to be a slave in America than free and in Africa. (Needless to say, the view was not subjected to very much empirical scrutiny.) Nor was it even as though slavery was a new institution in Africa. Far from it. Slaves had long been taken in war and sold within Africa, or across the Red Sea to the Middle East. The 'white men, with horrible looks, red faces and loose hair'* merely represented a new market for a long-established industry.

This was the commerce in which Jobson so roundly refused to take part, yet the true significance of his voyages lay less in his personal integrity than in his investors' bottom line. Aside from slaves, Africa offered gold, ivory and Guinea pepper, yet not one of Jobson's three slaveless trips to Africa made a profit. Slaving made money, compassion did not.

From small beginnings, the British trade started to grow. At the conclusion of the War of the Spanish Succession in 1714, Britain won, among other things, the trading concession, known simply as the contract or 'asiento', to sell slaves to the Spanish Empire. The asiento was promptly sold to the South Sea Company as part of a complex transaction that effectively reduced the stock of government debt. Most famous now for its stock market boom and bust, the South Sea Company was in essence a slaving corporation, backed by the highest in the kingdom. A majority of the House of Commons bought shares. So did half of the House of Lords. So did every member of the royal family, royal bastards and mistresses not excepted.

* The quote is from the remarkable Olaudah Equiano, who was enslaved in Gambia, transported to the British West Indies and survived to write a notable account of his experiences.

From the start, the British broke the restrictive terms of the *asiento*. In a kind of semi-legal twilight, British slaving flourished. Even after the South Sea Bubble had well and truly burst, the fundamentally profitable trade continued. All major European trading nations participated. Over the centuries, Portugal carried the most slaves, transporting about 4,650,000. (The numbers are guesstimates only. Reliable records were never kept.) Britain carried about 2,600,000, with British North America, later the United States, accounting for a further 300,000. France transported 1,250,000, Holland around 500,000. Catholics and Protestants were involved in the trade. So was every Protestant denomination. So were the royal families of every trading nation.

The trade caused misery and violence wherever it touched: in the African interior, where it fuelled war and kidnap; on board ship, in the notorious Middle Passage, where death rates averaged around 15-20 per cent in the earlier years, falling to more like 10 per cent later on; in the cane fields of the New World, where conditions were brutal and lives short. Unexpectedly, perhaps, the trade also sowed death and destruction among Europeans, the death rates for crew members being higher than they were for the slaves themselves.

The trade inflicted a kind of moral brutality too, coarsening and numbing those who participated. Euphemism and silence cloaked the industry. Nobody referred to the business by its name. There were no traders in slaves, only adventurers in the Africa (or Guinea) trade. There were no shackles, only 'collars'. For four decades, the chaplain at Cape Coast Castle was a black Anglican, named Philip Quaque. During that time, not one single officer attended Holy Communion. The problem, wrote Quaque, wasn't racism, but guilt: 'The only plea they offer is that while they are here acting against Light and Conscience they dare not come to that Holy Table.'

At home, public opinion didn't reflect much on the trade, but when it did, it was mostly supportive. When Dr Johnson argued that 'no man is by nature the property of another', he represented a minority. Boswell's own view was commoner by far: 'To abolish a status which in all ages God has sanctioned … would be extreme cruelty to the African savages, a portion of whom it saves from massacre or bondage in their own country; and introduces into a much happier state of life … To abolish this trade would be to shut the gates of mercy on mankind.'

Thus far, there is nothing remotely exceptional in the English or British record. It's true that, from the mid-eighteenth century onwards, Britain was the leading slave-trading nation, but leadership came about from commercial and naval primacy more generally, not from any particular zeal for this trade over others. All the same, exceptional or not, Britain's participation in the commerce was arguably the ugliest episode in a history that's had its full share of ugliness. Though there have been occasions when Britain has been involved in a much greater loss of life (the Indian famine of 1770, or the violence of the 1947 Partition, for example), the slave trade lasted for centuries, was plainly murderous and was wholly avoidable. Comparisons with the Nazi holocaust are justifiable, not because the trade was genocidal (it wasn't), nor because it was intrinsically racist (ditto), but because ordinary men persisted in a course of action that they knew to be grossly wrong, and wrong on a colossal scale.

Finally, however, the code of *omerta* proved unsustainable. In France, Britain and parts of the new United States, public opinion began to turn – or more accurately, began to get a true sense of what was involved. In 1781, the Liverpool slaveship *Zong* mistook its course and ran low on water. The captain argued that if slaves died of natural causes, the loss would be borne by the vessel's owners. If, on the other hand, considerations for the crew's safety made it necessary for the slaves to be 'thrown alive into the sea, it would be the loss of the underwriters'. Against the protests of the first mate, 133 slaves were thrown overboard and left to drown. When the case finally came to court – not as a prosecution for murder, but by way of an insurance dispute – public uproar ensued.

Out of uproar, action. In 1785, a Cambridge student, Thomas Clarkson, won a university prize for an essay on slavery, written in Latin. Yet the essay was, to begin with at least, no more than the party-piece of a gifted student; a piece of brilliant writing, nothing more. Then, making his way to London to arrange for an English-language publication of the essay, Clarkson was struck by a sudden thought. In his own words: 'I sat down disconsolate on the turf by the roadside... Here a thought came to my mind, that if the contents of the Essay were true, it was time some person should see these calamities to the end.' That person, thought Clarkson, might as well be him.

His weapon was truth. Travelling to the major slaving ports of Bristol and Liverpool, he sought out those who knew the trade. Few were willing to speak, but enough did. In Bristol, he recorded stories of torture and murder. In Liverpool, he was given shackles, thumbscrews and a tool for force-feeding salves. Better still, he obtained a diagram of how slaves should be stowed, 482 human beings treated worse than any cattle. He made these things public. He carefully and cleverly broadened the anti-slavery lobby from its Quaker base to include leading representatives of every tier of the British establishment. He organized the first effective mass consumer boycott of sugar, a boycott that came to involve at least 300,000 people.

The blood-red tide had turned. In 1803, Denmark became the first country to abolish the slave trade,* but Denmark was hardly a major player. Britain was; and when, in 1807, Britain abolished the commerce, it put blood and treasure behind the abolition. From 1807 until the outbreak of the First World War, the Royal Navy pursued the slave trade with relentless zeal. British-owned slavers could simply be pursued and boarded, but the government's aim was to exterminate the trade generally, not simply the British share of it. Yet if Royal Navy vessels intercepted and boarded slavers of third-party nations, then the act could easily be interpreted as one of war. While the navy was willing to push the rules of diplomacy to their very limits, it was reluctant to indulge in overt aggression against third-party vessels.

Nevertheless, and despite these restrictions on their freedom of action, the British persisted. Even during the height of the Napoleonic Wars, when the Royal Navy had a few other things on its mind, there were British anti-slave ships stationed in West Africa. By the 1830s, there were fourteen vessels on permanent duty; by the 1840s, well over thirty. Behind naval might lay political will. When Brazil signed a treaty banning the trade but then refused to enforce it, the British prime minister, Lord Palmerston, dispatched a naval flotilla to bully the country into submission – gunboat diplomacy of the most benevolent kind. If thuggery didn't work, then bribes probably

---

* France, with the temporary fervour of revolution, had done so briefly in 1794. A few northern states had already done so in the USA.

would. Britain paid more than three million pounds to Portugal and a further million to Spain to cease the trade. In 1862, the Civil War in America forced President Lincoln to accede to British demands for stop-and-search rights of American flagged vessels. France (as ever) was a peculiar and difficult case. On the one hand, the anti-slavery lobby had once been as powerful there as it had been in Britain. On the other hand, French national pride was unable to accept any British role in enforcement – so while the trade was banned in theory from 1815, it flourished happily nonetheless.

Finally, finally, the British won through. The Atlantic trade effectively ended, the navy shifted its attention to East Africa, and British steam power finally drove out the slave traders there too. Slavery does still exist in parts of Africa and elsewhere, and campaigns to extirpate it are ongoing, yet the problem is less than it used to be. Boswell's 'gates of mercy' may finally be closing.

From the point of view of British exceptionalism, it needs to be stated that the British campaign against the slave trade was, historically speaking, remarkable. Never before had any country, for purely moral reasons, committed so much money, men and diplomatic capital to a cause so positively injurious to the national economic interest. Even today, with the rich world overflowing with material plenty, it seems oddly difficult for most wealthy countries to meet their self-imposed target of making 7/10 of one penny in every pound available to the developing world. To state a fact, however, is not to make a moral judgement. If a school bully spends an hour thumping someone in the school playground, he does not all of a sudden cover himself in glory for finally choosing to stop.

The British may have been slow to acquire the taste for muscular do-gooding, but it's a taste that lingers still today. There are nations more generous than we are when it comes to handing out development aid, but not one that commits a greater share of national income to military-backed peace-keeping and humanitarian missions. Our taste for combining military force with moral intent is one that our forebears would certainly have recognised. Lord Palmerston – the Victorian anti-slaver and gunboat diplomat – would surely be proud.

THE RELUCTANT FATHER

In 1850, the scale of British global leadership was at an all-time high. In industry, commerce, finance, technology and sheer naval muscle Britain was the world leader. Furthermore, British ascendancy had been around a long time. France's imperial and naval challenge had more or less been ended by the conclusion of the Seven Years War in 1763 (the American war proving to be a nasty, but temporary, setback). Britain's industrialization had enjoyed a headstart of at least fifty years over its war-torn European rivals. Knowing all this, you might well be inclined to guess that the British Empire would be pretty much at the peak of its power too. More colonies might tumble into the bag later on, but the colonial knapsack would already be bulging with goodies.

That picture is entirely true – or rather, entirely false. Or, if we're to be entirely honest, then it's both true and false, utterly precise and wholly misleading. If that explanation hasn't yet completely clarified things, then perhaps some geography will.

At first glance, the striking fact about the map of Britain's possessions in 1713 is that it's not all that different from the same map 140 years later. There have been substantial territorial gains (in Canada and India) and one major loss (the breakaway American colonies). Australia, however, was still

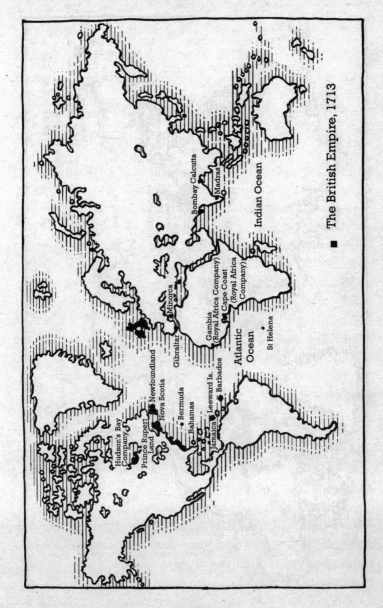

The British Empire, 1713

Indian Ocean

Bombay Calcutta

Madras

Gambia (Royal Africa Company)

Cape Coast (Royal Africa Company)

St Helena

Minorca

Gibraltar

Atlantic Ocean

Hudson's Bay Company

Prince Rupert Land

Newfoundland

Nova Scotia

Bermuda

Bahamas

Leeward Is.

Jamaica

Barbados

* Naval Bases and Depots
■ The British Empire 1850

Norfolk Island
New Zealand
South Wales
New
Van Diemen's Land
Hong Kong *
Singapore
Calcutta
Ceylon
Seychelles
Mauritius *
Bombay
Aden *
Bahrain
South Africa
Cape Colony
Natal
Simon's Bay *
Iontan Islands
(to Greece 1860)
Malta *
Gold Coast
Gambia
Ascension *
St. Helena
Rio de Janeiro •
Falkland Islands
Gibraltar *
Newfoundland
Halifax
Bermuda *
Bahama Islands
Leeward &
Windward Is. *
Trinidad
Sierra Leone
British Guiana
Jamaica
Canada
Callao *
Valparaiso *
Esquimault
Victoria

largely unsettled; Britain's African colonies little more than spots of colour on the coasts; Canada divided between its east and west coasts. Even in India, the 1850 map is somewhat deceptive. The country wasn't a colony, in the fairly straightforward way that the American states had been colonies. Much of India was still run by theoretically autonomous princely states. The rest of it was not run by Whitehall, or any Whitehall agency; it had been taken over and was still run by private enterprise in the shape of the East India Company, whose shares could be bought and sold on the stock market. (Because this last fact is a reasonably familiar one, it's easy to overlook its tremendous oddness. In principle, if you'd been rich enough, you could simply have made a dawn raid on the stock market and bought India. Since the country accounted for roughly one fifth of the world's population in 1850, and one seventh of world GDP, that's roughly equivalent to being able to buy China today.)

Overall, then, in 1850 the geographical extent of the British Empire as acquired by and administered from Whitehall was little changed from 1713. Arguably the lost American colonies represented a bigger loss than could be offset by the (limited) gains made in Australia and the (chilly) ones made in Canada. Viewed in that light, Britain's long period of world dominance seems to have profited her, in geopolitical terms, almost nothing. What in hooting heck had she been doing?

The answer is simple: Britain had been consciously, carefully and brilliantly building the most extensive empire in the history of humanity – but the empire she built so busily was strategic and commercial in nature, not primarily territorial. Glance back at those maps. The most striking difference between the two is both obvious and easy to overlook: it's all those tiny little dots and splodges of colour – Malta, Gibraltar, Ascension Island, St Helena, Bermuda, the Leeward and Windward Islands, Rio de Janeiro, the Falkland Islands, Aden, Cape Colony, Mauritius, Singapore, Hong Kong, Sydney and the rest. In geographical extent, those fine places may have amounted to little more than a handful of Iowa cornfields, but in strategic terms, in the age before mechanized land transport, they dominated the world. Through the era of the Pax Britannica, until the dawn of the twentieth century, no other country in the world operated a naval base outside home waters. Britain had almost forty, including all the most important ones.* It didn't simply have the strongest navy in European waters; it had the strongest navy in every other ocean of the world as well, including the Pacific. This, in effect, was Britain's first empire, the strategic empire, negligible in territory, vast in consequence; the empire upon which everything else depended.

That string of naval bases had two purposes. First, they enabled Britain to impose her Pax Britannica on the rest of the world, whether the rest of the world liked it or not. Second, they kept the sea lanes clear of warfare and piracy, so that everyone could get down to the one thing that, in British eyes, genuinely mattered: the ordinary, everyday business of making shedloads of money. In the mid-nineteenth century, Britain was not merely the world's most evolved industrial economy, she was also, by far, its most international. European countries didn't trade as much, and they traded mostly with each other. Not

---

* 'Five strategic keys lock up the globe,' gloated Admiral (later First Sea Lord) Jackie Fisher, and Britain had them all: Dover, Gibraltar, the Cape, Alexandria and Singapore.

so Britain, for whom Europe accounted for little more than a third of imports and exports. The rest of the trade was with the world: with the United States, India, Latin America, everywhere.

This, then, was the second empire, the commercial empire, invisible, omnipresent, lucrative. If the strategic empire was the one that mattered geopolitically, the commercial one was the bit that brought home the bacon. As for the third possible form of empire – an empire of territory and dominion – who on earth would want such a thing? The American colonies might have been lost, but trade and investment with the new United States had vastly increased. Just as important, all the expense and bother of government were now someone else's headache. Instead of throwing British tea into Boston harbour, those plaguey Americans now had to tax themselves, police them-selves, defend themselves, make hard political choices themselves. From the British perspective, it was a win-win outcome. So deeply ingrained was the British opposition to acquiring needless overseas territories that the word 'empire' was almost never used. Napoleon Bonaparte had been an emperor; the very word now connoted tyranny, the antithesis of British values.

Obviously enough, something changed. By the end of the century, huge swaths of Africa lay under the British flag. The colonies in Canada and Australia had filled out to the maximum limits of geography. India was now ruled direct from Whitehall, the Queen had become its Empress, and further territories had been added to the north, east and west of the country too. The ideology had shifted as well. No longer did empire suggest something suspiciously French; empire now was Britain's crowning glory, her chief strength, the prime

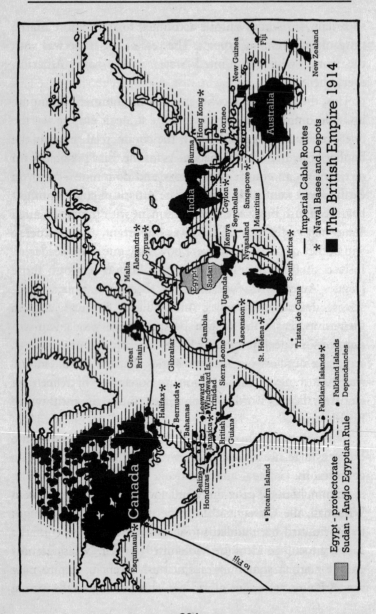

The British Empire 1914

— Imperial Cable Routes

✳ Naval Bases and Depots

■ The British Empire 1914

Egypt – protectorate
Sudan – Anglo Egyptian Rule

• Falkland Islands
  Dependancies

New Guinea
New Zealand
Fiji
Australia
Hong Kong ✳
Burma
Borneo
India
Ceylon ✳
Singapore ✳
Seychelles
Mauritius
Kenya
Nyasaland
South Africa ✳
Egypt
Sudan
Uganda
Alexandra ✳
Cyprus ✳
Malta
Gambia
Ascension ✳
St. Helena ✳
Tristan de Cunha
Great Britain
Gibraltar
Sierra Leone
Falkland Islands ✳
Halifax ✳
Bermuda ✳
Bahamas
Leeward Is. ✳
Jamaica ✳ Windward Is.
Trinidad
British Guiana
Belize
Honduras
Pitcairn Island
Canada
Esquimault ✳
to Fiji

vessel for her God-given role as bringer of civilization. To the progenitors of this new imperial culture, the more elephants, tigers and dancing tribespeople, the better. (An attitude the Queen still pays for today. A British monarch? She must love dancing tribespeople. Can't get enough of them. Bring on the bongo drums.)

It would be all too easy to interpret the change as simple hypocrisy, to assume that the powerful will always be greedy for territory, no matter what the rhetoric might claim. Yet such an explanation falls wide of the mark. The strange, counter-intuitive fact is this: the British Empire was born of weakness, a response to competition, the defensive reaction to a changing world.

The examples are too numerous to list in full, but a handful of cases (mostly from the 1870s and 1880s) will make the point. Afghanistan and Baluchistan were folded into the British Empire, for fear of the Russians. Burma was invaded and incorporated for fear of the French. Egypt was made a protectorate, largely because of worries over French influence. Territory was snatched in South and East Africa, because of fears over Germany. Islands in the western Pacific went the same way and for the same reason, New Guinea being divided half and half between the two countries. In West Africa, Nigeria sprang into being as a result of British alarm over French and German acquisitions.

In almost every case, the result for the British government was worse afterwards than it had been before. Nice as it might be for Edwardian schoolkids to drool over their pink-coloured maps, the simple fact is the world in 1913 was a far less friendly place for Britain than the world of 1850. In that earlier, happier world, for example, East Africa had been under the influence of the sultan of Zanzibar. The sultan knew that he needed to keep the British sweet, and so he did. The British could trade as they pleased with the whole of East Africa; they had all the security they needed, and zero expense, zero responsibility. Scroll forward fifty years, and Britain had lost in every conceivable way. Trade with what is now Tanzania had disappeared because it had become a German colony. Trade with the rest of East Africa continued, but now had to be paid for with all the troubles and expense of colonial administration. This third empire – an empire of territory, government, expense and responsibility – was precisely the one that Britain had sought to avoid.

The most obviously exceptional fact about the British Empire is its sheer extent: one quarter of the land and population of the earth; domination of the oceans; the sun never setting and all that. Just as exceptional, though, was the way in which empire came into being: from private enterprise more than public intention (in the early period); from growing weakness more than growing strength (in the later). Britain never, as the Victorian historian Sir John Seeley put it, acquired her empire 'in a fit of absence of mind', but that's not to say that the empire she'd ended up with was the one she'd wanted. Britain had wanted, and carefully built, her first empire, the one of naval bases and dominance of the sea lanes. She had also wanted, and wanted badly, her second empire, the one of trading and investment. The third empire was never quite like that. As the historian Bernard Porter puts it:

There was no deliberate intention on the part of the Foreign or Colonial Offices to colonise the world in order to make things easier for the British capitalist – rather the reverse. Britain would much have preferred to extend her trade without extending her political control. But things seemed to be taken out of her hands. The area of British economic interest in one or two places hardened into areas of overt colonial or near-colonial domination, by a natural process, almost, of reaction and counter-reaction. Victorians grumbled at the responsibilities thus incurred, but they had about as much right to complain as a reluctant father-to-be. They did not want what happened, but they had wanted the thing which had made it happen in the first place.

Chastity, unsurprisingly, was never an option.

BOMBAY DIRECT

I am just celebrating my fortieth birthday, I've got enough socks and I don't wear ties. Faced with the alarming prospect of finding me a present, my parents-in-law struck on an inspired solution: an original copy of *The Times* dating from April 1860, and a copy of the *Sun* dating from April 1797.

The *Sun* is the more obviously interesting one of the pair. In April 1797, the country was at war with revolutionary France, the mutiny of the fleet at Spithead was in full swing, and the newspaper contains the full text of Admiral Bridport's address to the seamen of the fleet. Here's a representative chunk:

> You have a father in your KING, who values your hitherto gallant Character – You have Friends in your Commanders, who have spent the prime of their lives in the honourable line of the *Wooden Walls of England* … Consider this Address as the overflowing of a heart panting for the preservation of the *Honour* and Happiness of his native Land of Liberty; and let me trust, when *next* my ears are saluted with Three Cheers, that I shall not be ashamed to hear that animating sound, *Rule Britannia*, and *God Save the King*.

They don't make admirals like that any more, more's the pity, though it would be better pay which got the seamen back to work, not panting hearts at the Admiralty.

Major as the mutiny was, however, it didn't make the front page, which was given over to advertisements – the universal layout for British daily papers up until 1900. The ads are much as you might expect. The land, goods and services being pitched include a new play, some grazing land, a book on stenography and the magnificent Cardiac Tincture ('In a stroke of the Dead Palsy I had the advice of the ablest Physicians ... [but] continued helpless, crawling upon crutches ... with Bilious Complaints and Costiveness and ... a general numbness in my flesh. In this deplorable condition, a friend brought me a Bottle of Cardiac Tincture and a Box of the Detergent Pills ...')

Sixty years on and the ads have changed. *The Times*' front page is crowded, dense with advertising, which indeed dominates the entire newspaper. The ads are grouped by theme, kicking off with some personal items ('LOST, April 8, a LIVER-COLOURED RETRIEVER ... TEN SHILLINGS and SIXPENCE REWARD') and continuing with notices for concerts, exhibitions, pleasure trips and suchlike. The most striking element of the front page, however, is two full columns, close printed, of advertisements by shippers offering to carry freight and passengers overseas, with a further column and a half on the following page. In this one randomly chosen newspaper, there are over 150 ships mentioned (nearly all of them 'splendid' or 'fine and fast-sailing'), sailing off to destinations including Bombay, 'Kurrachee', Calcutta, Madras, Hong Kong, Shanghai, Sydney, Adelaide, Melbourne, Auckland, Wellington, Alexandria, the Cape of Good Hope, Port Natal, New York, Canada, California, Vancouver Island, Brazil and Argentina.

These ships represented the commercial muscle of the world's most impressive trading nation. They also, however, represented something just as important, and much less spoken of: the British willingness to jump on a ship and set sail for foreign shores. The outward migration started small. From Columbus's 1492 landfall to 1820, most migration to the Americas was coerced, with roughly three slaves arriving (8.7 million in total) for every one free European (2.7 million). Those Europeans divided into roughly equal thirds of English/British, Spanish and Portuguese, but the crude totals conceal different trajectories. Iberian emigration started earlier, peaked sooner and declined; while English/British emigration started later and went on growing. Through the seventeenth and eighteenth centuries, Britain was the largest source of emigrants in Europe, with an annual average of 3,500 people leaving, mostly for the New World (some sources put the total nearer 6,000). The migrants were mostly Scots and Irish, mostly men, mostly in the prime of their life.

These outflows may have been small, but they mattered. In 1756, the Seven Years War broke out between Britain and France, a battle for global supremacy, with the whole of North America up for grabs. As we know, Britain won that struggle, thanks to Pitt's leadership, the navy and British financial might. But there's another explanation, every bit as important. The population of British North America was over one million, the entire population of 'New France' just fifty thousand. New France may have looked enormous on the map, but it was a huge sweep of emptiness, a bold idea signifying nothing. If you want to build an empire, you need to be prepared to leave home.

Those million anglophone Americans were enough decisively to alter the tide of history, but their numbers provided little clue

to the deluge that was to follow. In the century between
Waterloo and the First World War, around 60 million
Europeans would leave for the New World, and still more for
Africa, Australasia and elsewhere. Britain's most significant
export over this period wasn't cotton, or iron, or arms, or ships,
but people. We lack detailed statistics for the emigration in the
early part of the century, but there's no doubt at all that Britain
was by far the most important source of European migrants to
non-European destinations. In the period 1846-50, for
instance, it's estimated that the United Kingdom accounted for
a gob-smacking 78 per cent of all emigration from Europe. In
the period before 1846, Britain's share was, if anything, higher.
Even during the second half of the century when other parts of
Europe started to catch up, the British and Irish wanderlust
remains impressive.

Migration rates	Decade ending					
(per 1,000 population)	1860	1870	1880	1890	1900	1910
Britain	58	52	50	70	44	65
Ireland	–	–	66	142	89	70
Austria-Hungary	–	–	3	11	16	48
France	1	1	2	3	1	1
Germany	–	–	15	29	10	5
Italy	–	–	11	34	50	108
Spain	–	–	–	36	44	57

The impulse towards mass migration is easy enough to
understand: a better life, plentiful land, new horizons. But why
was Britain so very different? What made the outflow so great?
Or rather, given that Italian emigration would eventually outdo
the British, what made it come about so *early*?

There are four principal answers. One, British wages were the highest in Europe and transport costs the lowest. Quite simply, if people wanted to leave, Brits were among the first to afford the trip. Second, during the critical phase of the early nineteenth century Brits were in the paradoxical position of being both wealthy enough to leave and poor enough to want to, the offer of free land in the USA still a significant enough factor to encourage the trip. Third, the British population boom came earlier and faster than it did elsewhere. As population cohorts reached their twenties, with farmland not freely available and industrial jobs hardly attractive, there was an inevitable tendency for that population surplus to head down to the nearest port and set sail for someplace new.

The fourth reason, however, would prove the most important. Emigration breeds emigration. If no one in your village has ever made the long voyage to New York, only the pluckiest, most intrepid sorts are likely to do so. But if your Uncle Joe and your Auntie Edna and your Cousin Flo and that ginger bloke called Ted who once kissed your sister are all already in the USA, then the move will seem far less daunting. We Brits never felt alone. That's why, during the decisive phase of mass migration, it was Brits, not Continental Europeans, who peopled the new worlds.

All this matters. Assumptions of inevitability have a habit of smuggling themselves into historical thought without anyone ever quite noticing. It's easy, for instance, to assume that because the *Mayflower* contained a bunch of English speakers, with recognizably English political, religious and cultural attitudes, then the modern United States was bound to end up retaining (in modified form) that outlook. The idea's nonsense, of course. If, in the decades and centuries following the

Mayflower, the French had emigrated *en masse* (or the Germans *in Massen* or the Italians *in blocco*) and the Brits had stayed at home, the world today would be a vastly different place. America would be utterly different in terms of politics, economy, science, culture and cuisine. Even its language might well have shifted, those early English-speaking Puritans becoming no more than a historical curiosity.

This parallel universe, of a French-speaking America peopled by French-speaking migrants, would be utterly different from the one we actually inhabit. The 'Special Relationship' could have tied America and France, with Britain watching jealously from the sidelines. There might be an anglophone secessionist minority in Canada; 400 million French speakers in India; a burgeoning swell of French speakers in China; and here at home, societies clamouring to protect the English language. This parallel universe might well be disconcerting, yet it wouldn't be all downside. After all, in such a world, we'd surely, finally, be able to thrash the Aussies at cricket.

SOLDIERS AND SLAVES

If you poke around on an internet video service such as YouTube, you'll be able to find video clips of the Japanese Parliament, or Diet, in action. At first glance, those videos are nothing so special: a whole load of blokes in suits, in a modernish assembly building, talking interminably in a language that few of us understand. Except that the blokes in question are clearly Asian not European, the clips might easily have been shot in Luxembourg or Slovenia or Denmark; or, for that matter, in Cardiff, Belfast or Edinburgh.

Yet familiarity ought not to blind us to the tremendous oddness of this sight. Here is the Prime Minister of Japan, addressing the Japanese Parliament, and he's wearing *British national costume*. The modern grey business suit, after all, is as traditionally Japanese as is jellied eel or pie and mash. The sight of an oriental prime minister in a suit should startle us every bit as much as if (God forbid) Gordon Brown were to come to the dispatch box wearing a silk kimono. The oddness, however, does not stop at a certain form of attire. The Japanese obtained their parliamentary constitution from the post-war American occupiers, whose own political thinking had its roots all the way back in the constitutional arrangements of the first Anglo-Saxon kings of England. That Japanese Parliament is bound by the rule of law, a concept whose practical origin can be traced back to the signing of Magna Carta by the banks of the River Thames. In short, Japan – a country that lies half a world away from Britain and for most of the past few centuries did much to prohibit contact with Europeans of any stripe – bears a British imprint, not merely in the superficials (those boring grey suits), but in the deepest elements of its political culture too.

The British way of doing things has been disseminated by a number of different means. One notable way has been emulation. During the eighteenth century, European countries noticed that the Brits somehow managed to operate their criminal justice system without either torturing the accused or bringing about the collapse of civilization. Consequently, the realization began to dawn that perhaps torture was not quite as needful as had long been thought. Equally, when British sailors started kicking footballs around on the beaches of Genoa or Rio de Janeiro, their games were interesting enough to be widely adopted.

A second means of transmission has been migration. The United States has English as its national language, because, early on, Brits were readier to emigrate there than anyone else. For the same reason, British political and legal concepts were more influential than French or Spanish ones in building the country which would become the twentieth century's most successful and influential superpower. As with the United States, so too with Canada, Australia, New Zealand, South Africa and (to a lesser extent) elsewhere too.

The third mode of transmission, however, has been just as potent, and morally far more uncomfortable. The British Empire spread British ways by means of the carronade and the cutlass, the musket and Maxim gun. Territory was acquired by force or the threat of force. Once acquired, it was held the same way. By the standards of empires, the British model was relatively gentle, relatively non-exploitative and relatively tolerant. Yet empires are unlovely things, and even a relatively good version of the breed remains brutal, exploitative and aggressive. Even a fairly short list of British imperial excesses would have to take in the enslavement of Africans, the genocide meted out to Native Americans, the displacement of Australian Aboriginals, the imperial campaigns of 'reprisals', the concentration camps of the Boer War, the rebels blown apart on the cannon's mouth following the Indian Mutiny, the massacres at Amritsar or Omdurman, the famines exacerbated by colonial rule, the bloodshed and inadequate government that often followed independence. The British Empire was morally implicated in all these things, and countless more such things besides. The ill-effects of colonial rule linger on today, not just in the poor countries of ex-colonial Africa, but in the in the most prosperous parts of the former empire too. Think of the unhappy situation of Aboriginals in Australia, or of Native Americans in the United States. Better still, think of the long and violent colonial legacy in Ireland, whose troubles may only now be drawing to their unlamented close.

It is conventional now – 'politically correct', if you will – to be anti-empire. I think that such conventional wisdom represents the only morally tenable position to hold. Anyone today wanting to argue the case in favour of empire will inevitably find themselves having to defend those things that it gave rise to and was built on: the enslavement, the genocide, the displacement and the rest. Yet to take a moral stance shouldn't blind one to some of the other legacies of the British Empire.

Take, for instance, the not so minor issue of democracy. British lip-service to liberty might have produced its share of belly-laughs, but the colonial system brought with it common law notions of the rule of law, habeas corpus, jury trial, and the rest. Democracy was held up as a goal – one that seemed to recede forever out of reach, but a goal nonetheless. In the white colonies of Canada, Australia and New Zealand, democratic self-determination was achieved with remarkable smoothness. Elsewhere, colonial rule and representative government were deemed simply incompatible, yet it remains a striking fact that virtually every larger country to have emerged from colonial rule as a continuously functioning democracy is a former British colony, India being the wonderful, pre-eminent example of the type.

Indeed, even the briefest consideration of twentieth-century history underlines the importance of the British democratic tradition. Depending a little on how you count, the only countries to have gone through the twentieth century as stable democracies are as follows: Australia, Britain, Canada, Iceland, Ireland, New Zealand, Sweden, Switzerland, and the United States. Of these nine countries, six are English-speaking. The other three – Iceland, Sweden, Switzerland – were not among the heavyweights of world affairs. Had it not been for the British imperial legacy, including, most importantly, the United States, the most prevalent model of government in the world today would most likely be taken from the versions offered by Hitler, Stalin, and Mao. As it is, the world, is in large part free and getting freer. In 1973, Freedom House, an American NGO, reckoned that just 29.7% of the world's countries were free, compared with 45.9% unfree. Today, those statistics have reversed: 46.9% of the world's nations are free, and just 23.2% unfree. (In both cases, there's an intermediate group of partly free nations too.) These free nations enjoy not simply representative government, but all the trimmings too: a free press, the rule of law, due process in criminal trials, and the rest.

Writing about the British Empire, historian Simon Schama has written:

> The irony that an empire so noisily advertised as an empire of free Britons should depend on the most brutal coercion of enslaved Africans is not just an academic paradox. It was the condition of the empire's success, its original sin … By the end of the eighteenth century … instead of an empire of farmers and traders the British Empire was overwhelmingly an empire of soldiers and slaves. The Americans who had taken the professions of liberty most seriously had flung them back in the teeth of Britain and gone their own way.

He's right. Brutality in all its forms was a necessary part of the imperial project, its original sin. Yet Schama is also right to call attention to the paradox of Empire, the contradiction embedded at its heart: those professions of liberty which, ludicrous as they often looked, nevertheless bore fruit. The world we live in today is increasingly free, increasingly democratic. That this is the case owes much to a liberty built on coercion, a dream of freedom given life by soldiers and slaves.

LIFESTYLE

THE BRITISH WAY OF DEATH

In one of his travel books, Evelyn Waugh speaks of meeting a 'very elegant Greek who wore an Old Etonian tie and exhibited an extensive acquaintance with the more accessible members of the English peerage'. According to Waugh, this anglophile Greek told him of a recent incident, in which one of the main ferries crossing the Bosporus had run aground on some rocks hidden by morning mist. The captain and chief officer had taken the only available lifeboat and made off in it themselves.

> Left to themselves the passengers, who were a motley race of Turks, Jews and Armenians fell into a state of mad panic. The only helpful course would have been to sit absolutely firm and hope for rescue. Instead they trotted moaning from side to side, swaying the ship to and fro and shaking it off the rocks on which it was impaled.

So far this is all run-of-the-mill Waugh: a less than wholly reliable anecdote, spiced up with disparaging remarks about foreigners – particularly those presumptuous enough to affect the wearing of that most sacred of English icons, an Old Etonian tie. But Waugh is still working up to his climax:

My informant [the Greek] sat frozen with terror … in expectation of almost immediate capsize. He was here met by a stout little man, strutting calmly along the deck with a pipe in his mouth and his hands plunged into the pockets of his ulster. They observed each other with mutual esteem as the frenzied workmen jostled and shouted round them.

'I perceive, sir,' said the man with the pipe, 'that you, too, are an Englishman.'

'No,' answered the Greek, 'only a damned foreigner.'

'I beg your pardon, sir,' said the Englishman, and walked over to the side of the ship to drown alone.

Did any such event ever happen? Was Waugh ever told this story in anything like the form in which he relates it? Quite possibly not. And even as told, the tale doesn't quite hang together. While Waugh is acerbic about the workers who 'trotted moaning from side to side', surely his Englishman's calm 'strutting' would have had exactly the same effect on the balance of the ship?

All this, however, is beside the point. In Waugh's world, an Englishman was expected to be calm, even imperturbable, in the face of his impending death. It is no coincidence that Waugh's Englishman is depicted as a stout, small, ulster-wearing pipe-smoker. Each of these attributes is designed to convey not an aristocrat or man of breeding, but the ordinary Englishman, a man of the phlegmatic middle classes, a John Bull type, solid in build, practical in dress, calm in temperament. Place such a man in a life-threatening situation, and this most ordinary of Englishmen would come out superior to even the showiest of well-born foreigners. (It's perhaps worth noting that when Waugh spoke of the 'English', he would have included any Scot, Welshman or Irishman who had the proper understanding of the important things in life: the flight of a cricket ball, the fall of a trouser leg, the correct use of a finger bowl, the right way to patronize a foreigner.)

Of course, Waugh was a snob, a bigot and a propagandist. To use his anecdotes as a means of assessing the British temperament would be as nonsensical as using *Pravda*, say, to assess the Soviet economy under Leonid Brezhnev. Better perhaps to use known historical incidents to prove the case. At the Battle of Waterloo, the dashing cavalry commander Henry Paget (later Lord Anglesey) had his leg hit by a cannonball. Paget is said to have exclaimed, 'By God, sir, I've lost my leg,' to which the Duke of Wellington replied, 'By God, sir, so you have.' Yet it's hard to build much of a case from scraps such as these. For one thing, this exchange may well have been polished in the telling. For another, the words as reported could as easily be the product of shock as of raw physical courage. For a third, every nation likes to burnish the martial lustre of its heroes and it would be impossible to find any nation on earth that didn't have comparable tales to tell.

All the same, Waugh was on to something real. Take, for instance, an incident that took place towards the end of the Russian Civil War in 1920. Admiral Kolchak, the leader of the anti-Bolshevik forces, had been captured and was to be executed along with Pepeliaev, a political ally.

> The lip of the escarpment was illuminated by the headlamps of the lorry that had brought the firing squad; its members were drawn up on either side of the bonnet, so as not to obscure the headlamps.
>
> In the still, freezing night ... the prison commandant led Kolchak into the funnel of yellow light. Pepeliaev had to be dragged. Both men were handcuffed.
>
> Kolchak was offered, but refused, a bandage for his eyes ... A priest was there. Both prisoners said their prayers aloud. Then they were placed, side by side, on the spot where many men, and some women, had looked for the last time on the stars. Pepeliaev's eyes were shut, his face livid. Kolchak was entirely master of himself: 'like an Englishman' – the analogy oddly recurs in an official Soviet account of the execution.
>
> The order was given, the soldiers fired raggedly, both men fell ... The corpses were kicked or prodded over the edge of the escarpment, down the short piste of frozen snow discoloured by the transit of their predecessors, into the water and under the ice.*

This is an extraordinary tale. Not that Kolchak was master of himself when he died, but that his executioners should report it in the way they did: 'like an Englishman'. Kolchak's executioners were Bolsheviks – communists – opposed to pretty much

---

* This passage was written by Peter Fleming, the brother of James Bond creator Ian Fleming. The two brothers offer a good case study in contrasts. Just as older brother Peter had a fondness for the old, restrained stereotype, younger brother Ian was developing a new model for a new era: unruffled for sure, but also ruthless, cynical, self-interested, sadistic.

everything that Britain stood for. The execution took place in Irkutsk, east Siberia, one of the remotest places on earth. None of the executioners could have had more than the haziest understanding of what Britain and Britons were actually like. Yet there it is: 'like an Englishman', a shorthand compliment for courage in the face of death. Nor was the comparison a one-off. Some backwoods partisans, on inspecting the quietly dignified officer in jail just a few weeks earlier, had made the exact same comment.

This courage, this stiff-upper-lippishness, remains part of the English mystique. (More English now than Irish, Welsh or Scots.) If you drop the words '*comme un anglais*' into Google today, you'll come across phrases like '*froid comme un anglais*', '*flegmatique comme un anglais*', '*arrogant comme un anglais*', '*digne comme un anglais*'. All these epithets, positive and negative, gesture at the same basic temperament – cold and arrogant on the one hand, phlegmatic and dignified on the other.

Yet these days these stereotypes are more false than not. If you doubt it, just think of *Big Brother* eviction ceremonies, the week of Princess Diana's death, the Britain of Elton John and Posh and Becks, the efforts of politicians to be touchier and feelier than thou. Surely if one were looking for dignity and emotional restraint, one would be more likely to look anywhere else in northern Europe than our own fair islands. And there's a point to all this. It's all too easy to generalize too widely from the past. There certainly was a time when Waugh's depiction of the phlegmatic Englishman carried more than a grain of truth – say, from 1800 to 1950, to give it some approximate dates. Before and after that time, the Brits were notable more for their rowdy gaiety than their restraint; more notable for their roaring, boastful courage than its quieter, more attractive cousin. In short, while history may certainly reveal some national characteristics that endure, many others – even those that were once considered to define the national identity itself – come, have their heyday and go again, leaving not a trace.

Which version of the breed should we prefer? Waugh's pipe-smoking Englishman, or his twenty-first-century, *Big Brother*-style grandson? Personally, I'm not in too much doubt. In crisis, of course, there's nothing to beat that stiff-upper-lip imperturbability. All the rest of the time, we ought to prefer its modern replacement: the occasional wobbling lip and a new-found capacity for honest, direct emotional expression.

YOBS

The word *yob* – a lame nineteenth-century joke, *boy* backwards – has a comfortable feel to it, suggesting the back row of the classroom, flicked ink pellets and the occasional surreptitious whack with a ruler. But the reality of British yobbishness is much uglier than this. It's binge drinking, fights after pub closing, knives in schools, teenagers mugging each other for their mobile phones. It's football hooliganism, louts urinating in public, casual vandalism, road rage.

And though certain newspapers would have us believe that there was a happier age, a time when crime involved cheerful cockneys 'alf-inching a wallet at the racetrack, or *Just William*-ish schoolboys swiping apples from an orchard, the truth is quite different. Our society has always been violent – usually much more so. Football hooliganism is probably only a few minutes younger than the sport itself. Victorian and Edwardian football witnessed crowds of 'roughs' fighting not just each other, but players and match officials too. In 1909, a riot broke out after officials refused extra time to settle a draw between Glasgow and Celtic. The riot involved six thousand spectators, injured more than fifty policemen, wrecked the ground and led to the smashing of every street light in the area.

Nor is the shocked foreign reaction to British ways anything new. A French visitor to eighteenth-century London, César de

Saussure, commented that it was verging on the dangerous for 'an honest man, and more particularly for a foreigner, if at all well dressed, to walk in the streets'. Such a person might be spattered with mud, called a 'French dog' or even pelted with dead dogs or cats. When a Portuguese visitor got into a fight with an English sailor, the mob nailed the Portuguese to a wall by his ear. When he broke away, leaving part of his ear still fixed to the wall, the mob raced after him, attacked him with knives and left him to die. As far back as the fifteenth century, a Venetian diplomat said, 'there is no country in the world where there are so many thieves and robbers as in England; insomuch, that few venture to go alone in the country, excepting in the middle of the day, and fewer still in the towns at night, and least of all in London'.

If all this sounds familiar, then so does the diagnosis. We like to blame our yobbishness on social disintegration: a sorry tale of decaying family structures, insecure employment, the loss of religion and a shared morality, and more. Louis Simond, a Swiss-American who came to Britain in the early nineteenth century, spent plenty of time noting the awfulness of English manners, before adding:

> Nobody is provincial in this country. You meet nowhere with those persons who were never out of their native place, and whose habits are wholly local – nobody above poverty who has not visited London once in his life; and most of those who can do so visit it once a year. To go up to town from 100 or 200 miles distance is a thing done on a sudden, and without any previous deliberation. In France, the people of the provinces used to make their will before they undertook such an expedition.

That last detail is perhaps the significant one. Restless, capitalist, internationalist Britain has long been a society more mobile than its neighbours, both literally and in social, familial and religious ways. That has its upside, of course, but the downside is yobbishness, violence, an undercurrent of disorder.

That sounds like a good conclusion. It was the conclusion I'd expected to come to as I researched this piece, and yet it's much more wrong than right. On the one hand, it certainly seems true that we Brits are characterized by a certain violent yobbishness. As regards de Saussure's comment that 'the lower populace is of brutal and insolent nature, and very quarrelsome', it would be hard to stand in a British town centre on a Friday night and find anything to disagree with. But the trouble with working from anecdotal evidence is that anecdotes are all you end up with. What's really needed are facts.

And where better to start than murder? Although murder statistics record only the very pinnacle of crime, they are strongly correlated with serious crime in general. Murder rates in Britain have tallied pretty well with the broader crime rate. Murder rates between countries tally pretty well with differences in overall criminality. In other words, if you want a broad gauge of British violence over time and compared with other nations, then the murder rate is the place to look. When criminologist Manuel Eisner did just that (excluding violent deaths from war) the results he came up with were these:

Murder rate per 100,000 people per year

Century	England	Netherlands	Scandinavia	Germany & Switzerland	Italy
13th & 14th	23.0	47.0	–	37.0	56.0
15th	–	45.0	46.0	16.0	73.0
16th	7.0	25.0	21.0	11.0	47.0
17th	5.0	7.5	18.0	7.0	32.0
18th	1.5	5.5	1.9	7.5	10.5
19th	1.7	1.6	1.1	2.8	12.6
1900–49	0.8	1.5	0.7	1.7	3.2
1950–94	0.9	0.9	0.9	1.0	1.5

These results are stunning. England was *by far* the least violent society in Europe as far back as we can see. In the thirteenth and fourteenth centuries, English homicide rates were at a level that wouldn't be seen elsewhere until about the sixteenth century. The sixteenth-century English homicide rate would have been the best in Europe one hundred years later. Only in the nineteenth century did north-west Europe (Scandinavia and the Low Countries) catch up with England. If we turn our attention to serious crime, rather than just the loutish behaviour of quarrelsome drunks, then it is Britain which has led the way towards a politer, more civilized, less violent society.

What made England so strikingly peaceful? Why did the quarrelling British become so much less likely to reach for the sword, pistol, knife or fist? The answer surely revolves around our systems of law and order. Not only were the courts available to sort out any quarrel, they were also there to punish those who chose to go about it through other means. That sounds obvious, but on the Continent a legal approach to resolving disputes was much slower to take hold, with family-mediated resolution common, and honour killings widely seen as appropriate. In contrast, English courts were seen as legitimate, the laws ancient, the trials fair, the verdicts final. When even the king needed to tiptoe around the laws of the land, the authority of the law received its highest possible endorsement. The strength of social infrastructure, from parish poor relief to the strength of parliament, must have encouraged people to gather behind the socially approved institutions for resolving disputes.

In the end, it just isn't true that modern Britain has gone to the dogs. What has happened, however, is that other Western societies have finally caught up with Britain's lead. Certainly we are more yobbish in certain sorts of behaviour: binge drinking and mobile phone theft. But we don't do vandalism like the Dutch, car-burning like the French, organized crime like the Italians, or thuggish right-wingery like (a small minority of) the Germans. Perhaps if there's one truly British characteristic in all this, it's the most ancient one of all: having a good old moan about the way we are now.

CLOUDS OF FECULENCE

In July 1855, the great physicist Michael Faraday conducted a simple but striking experiment, which he reported to *The Times* in the following words:

> Sir, I traversed this day by steam-boat the space between London and Hungerford Bridges between half-past one and two o'clock; it was low water, and I think the tide must have been near the turn. The appearance and the smell of the water forced themselves at once on my attention. The whole of the river was an opaque pale brown fluid. In order to test the degree of opacity, I tore up some white cards into pieces, moistened them so as to make them sink easily below the surface, and then dropped some of these pieces into the water at every pier the boat came to; before they had sunk an inch below the surface they were indistinguishable, though the sun shone brightly at the time; and when the pieces fell edgeways the lower part was hidden from sight before the upper part was under water ... Near the bridges the feculence rolled up in clouds so dense that they were visible at the surface, even in water of this kind.
>
> ... the whole river was for the time a real sewer.

So indeed it was. In previous generations, sewage in London had drained into cesspools, which were emptied by 'night-soil men' who would take the solid waste to sell to farmers based around the capital. Although there was a system of under-ground sewers, these were designed to drain surface water into the Thames or one of its tributaries.* Drinking water came either direct from one of these rivers, or from one of London's many wells (remembered now as Clerkenwell, Holywell, Well Court, and so forth). These old arrangements had been overwhelmed by the speed and scale of London's nineteenth-century expansion. Sewage was increasingly being dumped straight into the Thames, even as water companies continued to draw from it. The effect of such arrangements was inevitable. Infectious disease was rampant. In 1848/49, cholera killed over 14,000 people in London alone, and would kill over 10,000 in another outbreak five years later. Prior to 1830, the disease had been unknown in Britain.

Threats on this scale were a new phenomenon for the English.† The country had long been one of the longest-lived nations on earth. In 1800, the life expectancy of the average English baby was over thirty-five years, more or less in line with the average of the previous 250 years. The high point came in 1581, where life expectancy reached almost forty-two years, the low point twenty years earlier when it fell to just under twenty-eight.

---

* Of which, by the way, there are many: you just can't see most of them. The largest of London's streams is the Fleet, which runs from Highgate Ponds on Hampstead Heath past King's Cross station then under the Farringdon Road to discharge just west of St Paul's. The stream is large enough that it used to be navigable as far as Holborn. Pirates once used it to attack King Edward II.
† There's been more work done on English life expectancy than on British life expectancy generally, hence the references throughout this piece to England, where you might expect Britain.

Dismal as such stats may sound to us, they were astonishingly good. Few societies since the Neolithic revolution could have boasted such a strong and consistent record. As for the global average life expectancy in 1800, it was certainly under thirty, and quite likely less than twenty-five. Even in prosperous western Europe, few countries matched the English. In France, in the fifty years ending in 1790, the average life expectancy for boy babies varied between twenty-four and twenty-eight; girls lived about two years longer. Rampaging infant mortality was the main cause of the huge disparity with modern life expectancies, but adults too lived less long then than adults of today.

Good as English life expectancies may have been, they had been achieved in the context of a largely rural society, where the few large cities that existed had evolved water and sewerage arrangements that worked, at least approximately. All that stood to be overturned, as traditional methods of supplying clean water and removing waste started to collapse under the strain of a fast-rising population. To make matters worse, doctors and scientists had no clear idea about the process of disease transmission. The germ theory of medicine wouldn't become finally accepted until the work of Pasteur and Koch towards the end of the Victorian era. Much more widespread was belief in the miasm theory: the notion that foul air spread disease and (depending on who you listened to) quite likely immorality too. This theory led to some dangerous conclusions. Florence Nightingale argued against laying drains under houses, in case foul airs escaped. Social reformer Edwin Chadwick, coining the slogan 'all smell is disease', thought it more important to make houses smell better than to remove sewage from the capital's major source of drinking water, the River Thames. Unsurprisingly, there were parts of London where the average expectation of life was just sixteen years. Michael Faraday didn't know it, but those clouds of feculence threatened a catastrophic reversal of all those hard-won gains in British health and mortality.

That catastrophe never happened. In fact, British life expectancies grew to around forty-one years by the 1820s, marked time for a while, then – from 1860 onwards – began to grow. By 1900, English life expectancies were around forty-seven years, just about as high as anywhere in the world. Still more impressive, Britain achieved this position despite being by far the world's most urbanized nation. Those other countries, such as Sweden, that were as long lived as England had the benefit of being largely rural societies. The trick of creating a healthy city was invented here first.

What worked the magic? Not doctors, that's clear. In 1976, a researcher named Thomas McKeown shocked the medical establishment by demonstrating categorically that the major killer diseases of early Victorian England had all but disappeared long before antibiotics, immunizations or chemo-therapies appeared on the scene. Take, for instance, scarlet fever. Mid-Victorian children were dying of this disease at the rate of almost 2,500 per million. By the time the disease-causing organism was discovered in the 1880s, the death rate was already down to under a thousand and falling fast. By the time the first semi-effective drugs had come along in the 1930s, and the first properly effective antibiotics had come along in the 1940s, the disease was killing only a few tens of children per million. If you look at a graph of scarlet fever mortality over time, you can't identify any impact from the introduction of drugs whatsoever. As for scarlet fever, so too for measles, whooping cough and others. In short, whatever caused the precipitous modern decline in mortality, it had nothing to do with the curative powers of doctors.

McKeown's own conclusion was a simple one. If doctors weren't responsible, then rising living standards must be. According to McKeown, higher wages meant better food meant better disease resistance. On this view, it was capitalists not doctors who had won the battle with death. There is certainly some truth in this argument. Past English longevity had been won on the back of productive agriculture, effective markets and high living standards. But more detailed examination of the data threw McKeown's claims into question. Although living standards rose in the first half of the nineteenth century, the average height achieved by English children began shrinking: a sure sign that higher economic living standards weren't translating into stronger, healthier, more disease-resistant kids. In effect, the deadly conditions in Britain's cities were more than balancing out any gains from higher wage levels.

So what happened? The emerging consensus today pushes a third breed of hero to the fore: the engineers, social reformers, municipal councillors and medical officers of health, who together constituted the public health revolution. London led the way, in part because the Houses of Parliament were situated on the river. With their Honourable Members appalled by the sheer stink coming from the river of sewage beyond their windows, it became clear that Something Had to Be Done. The man doing it would be Joseph Bazalgette,* not the most famous of Victorian engineers, but surely the most influential.

---

* Also, by the way, the great-great-grandfather of Peter Bazalgette, the man responsible for the UK version of *Big Brother*. Feel free to invent your own joke about one man removing sewage, the other putting it on the telly.

Bazalgette's brief was awe-inspiringly daunting: to remove all sewage from the River Thames. By the time he was finished, he had not simply met his brief, he had made the Thames the cleanest metropolitan river in the world, a distinction that it still possesses today. Bazalgette's design involved building a series of massive intercepting sewers running broadly west to east across London. The ones in the northern half of the city run roughly: Kentish Town-Stamford Hill-Hackney; Bayswater-Oxford Street-Bethnal Green; Hammersmith-Chelsea-Victoria Embankment-Limehouse. Those three huge thoroughfares of sewage come together between Bow and West Ham, and have outfalls in the Isle of Dogs and Beckton. A similar system was built south of the river too.

These sewers still exist; they are still the main way in which London's waste is removed. When you walk along the Victoria Embankment, you are walking *beside* one river, the Thames, but *over* another one, and one carrying a very different sort of fluid. The whole embankment called for fifty-two new acres of land to be reclaimed from the Thames, and brilliantly succeeded in engineering a honeycomb of rail, water, sewer and other services within spitting distance of a huge, powerful and tidal river.

The effects of Bazalgette's masterpiece were plain to see. Once his sewers had been commissioned, there were no further outbreaks of cholera in London. None. Nor typhoid. Deaths from diarrhoea and dysentery declined sharply too. In 1872, the annual death rate in London had fallen to just 21.5 per 100,000 people. That was a death rate lower than that of any major city in Europe or America – despite the fact that London was by far the largest city in the world, and therefore the one facing by far the biggest public health challenge.

Where London led, other cities followed. The Public Health Act of 1872 made more cash available to municipalities; it forced all councils to take sanitation measures seriously and appointed qualified officials to lead the charge. A steady decline in British mortality was the result. The country that had long been one of the leaders in life expectancy during the Age of Agriculture had proved – by a considerable distance – to lead the way during the Age of Industry too.

Historians spend a considerable time rehearsing the mantra that 'nothing in history is inevitable'. They're right to do so. Things could always have been otherwise. If Harold hadn't taken an arrow in the eye at Hastings? If Catherine of Aragon had produced a string of bonny baby boys for her husband, Henry VIII? If William of Orange had faced the expected equinoctial gales in autumn 1688? Everything always could have been other than it was.

Yet assumptions often lurk where we're least expecting them. It's easy for us to think of Victorian public health as part of the inevitable adaptation of an industrializing society to new conditions, as part and parcel of modernity itself. It was no such thing. All kinds of other responses could have been possible. Rich people could simply have procured clean water and stink-free neighbourhoods for themselves. The Houses of Parliament could simply have relocated to somewhere less pongy. Grand plans could have fallen apart in bickering over cost overruns (which were extensive) and delays (ditto). Central government need not have thrown money and resources at the national problem. Even if it had done, those municipalities could have wasted the money in corruption or bad practice.

In the end, Victorian society solved a potentially lethal problem because of the strengths that it possessed to a high degree: engineering excellence, clean government, the willingness and ability to tax and spend on a large scale, and an ability to innovate not only in engineering terms but in contractual and economic ones too. Behind these obvious virtues lay a further one: British (and previously English) society had long been protective of its poor. This was a society unprepared to solve the problems of the wealthy and leave those of the poor unattended. It is a very striking fact that the rich of Chelsea got their sewers no earlier than the poor of Stoke Newington: the sewers were built at the same time, by the same men, from the same pot of money. No sooner had the capital accomplished something remarkable, but the same life-saving technologies were rolled out to all the rest of the country too. All this might not have been.

Joseph Bazalgette is almost forgotten today. His only monument is a small bust hidden down by Charing Cross railway bridge, amidst the roar and blast of traffic along the Embankment. A Latin motto says, rather feebly, *Flumini*

Vincula Posuit ('He placed chains on the river'). If this paltry commemoration of Bazalgette's achievement is all he's to get, then perhaps at least the motto could be changed. The architect of St Paul's, Christopher Wren, lies under a plain black marble slab and a nearby plaque says simply, '*Lector, si monumentum requiris, circumspice*' – 'Reader, if you seek a monument, then look around you'. Perhaps the words on Bazalgette's own modest memorial should be rephrased: '*si monumentum requiris, despice*' – if you seek a monument, look under your feet.

GREEKS

And can any good thing come out of foreign parts? In matters
of sport is the world not divided into two parties? – the one
Greeks, the other barbarians; we being the Greeks and all other
nations whatsoever the barbarians.

REVEREND J.G. WOOD, *The Boy's Modern Playmate*, 1868

In the twelfth century, one William Fitzstephen observed that
'After dinner all the youth of the city goes out into the fields for
the very popular game of ball. The scholars of each school have
their own ball, and almost all the workers of each trade have theirs
also in their hands. The elders, fathers and men of wealth come
on horseback to view the contests of their juniors, and in their
fashion sport with the young men.' The game that was being
played would have had no formal rules. It might have been fifty
or more a side. Propelling the ball with hands or sticks may have
been permitted. Good-natured physical brawling was certainly a
core part of the entertainment, with injuries commonplace.

Such a game strikes us as so obvious, so elemental, that it
must have been as universal in human history as war-making,
say, or adultery. Not so. Although records exist of other foot-
and ball-based games, such as the Chinese *cuju* or the Japanese
kemari, the forerunner of football seems to have been largely
concentrated in Celtic and Anglo-Saxon areas, and it seems

more than likely that the Anglo-Saxons took the game from the Celts. By medieval times, the game was popular enough that it had to be banned. Often. Edward II, Henry V, Edward IV, Henry VII and Henry VIII all sought to ban or restrict the sport, with obvious lack of success. The sport continued – rough, fast, unlegislated – into the nineteenth century, played by the working classes of town and country, and by the public schoolboys who aped the same sports. There were no fixed rules to these games, beyond certain local customary forms. Some variants of the game involved plenty of handling, other variants less. There was no such thing as a foul and 'hacking', or chopping away at an opponent's shins, was a core part of the sport's delights. The delicate skills of a Cristiano Ronaldo, say, would have been no more suited to that version of the game than a sports kit consisting of ballet pumps and tutu.

At the dawn of the nineteenth century, it wasn't remotely clear that there was much of a future for the sport. Georgian aristocrats, on the hunt for recreations that could also serve as outlets for their gambing addictions, had started to formalize a variety of other sports. The Duke of Richmond had founded one of the earliest cricket clubs in 1727. The prizefighter and promoter Jack Broughton had devised rules for boxing in 1743 which brought both humanity and superior betting opportunities to the previously chaotic – and often life-endangering – fights. In 1752, the Jockey Club had taken the ancient pastime of racing horses and organized it into a formally rule-bound sport. Two years later, and following the example of an earlier Edinburgh-based club, the 'Royal and Ancient' St Andrews Club became home to the sport of golf. By the late eighteenth century most larger cities had well-organized, feverishly contested rowing regattas.

All this activity, however, left football looking boorish and unmodern. Derbyshire Council frowned on such nonsense as the annual Ashbourne Shrovetide 'football' game, calling it, accurately enough, 'the assembly of a lawless rabble, suspending business to the loss of the industrious, creating terror and alarm to the peaceable, committing violence on the person and damage to the properties of the defenceless poor'. (The game still goes on; windows in the town centre are still boarded up; but, hey, at least there's a rule that says players aren't allowed to kill each other.) When Joseph Strutt surveyed the sports of England in 1801, he said of football that 'the game was formerly much in vogue among the common people, though of late years it seems to have fallen into disrepute and is but little practised'. Overlooked by aristocrats, disliked by urbanites, reduced by rural depopulation, campaigned against by Methodists, the game seemed destined to peter out.

What saved it was the collision between the emerging Victorian ethic of Christian manliness and the unreconstructed thuggishness of those public school sports. Thomas Arnold, headmaster of Rugby school from 1828 to 1842, launched the reform programme for public schools generally, though he himself had little interest in sport. Nevertheless, some of his key disciples became evangelical on the topic. Sports, properly organized and played, might turn those individualistic thugs into responsible team players; God

would surely prefer honest, rule-bound, collective endeavour to all that physical scrapping; and, just possibly, if all those hormonal teenagers could be rendered tired enough, then they might keep their hands away from their own (or each other's) private parts. While it's safe to say that not every one of those hopes was fulfilled, public schools suddenly found a passion for sport which had never once been there before.*

As the new generations of public schoolboys made their way on into the universities and armed forces, the philosophy spread, and as it did so one particular problem became prominent. It was all very well for one particular school to fashion its own particular rules for its own particular game, but what if one school team wanted to play another? Worse still, what game would be played by a mixed bunch of Old Harrovians, Etonians, Wykehamists, Carthusians and so on once they got to Oxford or Cambridge? Compromise was both required and hard to find. For decades, the problem lingered on, unresolved, plagued by issues of tradition and prestige. Finally, in 1863, a group of former public schoolboys met in London to hammer out a common code. The two principal difficulties arose from the dispute between those who favoured a kicking/dribbling game and those preferring a catching/running one, and between those who favoured 'hacking' and those who wanted to ban such physical contact.† Finally, and after compromise with

---

* That's why the Duke of Wellington almost certainly didn't say that the Battle of Waterloo was won on the playing fields of Eton. In his day, those fields had hardly mattered.

† One sportsman said, disgustedly, that if hacking were banned, then 'you will do away with the courage and pluck of the game, and I will be bound to bring over a lot of Frenchmen who would beat you with a week's practice'. True enough, except that it took more than a week.

a near-simultaneous codification effort based up in Sheffield, the Association Football rules weren't simply agreed on paper, but on the mud and turf of the nation's pitches. In 1871, the aficionados of handling set up their own Rugby Football Union.

The rest is history, but like so much history it took its own unpredictable course. For one thing, the sport was very quickly dominated by the urban working classes. The game that most signally marked the changing balance of power was the 1883 FA Cup Final, in which Blackburn Olympic beat Old Etonians by two goals to one, the winning goal coming in extra time, after the working-class Northerners had asked to complete the game then and there, as they couldn't afford a rematch. For another thing, you might well have expected the empire to be the main agent of football's propagation, yet in fact resentment of British imperialism rendered the game *weakest* in all the countries of empire, and strongest in the countries of Europe and Latin America where British influence was pervasive, but not usually accompanied by soldiers.

The conventional story of British sport dwells at length on the story of football, makes further reference to other well-known British inventions (tennis, golf, rugby, cricket), then hangs up its boots in favour of a warm bath and changing-room banter. Yet dominant though football has now become in global terms, the most remarkable aspect of the whole tale is not that Britain produced the most globally significant sport, but that it produced virtually every other sport as well. What's more, although the muscular Christianity of the Victorian era certainly saw an uprush of interest in sports of every kind, that interest had hardly been lacking before. Think back to those aristocratic Georgians, who first formalized the sports of boxing, rowing, horse-racing, golf and cricket. Those same Georgians had also developed billiards, baseball* and skating, and nurtured the much older traditions of lawn bowls and archery. In fact, if you want an even vaguely complete list of the sports first formalized by the British (including by British colonials overseas), you'd need to include at least the following:

Football-based games
Football, Rugby Union, Rugby League, Gaelic football, Australian Rules football.

Other games of Celtic/Anglo-Saxon origin
Cricket, hockey, ice hockey, golf, curling, baseball.

European-derived games
Tennis, squash, rackets, fives, hardball, fencing, billiards, snooker, croquet, lawn bowls, tenpin bowling, downhill skiing (yes, really), slalom skiing (ditto).

Non-European derived games
Lacrosse, polo, canoeing.

Sports deriving from universal human activities
Boxing, swimming, rowing, archery, horse-racing, yachting, skating, mountaineering.

Invented sports
Water polo, table tennis, cycling, badminton, motorcycling.

* The first printed reference to baseball comes in a 1744 English publication entitled *A Pretty Little Pocket Book, Intended for the Amusement of Little Mister Tommy and Pretty Miss Polly.*

If this list doesn't smack your gob, then your gob is pretty much unsmackable. When we say 'we invented sport', the statement comes as close to literal truth as it's possible to get. Time after time after time, and irrespective of a pastime's geographical origin or climatic suitability, it was the British who turned diversions into sports. To be precise, recreations, which had previously existed only in the unlegislated, informal, chaotic manner of pre-FA football, were turned into organized, regulated, formal competition by the British.

Take lacrosse, for example, which was most likely (and bizarrely) a Viking sport that became naturalized in North America just as it died out in Scandinavia. Though there had never been any tradition of the sport in Britain, it took British colonials in Canada to observe the native sport and codify it, setting up the first ever lacrosse club in the process. Subsequently, British Britons, snobbish about the codification prowess of any mere Canuck, rewrote the rules and thereby laid down the basis of the laws by which the modern game is now played. In sport after sport, the same thing occurred. Even where Britain was not involved directly, it was typically the major influence, either as something to emulate (notably in de Coubertin's creation of the modern Olympics) or as something to resist (notably in the desire of American universities to hammer out their own code of football).

In short, the scale of British leadership in the creation of sport seems so extreme – as great or greater even than our one-time leadership in the realms of industry, agriculture or the navy – that something extraordinary seems needed to account for it. So what does? Well, first of all, it does seem clear that we Brits have always enjoyed physical activity. The Celts seem to have originated much more than their fair share of sports, the

Anglo-Saxons being highly enthusiastic adopters. So in part, we created sport because we may have been keener than most on its rough-and-tumble predecessors. We also seem to have had a knack of creating decent games, simple in conception but wonderfully complex in the playing.

It's also clear that from a certain point, around 1830 or 1840, the British began to idolize sport in a way that no other country came close to matching. The creation and codification of sports became a national obsession. Indeed, the plethora of games created by the Victorian Brits is hardly done justice by the list above. After all, it contains only those sports that survived into the present. The brutal process of natural selection had spelled extinction for dozens of others. Yet though the Victorian period certainly represented the pinnacle of British sport-making, it's clear enough that that pre-eminence in sport-building arose long before public schools built a philosophy around thrashing foot, squash, tennis, rugby and every other kind of ball.

Perhaps those universal activities – archery, horse-riding, sailing, rowing – provide the crucial clue. Most societies in the world used bows and arrows, yet Brits were the first to set up archery clubs and tournaments for fun. Though countless people have ridden horses, it took Brits to think that clubs and rules were essential. In sailing and rowing too, the same thing happened. All the oldest sports clubs in the world are British: the Southampton Town Bowling Club (1299), the Society of Kilwinning Archers (1483), the Guild of the Fraternity of St George (1537), the Kilsyth Curling Club (1716), the Royal Cork Yacht Club (1720), and the Edinburgh Skating Club and the Honourable Society of Edinburgh Golfers (both 1744). As soon as you have clubs, you need rules: what's permitted?; what's not permitted?; how should competitions be organized?; who can our club compete against? That habit of clubbishness is the clue, the reason why the pastimes of others became sports of ours.

So why were we so very clubbable? The answer must surely lie in how very organized the country was. From Anglo-Saxon times on, the country was ordered, from national parliament down to local parish or manor. Members of Parliament were appointed or elected; laws were made, were locally applied, were enforced through the courts. Nowhere else was society as minutely ordered; nowhere else was that order so little disrupted by war, conquest or revolution. Nowhere else was physical roughhousing less likely to spill over into serious crime.

And perhaps that's the secret: British love of rough-and-tumble games plus British clubbishness equals the British creation of sport. If so, it would be tempting to do as most historians have done, and relegate the whole story of sport to little more than a colourful footnote to the main story of Britain. Tempting, but wrong. Clubbishness *matters*. It's the insight of Robert Putnam, an American social scientist, whose book *Bowling Alone* traced the vast amount of social capital stored in a nation's clubs and associations. That social capital manifests itself as economic success, better health, social cohesiveness – all the good things a society seeks. If Britain was vastly more associative as a nation than others, then it almost certainly had way more social capital too. That's no mere footnote; that's an observation that goes to the heart of what has made Britain distinctive, what has shaped British national success.

The thought is a comforting one. If the most remarkable thing about Britons and sport is how many games we've invented, the second-most remarkable thing is how adept we've been at losing (the snobbish cult of Victorian amateurism being greatly to blame). Fortunately, though, social capital doesn't come from being good at something, it comes from doing it together. We Britons may have bowled badly, but we've never bowled alone.

VERY FINE LINEN

No perfumes, he used to say, but very fine linen, plenty of it, and country washing.

HARRIETTE WILSON of GEORGE 'BEAU' BRUMMELL

In July 1791, the Prince of Wales came to Eton College. He wore:

> A bottle green and claret-coloured striped silk coat and breeches and silver tissue waistcoat, very richly embroidered in silver and stones, and coloured silks in curious devices and bouquets of flowers. The coat and waistcoat embroidered down the seams and spangled all over the body. The coat cuffs the same as the waistcoat. The breeches likewise covered in spangles. Diamond buttons to the coat, waistcoat and breeches, which, with his brilliant diamond epaulette and sword, made the whole dress form a most magnificent appearance.

Magnificent indeed, but tasteful? The outfit sounds like a pearly king outfit, only with diamonds for sequins. Or perhaps the right comparison would be with some modern-day rap artist: all bling and Rolexes.

It wasn't that the prince was some mere victim of royal fashions, meekly donning whatever court etiquette thrust his way. On the contrary. He loved his clothes. When he was made colonel-in-chief of his own regiment, the 10th Regiment of Light Dragoons, 'The Prince of Wales's Own', he took the opportunity to design not only his own uniform, but those of every man under him. He chose extravagantly braided, frogged and epauletted jackets and a fur pelisse or cloak, all adorned with lashings of white silk and silver facings. In case the effect wasn't splendid enough, the ensemble was topped off by a 'Tarleton' – a helmet that threw together a leopardskin turban, a peaked leather cap, a silver clasp and a Roman-style crest of real fur. One single outfit alone could easily cost £300, or £20,000 in today's money.

Excessive as these fashions were, they represented only the latest effusion in a long line of male ostentation. Indeed, the only real challenge to such excess came from the two great revolutionary societies of the age, France and America. In both places, a new, pared-down, consciously democratic style had emerged, based (curiously enough) on the look of an English country gentleman: riding boots, close-fitting breeches, buff waistcoat, blue coat. To wear such things in any fashion-conscious spot in Britain was to make a deliberately political gesture, and one hardly likely to be endorsed by the extravagant heir to the British crown.

Yet Britain had its revolutionaries too, and one in particular: George Bryan (later 'Beau') Brummell. Brummell had been at Eton in 1791. He'd secured a junior commission in the 10th Light Dragoons in 1794, where he had come to be on intimate terms with the prince himself. When the prince got married the following year, Brummell was one of his three best men.* Brummell's army career was short-lived, however: he left the

---

* After his wedding night, the prince boasted to Brummell and others that, on first seeing him naked, his new wife had exclaimed, '*Mon Dieu, qu'il est gros!*' But was it appropriate to boast? The phrase might mean one of two very different things: 'My God it's big!' or 'My God, he's fat!'

regiment in 1798, and shortly thereafter took a house in a fashionable area of London. And then, he dressed. He dressed in his own particular style, in his own inimitable way. And almost everything he did overturned convention, challenged the foppishness that had ruled from the royal court down.

For one thing, he washed. All over, every day. He came to avoid perfume altogether. He shaved himself. Meticulously, using tweezers to pluck any stray offending hairs. In an age of no plumbing but plentiful manservants, all this was strange enough, but it was his style of dressing which really seized the imagination of the young, rich and fashionable. Brummell's dress code was revolutionary in its simplicity. He wore white shirts, white neckcloths, a white or pale waistcoat, tight-fitting pale-coloured breeches or pantaloons, and black riding boots. Topping off the ensemble was a coat in dark blue, cut high at the front, and forming tails at the back. That was it. White, black and dark blue. No bottle-green, no claret-red, no primrose-yellow. No silver facings, no gilt frogging, no emeralds or diamonds, no swags and festoons of braiding.

The style relied on perfection in detail. That white linen had to be scrupulously white to pass muster. That was why Brummell insisted on 'country washing': town-dried linen risked being speckled with coal smoke. Even so, linen needed frequent changes to maintain the look and keeping it simple didn't mean cheap. As one German visitor to London complained:

> An elegant then requires per week, twenty shirts, twenty-four pocket handkerchiefs, nine or ten pairs of 'summer trousers', thirty neck handkerchiefs … a dozen waistcoats and stockings à discretion. I see your housewifely soul aghast. But such a dandy cannot get on without dressing three or four times a day …

Brummell himself probably exceeded these basic requirements. A neckcloth had to be tied absolutely right to be acceptable. The line of the cloth against the neck, the tie of the knot, the fall of the ends – all had to be perfect. If one attempt failed, it was no use having another go with the same cloth, as creases would reveal the short cut. As Brummell became ever more widely known, it became a fashionable pastime to come and watch him dress – so fashionable, indeed, that the portly prince himself was often to be found in Brummell's rooms at Chesterfield Street, watching the ritual and mixing with others in the first rank of London society. With an audience, the theatricality of the performance increased. Robinson, Brummell's valet, used to leave his master's room with an armful of rejected neckcloths, saying sadly to the inquisitive, 'These, sir? These are our failures.'

If the style was limited in palette, it was remorselessly classical in cut. If the classical statuary of Greece and Rome revealed perfection in the male body, the purpose of Brummell's tailoring was to bring out that perfection in clothes: revealing what was best to reveal, disguising or flattering what was imperfect. Coats were padded, stitched, cut and sewn to produce the perfect form, always suggesting the musculature that lay beneath. Collars came to be cut separately from the coat and sewn on, so that the fabric of the collar would sit in line with the wearer's neck muscles. Lapels thrust out from the chest like imitation pectorals. Shoulders were carefully but subtly padded. The cut-away bottom of the coat emphasized a narrow, athletic waist.

Nor did such subtle flattery stop at the crotch. On the contrary, pantaloons or britches were worn almost painfully tight. Corset-style stitching at the back kept the fabric taut in one dimension. Braces (an innovation of Brummell's) and stirrup straps beneath the feet kept the fabric taut in the other. The effect, of course, was to emphasize a gentleman's equipment (and no doubt his socks too, if the equipment was lacking). The modern pair of trousers is a direct descendant of those pantaloons.

Brummell wasn't a particularly wealthy man, given the circles he moved in. His fortune – about £2.5 million in modern terms – was soon supplemented by gambling. When the gambling winnings turned into losses, and perhaps as his syphilis started to act on his mind, his place in the first flight of society began to slip. He allowed petty quarrels with the prince to escalate out of control. The *coup de grâce* came when the prince came to one of Brummell's parties without acknowledging his host. Brummell called loudly to the prince's companion, Lord Alvanley, 'Alvanley, who's your fat friend?' The prince never forgave him. When, finally, Brummell became unable to pay his gambling debts, one of his creditors went to his club and told everyone there that Brummell had behaved in an ungentlemanlike manner. The message was clear: pay up, fight a duel or leave the country. Brummell left for France, never to return. He died ill, poor and half mad with syphilis in 1840.

But his style is with us still. In the capital city of the world's most influential nation, Brummell's London-made fashions set the tone for Europe and beyond. His severely restricted colour palette still sets the global standard today. His neckcloths evolved into collars and tie. The waistcoat gradually faded away. Pantaloons became trousers. The emphasis on tailoring not ornament, classical form not romantic showiness, has remained unaltered. The style of the modern business suit is Brummell's style, brought quietly up to date. For all that men's fashions have relaxed and expanded over the last few decades, it's still unthinkable that the predominant style in the board-room, parliament or a night at the opera should be any-thing other than a subtle variant on Brummell's tailored monochrome – so much so that we have quite got used to the extraordinary sight of Japanese businessmen and African politicians walking around in British national dress.

It's not just the business suit in which you can see his mark. James Dean's *Rebel without a Cause* seems as far from Regency London as you can get. But is it? Dean's character wore clothes in Brummell's own colours: blue jeans, crisp white T-shirt, black leather jacket. The look was, as Brummell's was, almost military in its spareness. It depended, as Brummell's did, on spotless whites and precisely the right cut for trousers and jacket. It called attention to the male physique – broad shoulders, tight waist, flat stomach. The fact is that Brummell so deeply influenced our concept of male costume that even when we think we escape it, we often turn back to it by a different route.*

* It was also a Briton who invented *haute couture* for women. The Briton was a Lincolnshire man, Charles Worth, who set up shop in Paris in 1858. Worth's innovation was to create collections of designs, from which wealthy customers could make their choice. Before that, every dress had been made to the customer's own specification. Worth and his sons are also credited with the invention of the catwalk show. For all that, the centre of women's fashion has always been Paris, never London.

And he did more than that. He created a certain masculine ideal which remains with us still. James Bond is Brummell's version of a hero: drily witty, sophisticated to the point of snobbery, impeccably tailored, unruffled. This masculine ideal has become worldwide in its scope, to such a degree that it's easy to mistakenly see it as nothing more than a universal archetype. There is something universal in the model, of course, but the precise twist is notably British all the same. Contrast Bond with, for example, the Bruce Willis character in *Die Hard*. The latter is carefully, deliberately anti-Bond. He's dirty, sweaty, rejecting refinement in speech or manners. What's more, Willis's hero is counterpointed by the effetely sophisticated, European baddie, played by Briton Alan Rickman. In effect, the film relates how the all-American Joe Six-pack fights and defeats the ghost of Beau Brummell. For all that Willis won that particular fight, Brummell's ghost lives energetically on.

CONCLUSION

AGE AND LIBERTY

There are many ways to tell a story. One biographer of Bill Gates might, for instance, want to write a biography slanted towards the more geeky, technical aspects of Gates's career; another might emphasize things financial; another might want to tell a corporate story, about the rise and rise of Microsoft; another still might be most interested in Gates's philanthropy, and want to leave aside any detailed account of where his billions came from. It would be hard to argue with any of these approaches. On the contrary, each, in its own terms, makes eminent good sense. Yet it would be almost impossible to imagine any halfway sensible biography of the great man which didn't at least make it plain (i) that Bill Gates was the world's richest man; (ii) that, in Windows, he'd built the world's most widely used operating system; (iii) that his company was one of the largest in the world; and (iv) that his charitable giving was greater than anyone else's ever. In short, any half-sensible biography would give due prominence to those things that make Gates special, those things that most justify the biography's very existence.

When it comes to biographies of individual human beings, this ordinary common sense is followed to the letter. When it comes to biographies of nations, however, good sense seems to fly out of the window. Perhaps because national populations are going to be interested in their own stories come what may, historians (and not just historians of Britain) don't spend much time looking sideways – asking what makes country X different from country Y, what individuates this particular national story from any other. Although there are some tremendous narrative histories which follow a basically traditional pattern, it's easy for we amateurs to grow dizzy after a certain point. Read a narrative history of medieval England, then quickly read one about medieval France, and most readers will admit to a certain seasickness. The sensation is of a carnival ride in which kings, popes, barons, plots, wars, mistresses, heresies, castles, crusades, uprisings, charters, plagues, murders, sieges, alliances and perfidies pass in a giddy whirl before our eyes. Century merges with century; country with country. The only antidote for this giddiness is perspective: what are the broad themes of change? What makes a country's particular national history distinctive?

In Britain's case, the answers to that latter question are unusually abundant. If one were asked to pick out the most salient single feature in human history since the birth of Christ, it would be hard to avoid picking out industrialization, first of the West, and increasingly now of the rest of the world too. Just below industrialization in importance, any number of historical developments clamour for attention. (I'm talking about the positives here, though there are plenty of negative ones too, notably the increasing destructiveness of weaponry and its international spread, a development that Britain has played a very full part in promoting.) These developments are partial, in the sense that many countries are still too little touched by modernity in its current Western democratic sense, but a partial change is still one heck of a lot better than no darn change at all. A non-exhaustive list of such tidal movements of history would surely include the following:

- The shift from low productivity, subsistence agriculture to a high-productivity, capitalist one.
- The rise of representative democracy.
- Government by the rule of law.
- The birth and development of science.
- The rise and rise of technology.
- The health transition, by which the average human lifespan has doubled or trebled.

Further below these matters in importance, but still hardly inconsequential, one might want to mention, among other things, the following:

- The development of secure property rights.
- The development of modern public finance.
- The globalization of trade and investment.
- The slow march of freedom of speech to its current position at the front rank of human rights.
- The gradual (and incomplete) abolition of torture and other non-reason-based methods of trial as a means of determining guilt or innocence.
- The gradual (and incomplete) abolition of slavery.
- The enormous reduction in homicide and other serious crime.
- The construction of effective governmental programmes for the relief of poverty and other forms of hardship.

- The British Empire and all that went with it.
- The birth of mass migration and the creation of the Western offshoot countries (the USA, Canada, Australia, New Zealand).
- The development and spread of a genuine global tongue.
- The reduction of warfare between the Great Powers.
- The diversion of young male testosterone into sporting rather than military or other violent activities.

I hope it will not have completely escaped the reader's attention that Britain played more than its share in every one of these developments, and in many cases its role was unquestionably the leading one. It seems to me that these facts are important enough to deserve mention in any biography of Britain, and yet they are also, typically, downplayed. Such things as the Industrial Revolution, empire and the slave trade will get their page space, of course – but what about the health transition? The scientific revolution? The reduction in homicide? The development of a free press and the associated commitment to freedom of speech and thought? The early English development of property rights? The common law's unique emphasis on the abolition of torture and the corresponding rise in reason-based methods of trial? The transfer of social protection from being a local, religious duty to a national, state one? These things are often mentioned only glancingly, if they're mentioned at all. Even with such major landmarks as Magna Carta, the discussion often alludes only to the charter's significance in Britain's constitutional history, as though the event were of purely local, domestic importance, when really it is better understood as marking the birth of one of the most important political developments anywhere, ever. Part of the point of *This Little Britain* is to call attention to the obvious, to relocate our own particular history in the broader sweep of world affairs, to remind ourselves of things we once half knew but have somehow contrived to bury.

To argue like this is to step instantly into the minefield of contemporary political divisions. Left-wingers are prone to see such arguments as covertly imperialist, intolerant, possibly even racist; hiding a refusal to regret the undoubted brutality inflicted by past Britons on other, less fortunate, peoples. Right-wingers, on the other hand, are likely to see these arguments as biffing those lefties where it hurts; flying the patriotic and – yes, perhaps even imperial – flag with pride. It's not that I do or don't agree with these positions, it's that I genuinely don't understand either of them. Why should a left-winger want to avoid honouring the abolition of torture? Or the huge and recent expansion in the human lifespan? Or the government's role in providing poverty relief? If the left doesn't want to honour such things – and that means in part by taking their history seriously – then what on earth does it wish to honour? My bafflement is equally acute when it comes to that sotto voce right-wing delight. That Britons should want to take pride in their past is understandable, but why should such pride have anything to do with contemporary political divisions? And the notion that celebrating, say, representative democracy should somehow let Britain off the hook for those other, less pretty sides to its history (slavery and all the other forms of colonial violence) is just plain nuts. Democracy was good; slavery was bad; the same country promoted both. Why should this be so hard either to say or to comprehend?

Since I obviously don't understand these issues, I'll return instead to the question that opened the book: *Who are we?* Britain has obviously been something of a historical oddity for quite some length of time, but what is it exactly that lies at the heart of its distinctiveness? The American economic historian David Landes, in asking that question about the narrower topic of industrialization, listed the social and political attributes that would, ideally, be manifested by an industrial or proto-industrial society: the need for personal liberty; for rights of property and contract; and for stable, honest, responsive, moderate and efficient government. Back at the birth of the industrial age, it was clearly Britain which came closest to meeting these needs. As Landes writes:

> Britain, moreover, was not just any nation. This was a precociously modern, industrial nation ... one key area of change: the increasing freedom and security of the people. To this day, ironically, the British term themselves *subjects* of the crown, although they have long – longer than anywhere – been *citizens* ...
>
> This was a society that shed the burdens of serfdom, developed a population of cultivators rather than peasants, imported industry and trade into the countryside, sacrificed custom to profit and tradition to comparative advantage. With mixed effect. Some found themselves impoverished but on balance incomes went up. Many found themselves landless, but mobility was enhanced and consciousness enlarged.
>
> England gave people elbow room. Political and civil freedoms won first for the nobles (Magna Carta, 1215) were extended by war, usage and law to the common folk. To all of these gains one can oppose exceptions: England was far from perfect ... But everything is relative, and by comparison with populations across the Channel, Englishmen were free and fortunate.

Landes's comments here are pitch perfect. Here, in a nutshell, are the common themes behind such things as Bazalgette's sewers, Newton's Royal Society, Pitt's tax collectors, Edward I's parliaments, Norfolk's farmers, Anson's navy, Henry II's judges and all the rest. By contrast with the rest of Europe, Britons were freer than most for longer than any.

This freedom wasn't the freedom of anarchy; it wasn't the freedom of the Wild West or Yeltsin's Russia. On the contrary, this freedom came with – and was intricately reliant on – a minutely ordered society. Those Victorian Britons decided that London would benefit from sewers, so they had them built. Then, on seeing their effectiveness, they rolled out the same public health innovations all across the country, doing so in a way that was legal, democratic and simultaneously attentive to costs and responsive to need. That combination of central consultative authority and disciplined local effect was equally visible in the Elizabethan Poor Law, Henry II's common law and indeed in the hundreds and shires of Alfred's England.

The mention of Alfred suggests the final triumvir of British distinctiveness: alongside liberty and order, we need to mention age. Our institutions are old. Alfred's England didn't just rejoice in its shires and hundreds, it had its sheriffs, courts, gelds and *fyrd*s too, each of which institutions survived the Conquest, and some of which are still going strong today. No other country has maintained, unbroken, such old state structures. We know something of the institutions of Alfred; much farther back than that, and our knowledge starts to dissolve into speculation. All the same, hints are there: early legal codes, early evidence of orderly and effective state power, early government through consultation, early evidence of land and service assessments. In short, the best guess is that our institutions and habits of mind have origins that are literally prehistoric.*

Ours, then, is a uniquely old, free and orderly country, which you'd think would be a fairly good recipe for a confidently positive sense of national identity. Yet there's a general sense, and I suspect an accurate one, that confidence in our identity has declined sharply over the past few decades. That decline is at the same time easy to understand and hopelessly inappropriate. As late as 1950, it would have been easy for any Briton to believe in British distinctiveness. That belief would hardly even have been a delusion. Certainly, the British Empire was reduced (after India) and much weakened, but it was still the world's largest such entity. Closer to home, with democracy still young in Germany and Italy, absent in Spain and Portugal, shell-shocked in France, then the depth of British democratic traditions must certainly have seemed distinctive, to put it mildly. Within a generation or two, however, the empire vanished and democracy triumphed utterly (inside 'old' Europe, anyway), as have the rule of law, industrial capitalism and all the rest.

After centuries of believing ourselves, with reason, to be different from 'abroad', Britain suddenly finds itself looking very much the same as our counterparts elsewhere in the rich

---

* Those habits certainly came with the Saxons, but one can't rule out the possibility that the Celtic Britons also knew something about how to run a state. To add to the long list of exceptionalisms noted so far in this book, here's a last one to add to the pile: by AD 500, 'barbarians' had taken control of every part of the Western Roman Empire, except one – Roman Britain, where an invasion was certainly in progress but still extremely partial. The invasion wouldn't be finally complete until Llewellyn's defeat by Edward I in 1282.

world. Though we're certainly a bit more American than most (think of our labour markets, our scientists or our jails), broadly speaking we're just the same as everyone else, a bit better here, a bit worse there, not really so distinctive at all. Indeed, we're also having to get used to the fact that some of our ideas and institutions haven't just been widely disseminated, they've been improved in the process and are being re-exported back, old friends in new clothes. A free press, for example, may have first taken root in Britain, but it took European legislators to enshrine freedom of speech in law, and it wasn't until 1998 – some three hundred years after the lapse of the Licensing Acts – that the right came to be enshrined in British law and actionable through British courts. Again, we may have invented the sport of football, but it's we who are seeking to emulate the technical gifts and tactical nous of our neighbours, not vice versa. In short, our ancient, cherished, much-vaunted uniqueness has vanished and is never likely to return.

Good. If we want to celebrate anything in our history, then nothing is more worthy of celebration than that loss of distinctiveness. To worry about it would be like a father getting upset by his son beating him at cricket, or a mother annoyed by her daughter's sparkling university grades. Over a period of centuries – a millennium and a half, at least – the inhabitants of the British Isles came slowly to hammer out a concept of modernity that was largely free, fair, technically advanced, prosperous and peaceful. That was their second-greatest achievement. The greatest was simply this: to have exported that model so widely and so well that it no longer looks British at all.

ACKNOWLEDGEMENTS

History, more so than fiction, is a collaborative sport. I've been hugely indebted to Maurice Keen, Prof Donald Read, Mary Welstead, and Tom Bingham for extensive comments on various drafts of the book. Between them, they've added wisdom and saved me from many an inaccuracy. Those that remain are my responsibility, of course. Thanks too to Simon Ager for his Shavian expertise, Victoria Whitworth for her Anglo-Saxon, David Franklin for his Latin and Joshua Rey for his forklift truck know-how. Bill Hamilton has been an outstanding agent, Mitzi Angel the best of editors. My thanks to them both, and to all at Fourth Estate.

SOURCES

A scholarly bibliography of the material covered in this book would be substantially longer than the book itself, and in any case good bibliographies on the various topics addressed are not hard to find elsewhere. I've therefore limited myself to listing sources for material directly quoted in the text. My thanks to all copyright holders for their kind permission to reprint their material. Where texts are readily available online, I've noted as much.

Introduction
Page xi, 'How about a couple of yobs ...': *The Times*, August 2005

Page xiii: 'British industry came to lead ...': Home Office, *Life in the United Kingdom*, TSO, 2004

Page xvi, 'Be advised ...': Seamus Heaney, *Open Letter*, Field day Pamphlet no. 2 1983

Page xviii, 'Many modern writers ...': N.A.M. Rodger, *The Command of the Ocean*, Penguin, 2004

Shaw's Potato
Page 11: Shavian alphabet: sample reproduced by kind permission of Simon Ager at Omniglot.com

Declining to Conjugate
Page 15, 'Ic selle the …': example quoted from McCrum, MacNeil & Cran, *The Story of English*, Faber, 3rd ed., 2002

A World of Squantos
Page 17, 'And for the season …': William Bradford, *Chronicles of the Pilgrim Fathers of the Colony of Plymouth from 1602 to 1625*, Alexander Young (ed.), Little, Brown, 1841. Available in full online

Lashings of Pop
Page 29, 'This is perhaps one way …': UNESCO website, 2006

Of Cows and Beef
Page 33, 'In off the moors …': Seamus Heaney (tr.), *Beowulf*, Faber, 1999

Page 35, 'Foy porter, honneur garder …': Guillaume de Machaut, 'Foy porter'. Available online

Page 35, 'Summer is y-comen in …': anon, 'The Cuckoo Song' in Helen Gardner (ed.), *The New Oxford Book of English Verse*, OUP, 1972. Available online

Page 36, 'I caught her with a rope …': Ted Hughes, 'February 17th', *New Selected Poems*, 1957-1994, Faber, 1995

Page 37, 'Yet fifteen years ago …': Philip Larkin, 'At Grass', *Collected Poems*, Faber, 1988

Half-Chewed Latin
Page 38, 'Priests cannot be found …': quoted in Simon Schama, *A History of Britain*, BBC, 2000

Page 38, 'were there a hundred popes …': Robert Vaughan (ed.),

Tracts and Treatises of John de Wycliffe, Wycliffe Society, 1845. Available online

Page 39, 'Blisful the man ...': this and other versions of the Bible referred to are all available online

The Rustics of England
Page 57, 'We hear that you forbid ...': quoted in Christopher Hibbert, *The Roots of Evil*, Weidenfeld & Nicolson, 1963

From the Same Mud
Page 71, 'As of auncient and long tyme ...': Thomas Harman, *Caveat or Warning for Common Cursetors, vulgarly called Vagabonds*. Available online

A Bettir Lawe
Page 80, 'Be it enacted by the Queen's ...': this and subsequent snippets can be found in Ronald Butt, *A History of Parliament: The Middle Ages*, Constable, 1989

Page 83, '[King Edwin] answered that ...': Bede, *Ecclesiastical History of England*, tr. J.A. Giles, HG Bohn, 1847. Available online

Page 86, 'So a cloth merchant ...': Simon Schama, *A History of Britain*, BBC, 2000

Page 86, 'The first kynge mey rule ...': Sir John Fortescue, *The Governance of England*, Clarendon Press, 1885. Available online

No Remote Impassive Gaze
Page 88, military manpower: data from Geoffrey Parker, '"The Military Revolution" – a Myth?' in *The Military Revolution Debate*, Westview Press, 1995

Page 91, 'a system of government which ...': N.A.M. Rodger, *The Safeguard of the Sea*, HarperCollins, 1997

Page 93, 'Jack ... turned aft ...': Patrick O'Brian, *The Far Side of the World*, HarperCollins, new edn 2003

Good King Frank
Page 96, 'Willy, Willy, Harry, Ste...': Most of this verse appears to be traditional – I haven't succeeded in locating an author. The last two lines are my own.

A Most Strange and Wonderfull Herring
Page 103, 'A most Strange and wonderfull ...': Fritz Levy, 'The Decorum of News', in *News, Newspapers & Society in Early Modern Britain*, Joad Raymond (ed.), Frank Cass, 1999

Page 103, 'Proude heart, wilt thou not ...': Quoted in *A History of News*, Mitchell Stephens, Penguin, 1989

Page 104, 'But now beholde ...': Quoted in *A History of News*, Mitchell Stephens, Penguin, 1989

Page 108, 'And though all the winds of doctrine ...': John Milton, *Areopagitica*, Clarendon Press, 1874. Available online

Page 109, 'Sirs unto me ...': 'The Character of a Coffee House', quoted by Joad Raymond, 'The Newspaper, Public Opinion and the Public Sphere', in *News, Newspapers & Society in Early Modern Britain*, Joad Raymond (ed.), Frank Cass, 1999

Invasion
Page 125, 'six or eight men ...': Adam Smith, *The Wealth of Nations*, Nelson, 1852. Available online

Page 130, single ship encounters: data from N.A.M. Rodger, *The Wooden World*, HarperCollins, 1986

How to Be a Superpower
Page 134, warships: data from Jan Glete, *Navies & Nations:*

Warships, Navies & State-Building in Europe and America, 1500–1860, Alriquist & Wiksell, 1993

Page 136–7, ship building and capture: data from 'The Eighteenth Century Navy as a National Institution, 1690-1815' by Daniel Baugh in *The Oxford Illustrated History of the Royal Navy,* J.R. Hill (ed.), OUP, 1995

Lacking Elan

Page 139, bellicosity: data reported in Niall Ferguson, *The Cash Nexus,* Penguin, 2001

Page 142, '[At the outset of war] it was starved …': General Sir David Fraser, *And We Shall Shock Them,* Cassell, 1983

Page 144, 'The effect was to maintain …': John Keegan, *The First World War,* Random House, 1998

Page 146, 'To read this story …': Niall Ferguson, *Empire,* Penguin, 2003

President Monroe's Trousers

Page 148, 'that we should consider any attempt …': President Monroe's *Annual Message to Congress,* 1823. Available online

The First Scientist

Page 157, 'Gilbert's work contains …': William Whewell, quoted in Pumfrey & Tilley, *William Gilbert: forgotten genius,* Physicsweb.org, available online

Page 157, 'To you alone, true philosophers …': William Gilbert, *De Magnete;* see *The Scientific Revolution: The Essential Readings,* Marcus Hellyer (ed.), Blackwell, 2003

Ex Ungue Leonem

Page 161, 'In November [1665, I] had …': Isaac Newton,

Correspondence – quoted in Rupert Hall, *The Revolution in Science 1500-1750*, Longman, 1983. Other Newton quotations drawn from *Isaac Newton*, James Gleick, HarperPerennial, 2004

Page 162, 'Spread over a series of years …': Rupert Hall, *The Revolution in Science 1500-1750*, Longman, 1983

Page 171, 'Nature was to him …' Isaac Newton, *Optics*, foreword by Albert Einstein, Courier Dover Publications, 1952. Available online

The Last Scientist

Page 174, 'I do remember a particular moment …': Michael Green, quoted in *The Elegant Universe*, presented by Brian Green, PBS, 2003. Transcripts available online

Raising Water by Fire

Page 187, '*All right, but apart from …*': Chapman, Cleese et al, *Life of Brian*, Handmade Films, 1979

Page 192, 'I was thinking upon the engine …': James Watt, quoted in Ben Marsden, *Watt's Perfect Engine*, Icon Books, 2002

Page 195, 'cannot boast of many inventions …': quoted in Peter Mathias, 'Skills and the Diffusion of Innovations from Britain in the Eighteenth Century', *Transactions of the Royal Historical Society*, vol. 25, 1975

Page 196, 'In short, in the history …': Joel Mokyr, *The Lever of Riches*, OUP, 1990

Colossus

Page 209, footnote 'The delta stream of …': Paul Gannon, *Colossus*, Atlantic Books, London, 2006

Page 210, 'They [Bletchley Park] didn't commission me …': ibid.

Page 211, 'The first modern electronic computers …': quoted in Georgina Ferry, *A Computer called Leo*, HarperCollins, 2003

Whose Land?

Page 221, 'In perusing the admirable treatise …': Montesquieu, *The Spirit of the Laws*, 1748. Available online

Page 223, 'Oh England, England …': Sir John Aylmer, *An Harborowe for Faithfull and Trewe Subjects*, 1559 quoted in Alan Macfarlane, *The Origins of English Individualism*, Blackwell, 1978

The Monster with 10,000 Eyes

Page 225, population and GDP: data from Angus Maddison, *The World Economy, Vols I & II*, OECD, 2006

Page 227, 'Taxes upon everything …': Sidney Smith, *Edinburgh Review*, 1820. Available online

Wheat Without Doong

Page 233, 'The power of population …': Thomas Malthus, *Essay on the Principle of Population, 1798*. Available online

Page 235, calories per worker: data from James Simpson, 'European Farmers and the "agricultural revolution"', in *Exceptionalism and Industrialisation*, de la Escosura (ed.), CUP, 2004

Page 236, 'Where peason [peas] ye had …': Thomas Tusser, 1573, quoted in Mark Overton, *Agricultural Revolution in England*, CUP, 1996

A Wave of Gadgets

Page 241, GDP change: data here and subsequently from Angus Maddison, *The World Economy, Vols I & II*, OECD, 2006

The Food of the People

Page 255, tariffs: Data from Bordo, Eichengreen & Irwin, 'Is globalisation today really different from globalisation a hundred years ago?' Brookings Trade Forum, 1999

Page 257, capital invested: data from Angus Maddison, *The World Economy, Vols I & II*, OECD, 2006

Page 259, 'How far, how just …': Richard Cobden, Speech to House of Commons, 1842. Available online

The Gates of Mercy

Page 270, 'many times by several nations …': Richard Jobson, quoted in Hugh Thomas, *The Slave Trade*, Picador, 1997

Page 271, 'white men, with horrible looks …': Olaudah Equiano, *The Interesting Narrative of the Life of Olaudah Equiano, 1789*. Available online

Page 272, 'The only plea they offer …': Philip Quaque, quoted in *The Economist*, Feb 2007

Page 273, 'no man is by nature …'; also Boswell: quoted in Hugh Thomas, *The Slave Trade*, Picador, 1997

Page 274, 'I sat down disconsolate …': Thomas Clarkson, *The History of the Rise, Progress and Accomplishment of the Abolition of the African Slave Trade*, 1808. Available online

The Reluctant Father

Page 286, 'There was no deliberate intention …': Bernard Porter, *The Lion's Share*, 4th edn, Pearson, 2004

Bombay Direct

Page 291, migration: data from Hatton & Williamson, *Global Migration and the World Economy*, MIT, 2005

SOURCES

Soldiers and Slaves
Page 298, 'The irony that an empire …': Simon Schama, *A History of Britain,* vol. 2, BBC, 2001

The British Way of Death
Page 301, 'Left to themselves the passengers …': Evelyn Waugh, *When the Going Was Good*, Penguin, 1990

Page 304, 'The lip of the escarpment …': Peter Fleming, *The Fate of Admiral Kolchak*, Hart-Davis, 1963

Yobs
Page 308, 'an honest man …': César de Saussure, *A Foreign View of England in the Reigns of George I and George II*, John Murray, 1902

Page 308, 'there is no country in the world …': unknown diplomat, *A Relation of the Island of England*, tr. Charlotte Sneyd, Camden Society, 1847

Page 308, 'Nobody is provincial …': Louis Simond, *Journal of a Tour and Residence in Great Britain*, 1815. Available online

Page 310, murder: data from Manuel Eisner, 'Long-Term Historical trends in Violent Crime', in *Crime and Justice*: *A Review of Research*, vol. 30. Available online

Clouds of Feculence
Page 312, 'Sir, I traversed this day …': Michael Faraday, *The Times,* July 1855. Available online

Greeks
Page 321, 'After dinner all the youth …': William Fitzstephen, *History of London*, 1175; quoted in Roger Hutchinson, *Empire Games*, Mainstream Publishing, 1996

Page 323, 'the assembly of a lawless rabble …': Derbyshire Council, quoted in David Goldblatt, *The Ball is Round*, Penguin, 2006

Page 323, 'the game was formerly much in vogue …': Joseph Strutt, ibid.

Very Fine Linen

Page 331, 'A bottle green and claret-coloured …': Quoted in Ian Kelly, *Beau Brummell*, Hodder & Stoughton, 2005

Page 333, 'An elegant then requires …': ibid.

Conclusion

Page 346, 'Britain, moreover …': David Landes, *The Wealth & Poverty of Nations*, Little, Brown, 1998

What's next?

Tell us the name of an author you love

| Harry Bingham | Go ▶ |

and we'll find your next great book.